CH01507548

Contents

EXODUS TOO

For my beloved wife and soulmate,
Lina Tamman

EXODUS TOO

THE STORY OF AN ORDINARY EGYPTIAN JEWISH FAMILY
IN EXTRAORDINARY TIMES

Gabriel Tamman

VALLENTINE MITCHELL
LONDON • CHICAGO

First published in 2021 by Vallentine Mitchell

Catalyst House,
720 Centennial Court,
Centennial Park, Elstree WD6 3SY, UK

814 N. Franklin Street,
Chicago, Illinois
60610 USA

www.vmbooks.com

Copyright © Gabriel Tamman 2021

British Library Cataloguing in Publication Data:
An entry can be found on request

ISBN 978 1 912676 80 4 (Paper)
ISBN 978 1 912676 81 1 (Ebook)
ISBN 978 1 912676 82 8 (Kindle)

Library of Congress Cataloging in Publication Data:
An entry can be found on request

Acknowledgements

Many thanks to everyone who supported and helped with this project, including my wife Lina, our three sons and all the family.

Thanks to the contributors whose narratives form such a valuable and useful appendix to this document, and who have been exceedingly kind and generous with their time, memories and information.

Thanks to my research and writing assistant, Deirdre Nuttall, who has been working with me on this project since its inception.

Finally, thanks to all those – Jews and non-Jews alike – who have helped, and continue to help, to keep alive the memories of the Jews of Egypt.

1

The Egyptian Jews in Ancient Times

The narrative of Moses's life in Egypt and the flight of the Jews from slavery is central to Jewish theology and identity: the Exodus; the giving of the Torah to the people; and the Mosaic covenant.[1] Therefore, Egypt – as a geographical place, an historical nation, and a metaphor for both terrible adversity and the development of a sense of nationhood – is fundamental to the Jewish experience. As the Jewish Egyptian historian Maurice Fargeon wrote: 'Entered in Egypt as seventy fathers of family, the sons of Israel went out of it as a people, so to become a kingdom of priests and a holy nation.'[2]

I well remember studying this story in preparation for my bar mitzvah, and discussing Moses with my teachers and my parents, including the story of the ten plagues that were visited on Egypt by God afterwards. We young boys, growing up in Egypt, and identifying strongly as Egyptians, were all fascinated by it, particularly because it was said to have occurred in a place that we knew well. We speculated as to what the Red Sea must have looked like as it parted, and when it closed again to destroy Pharaoh's army.

I write as one of the few Egyptian Jews from my generation who is still alive. Born in 1932, I lived through the end of the golden age of Egyptian Jewry, the Second World War, and then a period of intense antisemitism and nationalism that saw the Jews erased from modern Egypt while, nearby, the nation of Israel went through its birth pangs.

Wanting to tell a story that both incorporates and goes beyond my own memories, I have consulted a large number of academic and other publications to relate the narrative of the Egyptian Jews – not just because it is deeply personal to me, but because it is an important story that the world should know, and that is as relevant today as ever.

As children growing up in Egypt, my generation could never have imagined how soon the long story of our people there would come to end. Today, only a few of us remain to relate it.

When I was a child, we were also often told stories of ancient Egypt. One of the great festivals was the ritual 'virgin sacrifice', said to commemorate an actual sacrifice performed by the ancient Egyptians each year, to ensure that the Nile would flood and fertilize the plains. On that day, the parks of Cairo were filled with families celebrating – Muslims, Jews, Copts, and everybody else – and the water was full of houseboats, on which many families held their festivities. Every year, Mum and Dad told us the story of the myth behind the celebrations. We always went to bed in a state of great excitement about what the following day would bring. We would wake up at four or five in the morning and go out. Many of the celebrating groups brought with them a doll dressed as a bride to represent the sacrificial maiden. The doll, which was the size of a human being, would be wrapped in chains and placed on a platform in the Nile as a symbol of the original sacrifice. The celebrations were a truly joyful experience for us children as we ran, played, and tried the traditional festive foods of our friends from different backgrounds: I remember with pleasure the eggs and the salted, marinated fish of the Copts, which were also enjoyed with great enthusiasm by the Jewish and Muslim children.

In general, Egyptian mythology lived on among the peoples of Egypt in the form of the superstitions and traditions that, as a diverse community, we carefully observed – many of them are still observed to this day. The history of the Jews in Egypt was also reflected in popular tradition. One example is the use of the number five to prevent harm from the evil eye, because the old story of Moses related that the Jews painted a handprint in lamb's blood on the door so that they would not be visited by the plague. According to the story, Jewish families were identified because they had been told to paint the number five on their doors, and therefore they were spared the plagues that were sent to punish the people – to this day, Jews paint the number five on or near their doors to keep the household safe.

We also celebrated the history of the Jews in the broader region, thus feeling a connection not only to our Egyptian predecessors but also to our remote antecedents. I recall in particular when we celebrated the Jewish festival of Purim, which commemorates when the Jews were saved from Haman, an Achaemenid Persian Empire official who was planning to kill all the Jews, as narrated in the Book of Esther. We children all dressed up as characters in the story – the girls as Esther, and the boys generally as villains – and acted it out in the local Jewish community centre for the entertainment of our elders. After the festivities, we shared traditional sweets and cakes made by our mothers.

Scholars of Biblical and historical sources believe that there was a Jewish presence in Egypt as early as the second half of the second millennium BCE,[3] and that some Jews were in the Egyptian army then. One of the best-known Jewish colonies, founded during the Saitic Dynasty, was officially known as the 'Jewish Garrison' and defended the southern border of Egypt from about 525 to 399 BCE.[4] We knew little of this but, as we grew older, at school we studied the Roman history of Egypt, and we knew not just about the Romans, but also about Egyptian Jews of that time. Of course, as we were children, we were taught a very simplified version of history, in which the Romans featured as the 'baddies', and the Egyptians (including the Egyptian Jews) as the heroic underdog.

Under Alexander the Great, whose campaigns conquered Egypt during the period 336-323 BCE, more Jews moved to Egypt, largely from Palestine. After the establishment of the Ptolemaic kingdom in 306 BCE, more Jews were introduced to Egypt, initially as captives, and later released, by Ptolemy the first.[5] Alexandria, in particular, then the largest city in the region, was home to a large, successful Jewish population, and Jews also lived in urban settlements along the Nile. At this time, high culture and learning were inextricably linked with Greek language and culture.[6] Jewish scholarship and learning were much admired by members of other cultural groups; documents of spiritual and historic value were translated from Hebrew into Greek, making them available beyond Jewish circles. By around 240 BCE, many Egyptian Jews were highly respected members of society, and some of the Roman aristocracy were interested in arranging marriages between their daughters and prominent Egyptian Jews.[7]

Julius Caesar landed in Alexandria with a few troops in 48 BCE. He could only withstand attack from multiple sources with the support of local Alexandrians, who were probably Jews. After his victory, the Bill of Rights established for the Jews of Alexandria formed the template for Jews' rights throughout the Roman Empire, including exemption from compulsory military service.[8] Nonetheless, the Roman period was often a very difficult one for the Jews, marked by ethnic conflict and frequent outbreaks of violence.[9]

In 32 CE, Aulus Avilius Flaccus was appointed prefect of Egypt. Under his rule, the Jews suffered terrible persecution. In 38 CE, when the Jews had hoped to improve their situation by sending formal congratulations to Caligula for having become emperor, Flaccus invalidated collective and individual Jewish rights, declared the Egyptian Jews foreigners, proposed that statues of Caligula should be erected in their synagogues,[10] and allowed vicious mobs to attack, rob and murder them. Many were evicted from their homes and forced to live in crowded and insanitary conditions, in which disease quickly spread.[11] When the leaders of the Jews were summoned, ostensibly to discuss a peace agreement, they were subjected to a public flogging. Thankfully for the Egyptian Jews, Flaccus was himself executed in 38 CE.

Under the reign of Emperor Nero (54-68 CE), the equal rights of Alexandrian Jews were cancelled, leading to a revolt that in turn led to the gruesome execution of three Jews and a Jewish counter-attack. Huge numbers of Jews were killed when the counter-attack was suppressed.[12] In 115 CE, Emperor Trajan went to fight the Parthians, who were threatening the western provinces of the Roman Empire. At this point, the Jews appear to have hoped that they would be restored to nationhood, perhaps with the help of the Parthians. Instead, many were slaughtered, and the great synagogue of Alexandria was destroyed. It would take over a century for the Jews in Egypt to show significant signs of cultural and economic revival.[13]

The Arab and Muslim conquest dramatically changed society. By and large, the Islamic attitude towards Jews was informed by the decisions taken by Muhammad during his lifetime. When he encountered Jews beyond the Arabian Peninsula, Muhammad generally granted them the right to self-rule, but also obliged them to pay a special tax or tribute to the Muslim nation state. Under Islam, Jews were allowed to function as a distinctive community, with formally recognized leaders, but they were also treated as second class citizens[14] and obliged to follow Muslim law in all but internal matters.[15] The special tax they paid entitled them to protection, and was expected to be paid not just voluntarily, but happily.[16] At this time, most Egyptian Jews lived 'as a tolerated minority... periodically subjected to harsh treatment'. During this period, very little is captured of the lives of ordinary people, Jews and non-Jews.[17] Consequently, the little writing of relevance to our topic that has survived is largely by Arab Muslims, who only discuss Jews and their culture and society where they were seen as relevant to Islam at the time.[18]

When Islam was first established in Egypt, it was an agricultural region, growing food for the Muslim armies in Syria and elsewhere.[19] Little is known of the Jews in the first three centuries of Islam, after which the record shows a well-established community in Egypt. Egypt had become the most important economic region for the entire Muslim world. Relatively large numbers of Jewish families with business interests had moved to Egypt, often from eastern Islamic countries,[20] to work in this vibrant environment.[21]

Under the Shi'ite Fatimid Caliphate (the Fatimids conquered Egypt in 969 CE[22]), there were two distinct Jewish Egyptian communities: the Rabbinites and the Karaites. The latter, probably founded in Baghdad in the eighth century,[23] largely rejected Rabbinical authority[24] in favour of the so-called 'Oral Torah', which is primarily comprised of handed-down traditions and beliefs.[25] Despite significant theological differences, the two groups intermarried, collaborated in business, and maintained friendly alliances,[26] as was still the case when I was growing up in Egypt in the twentieth century, more than nine hundred years later.

Levels of literacy among Jews were relatively high by the standards of the time, and they maintained their network of social and business relationships across a wide area by engaging in letter writing. Many of these letters, along with other documentary material, were stored in the anterooms of the Ben Ezra synagogue in Fustat, where the climatic conditions preserved them. These papers, collectively known as the Cairo Geniza, were a source of great pride to Jewish Egyptians when I was growing up. They provide much information about the daily lives of Egyptian Jews in this period.[27] We learn of the Jews' involvement in the medical and pharmaceutical worlds; Egyptian Jews handled a wide range of medicinal substances available either from the local environment or by way of trade from the port cities, such as Alexandria.[28] We also learn that attitudes to divorce were relatively liberal and that (whether because of divorce or widowhood) about half of the Jewish women in Egypt at that time married at least twice. In urban centres in Egypt at that time, people typically lived on the upper storeys of buildings serving multiple functions, with shops below, and a communal interior courtyard at the ground level. It was common for Egyptian Jews, Christians, and Muslims to be neighbours, with majority and minority families often living side by side in apartments in the same building, and sharing the same courtyard.[29] Again, this was still the case when I was growing up, many centuries later.

From about 980 to about 1030, the Fatimid Caliphate had grown in power and influence and Cairo had become an important economic and cultural centre.[30] Among the Jews, their leadership had hitherto primarily centred on Jerusalem and Baghdad, but now prominent Jews in Cairo acquired a more dominant role. Jews in other regions, such as Iraq and Palestine, increasingly looked to the Egyptian Jews for political and economic leadership.[31] Jewish businessmen fostered close relationships with one another across even tremendous distances, with regular, friendly communications between individuals working in Egypt and their counterparts in places including Tunisia and India.[32] This was still the case when I was growing up, and even today, Jews from all over the world always support one another.

While this was, broadly speaking, a positive era for the Egyptian Jews, there were setbacks. For a period, under the Caliph Al-Hakim, Jews and Christians in various areas were persecuted and subjected to forcible conversion. Jews were forced to wear distinctive clothing in the form of black garments, with a wooden block suspended around their necks (it should be noted that the primary target of this specific repression was the Christian community, with the Jews effectively experiencing it as collateral damage).[33] As the Karaites had established a positive relationship with the government, Jews from all over the region petitioned them to use their influence.[34]

Towards the end of the eleventh century, the eastern Mediterranean experienced a turbulent period. The Seljuks won Jerusalem in 1073, and the Fatimid won it back in 1098, only for the Franks to win it in 1099. Meanwhile, the Jews of the broader region were increasingly concentrated in Tyre, Damascus, and eventually Fustat. The chaos did not have a negative impact on their internal organization, and by the end of the millennium, the Jews of Egypt were in a powerful position, with the local Jewish administration of the entire region centred in Egypt.[35]

In 1071, the tide turned for the Fatimid Caliphate. The Seljuk conquered its northern territories, and the Fatimid gradually lost most of their foreign lands. However, during the eleventh and twelfth centuries, Egyptian Jewish communities continued to thrive. The Jews noted the gains made by Egyptian Christians and ensured similar rights for themselves, such as the right to represent themselves to the ruling authorities.[36]

By 1100, the Jews of Egypt had centralized a hierarchy of leadership, which oversaw responsibilities such as the appointment of judges and local officials. In 1100, that leader was the Cairene Mevorakh ben Saadya.[37] Over the next seventy years or so, all the Jews in the region respected the authority of a succession of Jewish leaders based in Cairo. The twelfth century was also the era of the great Jewish philosopher Maimonides, who lived in Egypt for most of his life and died in 1204.

Maimonides was one of the Sephardi, or Spanish, Jews who fled the anti-Christian and anti-Jewish al-Muwahhid regime, which then prevailed in Spain and Morocco,[38] and which led to the destruction of the rich cultural life that had been developed by the Jews of Iberia.[39] The Sephardis brought with them to the Middle East their Ladino dialect (which was also spoken by a number of my direct ancestors, who came to Egypt at a later point), which came to be spoken widely in the region,[40] and the term 'Sephardi' persisted and is still used by many Jews of Egyptian and Sudanese origins to describe themselves.[41]

Both formal and informal writings from Maimonides survive, giving us some insight into the role he played in his community,[42] and how he was received in Egypt by the majority population. At one stage, a Muslim visitor from Morocco attempted to denounce Maimonides as an apostate from Islam - a very serious charge, for which the penalty was death. The Egyptian authorities ruled that a forced conversion, such as those suffered by the Jews in Iberia, could not be considered valid and therefore that there were no legitimate grounds for accusing him of apostasy;[43] this was a very liberal judgement by the standards of the day.

Maimonides was greatly preoccupied with issues of social justice, and one of his great works was the codification of Jewish law on issues of charity, gathering together all of the relevant edicts in the Torah and in post-Torah Jewish writing. The resulting Code, the Mishneh Torah, formed a basis for Jewish social justice in the years that followed.[44] To put his teachings into the social context of the day, Maimonides stressed that marriage should not be forced, and that women, as well as men, should freely consent to any marriage that was proposed for them; previously, marriage was often arranged for girls, including very young girls, without their views being taken into consideration.[45] Maimonides was therefore not just a scholar, but a liberal and progressive voice by the standards of his day.

Like many learned men of his time, Maimonides also had some knowledge of medicine. For many educated Jewish men, being able to give medical advice and prescriptions was a great benefit not just within their own communities, but also in their interactions with the majority. Maimonides also wrote a glossary outlining the various names by which plants and other medicinal substances were known.[46] Jewish doctors in the time of Maimonides were much sought-after by wealthy members of the majority society, because - as minority figures - they were seen as having a limited power base in society, and therefore as being more trustworthy.[47] Maimonides himself provided medical services to the Sultan and his circle at the court in Cairo.[48]

For most Egyptian Jews at this time, it was possible to enjoy a good standard of living. Commerce was widespread throughout the Mediterranean region, and the Jews of Egypt - like other Egyptians - had access to products such as cheese and wine from Italy, as well as a wide range of local foodstuffs suitable to eat according to kosher regulations.[49]

While there were no significant barriers to Rabbinical and Karaite Jews intermarrying, the community went to great effort to ensure that Jews only married other Jews. Powerful families could consolidate their authority by means of strategic marriages. Marriages were typically arranged not by the couple in question, nor only by their immediate families, but by the broader community. Marriage between families who already knew one another well - and who were often themselves related through blood and marriage - was often preferred.[50] Traditions around marriage were broadly similar in the mid-twentieth century, when I was young.

As the Middle Ages advanced, the situation facing the Jews in Muslim lands tended to deteriorate. In Egypt, a relatively tolerant civil government was replaced by a military regime and more discriminatory official attitudes. There were fewer opportunities for Jewish and Muslim scholars to interact, and a significant decline in scholarship.[51] Egyptian Jewish scholarship advanced again when printing was introduced to the Muslim lands[52] by the Sephardim. Literate Jews were now able to disseminate written material to many more people, and levels of literacy and learning increased.

There was a continuous Jewish presence in Egypt throughout the late medieval and early modern period. This was a time of rampant anti-Jewish sentiment and legislation in Europe, and many Jews found a much more welcoming environment in Egypt. After the Edict of Expulsion of the Jews was declared and signed in Granada on 31 June 1492, all Jews had to accept baptism or leave the kingdom.[53] The Sephardim of the Iberian peninsula, who fled at this time, were the ancestors of many of the Jews of Egypt and other Arab lands. When I was growing up, we remembered their story in particular when we celebrated Passover.

Of course, Passover is the Jewish festival when we commemorate the original flight of the Jews from Egypt. We eat unleavened bread, because the story relates that the people had to flee so quickly that they did not even have time to leaven their bread. We descendants of the Sephardim also remember that the same thing happened in 1492, when our more recent ancestors had to flee Spain and Portugal. Thus, when we repeated the curses of Moses against Pharaoh, as we celebrated Passover in my childhood, we were also thinking of more recent persecutions – and perhaps also of the fear, ever-present in the mind of all Jews in all places – that they may once again be forced to flee.

The Sephardim from the Iberian peninsula, who were used to Islamic law and custom, adapted quite quickly to life in Egypt.[54] They were typically also fluent speakers of Arabic, and those who were literate could also read and write Arabic.[55] Many Jews in Arab countries conceptualised themselves as both Jews and Arabs;[56] confident in their religious and ethnic identity, and also sharing many cultural and other interests with their Islamic counterparts. Of course, over the years, some Muslim practices influenced Jewish traditional culture – and would do so until modern times. For example, during Eid, at the end of Ramadan, Muslim families would sacrifice a sheep, and the children's faces would be daubed with blood, while the meat was distributed to the poor. When I was a child, Jewish Egyptian families also sacrificed a sheep for important feast days and holidays, and gave the meat to the poor, as well as eating it themselves, although of course this had no religious significance for them, as it had for their Muslim neighbours.

In the sixteenth century, Ashkenazi Jews, fleeing persecution in Ukraine, also arrived in Egypt.[57] The Ashkenazim were gradually absorbed into the larger Jewish community,[58] although when I was a child, the Ashkenazim were still associated with a specific area of Cairo, where many of the descendants of these original arrivals from Ukraine still lived. Their numbers would be swollen again in the eighteenth century by Ashkenazim fleeing Russia. In the twentieth century, this community was still well-known for its characteristic baked goods and its marinated fish.

In the sixteenth and seventeenth centuries, the Ottoman Empire, which had been founded in 1517,[59] was at the height of its powers. The Jews of Egypt, now living within this empire, flourished. They benefitted from the expanded rights the empire gave them, as they were granted the same rights offered to Jews living elsewhere under Ottoman rule. The ongoing expansion of the empire provided businessmen with many opportunities, while the cultural exchange between Jews of European and Jews of Eastern origins created a lively, dynamic community fully integrated into the empire[60] and also able to act as a sort of cultural bridge between Europe and the Islamic world. Jews in sectors such as banking were regarded as particularly reliable; as a minority, they were considered less vulnerable to corruption or patronage.[61] Egyptian Jews also had extensive links with Jewish communities elsewhere in the Mediterranean region and beyond. Many filled roles in government administration, frequently in collating customs revenues.[62]

General knowledge of the teachings of Maimonides had waned since his day, but during the early modern period, there was a revival of intellectual interest in him and his work. This knowledge persisted beyond this period into the present. Maimonides was frequently discussed when I was growing up, and I would even say that the stories of him were rooted in the epicentre of Jewish Egyptian life at that time, in the middle years of the twentieth century. There was a synagogue dedicated to him in Haret al-Yahud, the old Jewish quarter, and he was also said to have been buried there – many people visited his tomb for the purpose of prayer and in seek of cures and help for all sorts of ailments and problems. Jews and Muslims alike used pictures of him in their folk medicine, putting an image of him under the pillow of the person who was unwell or unable to sleep.

In the early modern period, Egyptian Jews engaged in organized efforts to support the poor and needy members of their community.[63] On top of their state taxes, Jews also paid internal taxes in the form of payments on foods that required certification as kosher and as contributions to the synagogue. Many left bequests in their wills to support the vulnerable. Community-owned homes and businesses were rented out to raise funds. Widows, orphans, and other vulnerable people could receive regular payments from these centralised funds, while exceptional payments supported costs associated with weddings, funerals, and so on. A common source of financial distress was the poll tax demanded by the Ottoman authorities from all non-Muslims; the poor were often given financial assistance to cover their contribution.[64] There were also formal organizations, or confraternities, with each devoted to a specific charitable purpose, such as providing medical care, furnishing poor girls with dowries, and so forth.[65] This keen emphasis on charitable works, and supporting one's fellow Jews, was still very much a part of my family's life in the twentieth century – and indeed persists to the present day. I consider this a fundamental aspect of my heritage as an Egyptian Jew.

Despite the fact that the Jews of Egypt originated in many different parts of Europe and the Middle East, by the start of the eighteenth century they had merged, with only the Karaites maintaining a sense of difference (and even they freely mingled and intermarried with other Jews). By now, the Egyptian Jews were a largely urban people concentrated in a number of fields, including gold and silver-smithing, trade, and banking, as well as the spice trade and the textile industry. To a very great extent, they had assimilated with the local population,[66] speaking Arabic fluently, contributing to intellectual and artistic life through Arabic, and sometimes even using Arabic names.[67] Egyptian Jews also maintained a strong devotion to their faith and a clear sense of their cultural distinctiveness. They remained firmly endogamous, marrying within their community, and maintaining close ties across extended families.[68]

Europe had become a dominant trade power by now. This offered many opportunities to Christian businessmen living under Arab rule. Europeans generally preferred dealing with Christians, and therefore this was a time when the power and influence of Jewish businesspeople in Egypt declined relative to that of their Christian counterparts.[69] However, Alexandria remained an important city not just for Egyptian trade in general, but for the Jewish community. Between 1750 and 1775, Jewish families from all over Egypt moved to Alexandria.[70] At the end of the eighteenth century, however, the local Mamluk rulers were trying to extricate themselves from the Ottoman Empire, and from about 1780, outbreaks of violence were common, as were periods of epidemic disease and famine.[71] Amid a severe financial crisis, the Jews were frequently mistreated and subjected to periodic confiscations of their property.

The dawn of the nineteenth century heralded a new, and increasingly prosperous and positive, period in Jewish Egyptian history, and forms the subject of the next chapter.

For those of us who grew up in Egypt, our knowledge of Jewish Egyptian history - both the formal history that we were taught in school and the popular histories, legends, and mythologies that we learned at home and in our communities - left us Jewish children in no doubt about our Egyptian heritage and our identity as Egyptians. While, in my case, my more recent ancestors had come to Egypt in about 1800, the long Jewish history in the region gave me a strong Egyptian identity, and great pride in the venerable presence of the Egyptian Jews about whom we were taught. Later, nationalists would try to paint all Jews as *arrivistes*, foreigners, and newcomers - but we had never felt that way, and our love of Egypt sprang not just from the happy childhoods that we spent there, but from our knowledge of a Jewish presence in the region that dated to remote antiquity.

Notes

1. Modrzejewski, 1995, 5.
2. Miccoli, 2015, 149.
3. Hermann, 1973, 7; 19.
4. Kasher, 1985, 2.
5. Ibid., 3-4.
6. Modrzejewski, 1995, xi; 50.
7. Kasher, 1985, 6; 11.
8. Ibid., 17; 78.
9. Modrzejewski, 1995, xiii.
10. Ibid., 169.
11. Philo, Against Flaccus, 55-6. Cited in Modrzejewski, 1995, 170.
12. Kasher, 1985, 25.
13. Modrzejewski, 1995, 217.
14. Bareket, 2013, 1; Krakowski, 2018, 82.
15. Dulska, 2017, 259.
16. Bosworth, 1972, 214.
17. Lassner, 2012, 201; 196.
18. Goitein, 1974, 91; 89.
19. Ibid., 113.
20. Cohen, 1980, 2.
21. Goitein, 1974, 113.

22. Cohen, 1980, 4.
23. Krämer, 1989, 22.
24. Lassner, 2012, 204.
25. Kalimi, 2005, 102.
26. Rustow, 2008, 27; xviii.
27. Ibid., 37-9; Krakowski, 2018, 4-5.
28. Lev, 2007, 276.
29. Krakowski, 2018, 45; 49.
30. Rustow, 2008, xxx.
31. Cohen, 1980, 5.
32. Goitein, 1974, 112.
33. Cohen, 1980, 53.
34. Rustow, 2008, 176.
35. Ibid., xxxii.
36. Cohen, 1980, 60; 77; 52.
37. Ibid., 79.
38. Beinin, 1998, 4.
39. Halbertal, 2014, 15.
40. Sachar, 2006, 19.
41. Goldberg, 2008, 166.
42. Cohen, 2005b, 10.
43. Lewis, 1995, 88.
44. Cohen, 2005b, 24-5.
45. Krakowski, 2018, 130.
46. Lev, 2007, 278.
47. Halbertal, 2014, 61.
48. Nadler, 2007, 236.
49. Rustow, 2008, 285-6.
50. Ibid., 239-41; 253.
51. Lassner, 2012, 210.
52. Lewis, 1995, 23.
53. Ibid., 34-5. Many years after the expulsion of the Jews from Spain and Portugal, writing in 1938, the Jewish Egyptian poet George Cattaoui (who was also the member of a prominent business family) wrote in praise of fifteenth-century Egypt and the Islamic government of the time for the welcome it extended to the Jewish people in those distant days. Miccoli, 2016, 18.
54. Krämer, 1989, 16; Sezgin, 2005, 218.
55. Stillman, 2018, 296.
56. Snir, 2012, 175.
57. Krämer, 1989, 18; Abdulhaq, 2016, 67.
58. Oppenheim, 2003, 414.
59. Hanna, 2003, 6.
60. Lewis, 1984, 112-16.
61. Lessner, 2012, 211.
62. Lewis, 1984, 132; Ben Israel, 1901 (orig. 1655). The Jews continued to dominate in this field until 1768, when responsibility for the customs was transferred from them to members of the Greek community. Crecelius, 1998, 65.

63. Cohen, 2005, 16.
64. Arad, 2017, 265-6.
65. Cohen, 2005b, 197.
66. Krämer, 1989, 12.
67. Gotein, 1974, 138-9.
68. Lassner, 2012, 159.
69. Lewis, 1984, 145.
70. Landau, 1969, 32.
71. Al-Sayid Marsot, 1984, 3-7.

2

The Making of a Jewish Egyptian Family – Memory and Context

As a small boy, growing up in Egypt and Sudan, I was often told stories about my ancestors, on both sides of the family. Like most Egyptian Jews, our family had come to Egypt in the nineteenth century, and we had roots in various places that linked us to one another, to a range of locations around the Mediterranean basin, and to many of the big events and great people of history. We felt deeply rooted in our homeland – Egypt and Sudan were essentially the same entity in those days – and it was fascinating to know that, nonetheless, our ancestors had actually come from various distant places.

My father, Joseph Tamman, was born in a small town in Egypt called Tanta, as was his father before him. Jews from Morocco, Spain, Italy, and other areas had settled in this region after the Napoleonic invasion, often choosing to establish themselves in areas where they already had some relatives and would therefore find it easier to set themselves up in business. From what we were told in our family, none of our ancestors who settled in Egypt at this time were fleeing discrimination, persecution, or poverty in their lands of origin; it was simply that Egypt offered opportunities at the time and was seen as a safe, economically lively environment where anyone who was prepared to work hard could settle down to do business and raise a family. The Tamman family never forgot their Italian roots, and maintained a strong sense of being culturally Italian at the same time as being Jewish.

My mother, Flora, was born in Cairo. Her family originally came from Baghdad and were Iraqi Jews. They had originally moved to Egypt in 1823, attracted – as so many were – by the possibility of getting a good job and building a safe and secure life there. My grandmother's brother, Solomon Ani, had already established himself in Egypt and, as things were going well for him there, he had called for his sister to join him in the business, which was also a general store. My grandfather and grandmother, therefore, moved to Egypt, after which my mother, Flora, was born into the Egyptian

Jewish community of Cairo. Before coming to Egypt, the family had spoken only Iraqi Arabic, and even many years later, they still retained a trace of their Iraqi accent.

To understand how it was that so many Jewish families like my own chose to move to Egypt and built their lives there, we need to take a glance at the history of the nineteenth century, as the events of that period opened up the territory of Egypt and Sudan, making it an attractive and welcoming place to which many Jews moved.

The modern history of Egypt and Sudan really begins just before the dawn of the nineteenth century, with the Napoleonic invasion, so that is where we will start:

Napoleon and his army had invaded the Nile Valley in 1798, heralding an era that saw dramatic changes in how the Muslim world interacted with Europe, and also how the Jewish community would interact with both Egypt and its many trading partners. After establishing a French administration in Egypt, the French took over the tax concessions and gained access to a large stream of income, granting concessions to those who supported their regime.[1] The French authorities interacted directly with the Egyptian Jews – who at this point were still mostly people descended from the indigenous Egyptian Jews, who had been there since antiquity – ordering them to organize themselves along the same lines as the Jews in France, with an institution called the *Consistoire*, led by two rabbis and seven councillors, who would take responsibility for the whole Jewish community in the case of crime, anti-social behaviour, or disturbances.[2] Napoleon is also said to have had cannons fired at a synagogue in Alexandria, ostensibly because it was in his way, but really because he was punishing the local Jewish community for failing to pay a fine that he had levied on them.[3] In response to Napoleon's arrival, the British sent an army under the leadership of Admiral Nelson,[4] thwarting his plans to establish a French empire in the Middle East and confining the French to Egypt.

Before the French expedition, power in Egypt had been effectively shared by the representatives and authorities of the Ottoman Empire, and the Mamluks and members of the militias (the Mamluk having been integrated into the Ottoman Empire after the empire fell in the sixteenth century). Under the French, Cairo soon started to resemble a European city, with its administration run by the most highly regarded men of the province. Napoleon set up a library, a chemistry laboratory, a health service, a botanical garden, an observatory, an antiquities museum and a menagerie, and encouraged learning and scholarship in the French language.

Napoleon's incursion into Egypt started a new chapter of Jewish history in the area. Even though Napoleon and his army were actually only in Egypt for a little while, this outing cemented a deep connection between Egypt and France, including a fascination in France for all things Egyptian, the beginning of French scholarship in the area of Egyptian antiquities and history,[5] and ultimately profound cultural links between the Egyptian Jews and all things French. One can reasonably consider the close links between Egyptian Jewish and French culture to have begun at this time and to have opened to the door to the arrival, later on, of the Alliance Israélite Universelle, which (as we will see) would have such a profound impact on Egyptian Jewish culture.

Speaking for myself, as an Egyptian Jew I have always felt close to France, and have a strong sense of affinity for all things French – and our family history in Egypt starts in the wake of Napoleon's Egyptian adventure. Like most Egyptian Jews, in my family we were brought up to be Francophiles.

By the time my family really started to put down roots in Egypt, the French in Egypt had been defeated in 1801, and Egypt had been returned to the Ottoman Empire. Together, Egypt and Sudan were considered as essentially the same territory, and referred to as 'the valley of Sudan and Egypt'. The commander, Muhammad Ali Pasha ('Pasha' is a term created during the Ottoman Empire, equivalent to 'Lord' in English; it is a Turkish term that was used in Ottoman circles for generals, dignitaries, and others of high status), initially remained as a governor appointed by the Ottoman leadership in Istanbul, but he would soon establish a dynasty.[6] In the short term, the resulting weakening of law and order in Egypt impacted negatively on Egyptian Jews, as some of them suffered from periodic local outbreaks of violence. However, it also added to their population; some of the French, Italian, and Armenian soldiers, and others who had accompanied Napoleon on his adventure, were themselves Jews, and remained in Egypt after the army had left, while others returned later on, after the collapse of Napoleon's empire.

The government under Muhammad Ali Pasha protected the Jews and their property, making it possible for them to develop in the areas of business, commerce, and learning,[7] and also favoured progressive causes, including the education of women, and less restrictive laws with respect to women's rights, creating an environment that was attractive to European (including Jewish) businessmen and their families,[8] who were generally more progressive in their views than the Muslim majority in Egypt (for example, Jewish women such as my great-grandmothers had much more freedom in the public arena, and more influence in their families, than their Muslim counterparts, which made it easier for them to play an influential role in their communities).

In general, Muhammad Ali was very favourably inclined towards the arrival and presence of foreigners in Egypt, as their expertise was required for factories and other businesses, and Egypt also benefitted from their links with a wide range of European countries. He had a particular interest in France, and turned to French experts for help with his plans for reform in the areas of administration and economics.[9] All of this made Egypt look very attractive to the Jewish and other minorities who decided to settle there at this time. Nonetheless, in the earlier years of the nineteenth century, Egyptian Jews tended to 'keep their heads down' and largely worked and socialised within their own communities. Jews (and indeed other minorities) in Muslim countries were prohibited from doing or saying anything that could be interpreted as a criticism of the Qur'ān or of the Prophet Muhammad. Clearly, this made them extremely vulnerable to misunderstandings and false accusations, and contributed to their desire to live and work within the Jewish community as much as was practical.

From 1820, Ali Pasha actively encouraged Jews to move to Egypt, particularly Jews from Greece and Italy.[10] That same year, Ali Pasha gained control of Sudan, an area that had ancient ties to Egypt. This was the start of a long period during which Sudan was effectively administered as part of Egypt, as a consequence of which the Jews of Egypt and the Jews of the Sudan can be viewed as the same people – and many of them, such as my family, moved freely between Egypt and Sudan and developed businesses in both entities. Therefore, when I speak of the culture and history of the Egyptian Jews during the period of the nineteenth century, I include the Jews of Sudan, because the Egyptian Jews and the Sudanese Jews were no different: they were the same people.

With the government's support, there was a dramatic increase in foreign- (including Jewish) owned businesses between 1822 and 1837.[11] More newly-arrived Jews could look to the long history of Judaism in Egypt and feel certain that they would find their place. This was the context into which many of my ancestors immigrated.

When my parents and grandparents told me stories about our family's past, I learned that we had not always been in Egypt, but had a rich and varied history in a number of places around the Mediterranean basin and the Middle East. My paternal grandmother, for example, came from a noble family based in Tetouan in Morocco, where they had lived under Spanish rule in a thriving community of about 30,000 Jews, at a time when the

Spanish culture and influence dominated in the area. When Tetouan was handed over from the Spanish to the Moroccans, there were fewer opportunities for the Jews, and many of them left at that time, in search of greater opportunities elsewhere. My grandmother moved to Egypt where my grandfather was already living, his own family having migrated there from Italy via Libya, in the wake of Napoleon's Egyptian adventure (the Italian connection would prove to be very important later on, as we will see).

Neither my grandmother's nor my grandfather's family maintained links with their families of origin for long, but rather assimilated quickly to life in Egypt and Sudan, then essentially the same territory, raised their children to feel very much at home there, and identified strongly both as Egyptians/Sudanese and as Jews.

While Egyptian Jews had a strong sense of belonging to Egypt, they also had a sense of connection to Europe, which was often more pragmatic than emotional in nature. For the Jews, identifying more closely with Europe, and specifically with France, seemed to offer them a way out of their 'dhimmi' status within a Muslim society, which kept them formally relegated to the position of second-class citizens,[12] no matter how integrated they were in other ways.

By the 1830s, many Egyptian Jews were flourishing, but one visitor to Egypt remarked that, while the Jews were less oppressed than they had been in previous times, many still lived in fear of being denounced as 'blasphemers' by someone with a grudge against them;[13] an ongoing latent fear that would have remained at the back of many people's minds. They remained vulnerable to arbitrary arrest, with release only possible after the payment of a fine. As a consequence, Jews were very careful to dress and behave in a modest and unostentatious manner, lest anyone should assume they were wealthy and in a position to pay a substantial fine.[14] Another observer commented on the wretched situation in which many of the indigenous Jews still lived, stating that the poor Jews were held in contempt by the Muslim majority, and that many of them lived in appalling circumstances and depended largely on whatever they could get from begging.[15] (In this context, it is worth noting that the jizya tax, levied on all non-Muslims, was only lifted in 1855, while Jews were also liable for both a special community tax, as well as the general taxes paid by everybody.)

This was a period when Jews in the Ottoman Empire had a certain amount of protection, while Jews in Russia and other eastern European areas were dealing with terrible discrimination. In this context, growing numbers of Ashkenazi (European) Jews started to settle in the region that is now known as Israel,[16] heralding the beginning of a movement that, later in the nineteenth century, would become Zionism. Others settled in Egypt, where they quickly assimilated and learned to love Egypt and to consider themselves Egyptians. It would take several generations before the Jewish settlement of Palestine began to impact significantly on the Egyptian Jews, who had many reasons to maintain focus on their life in Egypt.

Nineteenth-century Egyptian Jews of all backgrounds worked in a range of areas, including money lending, trade in a wide range of products, and often in the textile industry,[17] at a time of rapid industrialization in Egypt, when large numbers of rural people were leaving the countryside for new, factory-based jobs in cities and towns.[18] At this point, as before, Jewish commerce and industry were closely linked to family relationships and connections, being 'clannish and family based, relying on personal acquaintance and confidence; well versed in both the European business methods and the Oriental ways of arranging affairs; resourceful; mobile; enterprising; and highly pragmatic'.[19] All of this was still true of my own family when I was born, a hundred years later.

In the mid-nineteenth century, legal reforms were passed, granting equality in the eyes of the law to all subjects of the Ottoman Empire, regardless of their ethnic or religious background. From 1849-54, Egypt and Sudan were ruled (within the Ottoman Empire) by Abbas Pasha, who oversaw the expansion of the country's transport infrastructure, and maintained an open approach to commerce and business.[20]

From 1858, foreigners were allowed to purchase land in Egypt, attracting foreign businessmen and investors, largely from Europe, some of whom were Jews.[21] In the 1860s, the American Civil War cut Europe off from supplies of American cotton, opening up opportunities for the Egyptian cotton industry to flourish, and making Egypt increasingly attractive to foreign investors and businessmen.[22] As many Egyptian Jews already worked in the textile industry, and were intimately familiar with the industry and the supply chains in the Egypt/Sudan region, this offered many opportunities to them, especially as international demand for Egyptian cotton continued to grow.[23] The situation with the cotton industry at this time attracted large numbers of immigrants from diverse backgrounds, including Greeks, Italians, Syrians, North Africans, Armenians and Jews from a variety of cultural and linguistic backgrounds.

In 1881, Muhammad bin Abd Allah, known as Mahdi, rose to prominence in Sudan. The local population was increasingly angry about how they were ruled, and Mahdi harnessed that resentment and created a movement predicated around a form of Sudanese nationalism and a mystical take on Islam that claimed that the prophet Jesus was going to return, and that Mahdi himself was the messenger of Prophet Muhammad. The Egyptian authorities attempted to repress Mahdi and his followers, but they were incredibly persistent and resilient, and had huge support from tribal people in areas of the north, west, and south. In 1885, Mahdi and his followers had actually managed to conquer Khartoum, and they captured and beheaded the British army officer Gordon, whose head they put on display in the branches of a tree to frighten anyone who resisted the rebels. Mahdi himself died of typhus six months after the capture of Khartoum, and his followers were finally defeated by the British under General Kitchener in 1898.

The violent Mahdi uprising was not the only difficult situation in the north-eastern part of Africa at this time. In 1895, the Abyssinian war broke out following the Treaty of Wuchale. The Italians claimed that the treaty meant that Abyssinia (which is now known as Ethiopia) was now an Italian protectorate, which meant that other European nations should not have direct diplomatic relations with it. Because my grandfather, Eli Tamman (who lived in Tanta at this time), was an Italian national and held an Italian passport, he was told that he would have to join the army and fight for Italy. He told me, when I was a little boy, all about how he dealt with that: after conscription, he simply ate and drank so much that he gained a huge amount of weight. The army doctors did not consider him medically fit for service because of his excess weight, and he was discharged! Apart from the fact that he had no interest in going to war, the war put him, and all Sudanese and Egyptian Jews of Italian origin, in a difficult situation: France had huge influence in Egypt at the time and was also fiercely opposed to the Italian goal of establishing an empire in Africa, starting with Abyssinia.

Before Britain seized control of Sudan, commerce in the area was very primitive; after the establishment of British control at the end of the nineteenth century, the economy in Sudan started to develop quite rapidly, and opportunities began to open up, making Khartoum increasingly attractive to Jewish Egyptian businesspeople, among others, who included Greeks, Armenians, and Italians. Soon there was a thriving business community in Khartoum, with a good quality of life, excellent schools, and an entrepreneurial spirit. Families who had only been able to afford modest apartments in Egypt, with no privately-owned outdoors space, found that in Khartoum they could buy large, comfortable homes on quite big plots of land where their children could play, and that they could also afford to pay for household staff to help with housework and childcare. Many of the families who settled in Khartoum at this time were hard-working, aspirational members of the working and lower-middle classes, who saw a chance to become socially upwardly mobile and to offer their children opportunities that they themselves had not enjoyed. The only downside to living there was the extraordinary heat, which could be oppressive at a time when there was no such thing as air conditioning.

The Jewish community in Sudan was relatively small, and seamlessly integrated with the larger Jewish community in Egypt. Sudanese Jews travelled to and from Egypt all the time, visiting their friends, extended family, and business acquaintances, and when girls and boys grew up and reached marriageable age, using the services of a matchmaker in Egypt to find a suitable spouse was standard practice, and many - if not most - families had branches in both Egypt and Sudan.

My mother's family, the Cohens, lived in Cairo, where they had assimilated quickly, and were proud to consider themselves Egyptians. Throughout this period, Tanta, where my father's family lived, remained a fairly rural town despite its population of about 30,000, and not at all like the increasingly sophisticated Cairo. There was a lively Jewish community there, with people of all walks of life speaking a range of languages. For example, my paternal grandmother spoke Ladino, which is a Jewish Spanish dialect, and also Arabic, while other family members also spoke Italian and French.

The local synagogues, which were regularly attended, were small and simple. They were just big halls lined with benches, without the expensive wooden fixtures that would embellish the grand synagogues that were constructed later on. They were carefully constructed with windows on either side that provided a draft of air that helped to keep the interior reasonably cool. In accordance with tradition, women and men worshipped separately. The men, who took care of the proceedings, were on the ground floor, and the women, together with the small children, were on the first-floor balcony, looking down on them. This did not mean at all that the women were considered second-class in matters of faith, or in any other way, but was simply the way that things had always been done.

The town of Mansoura was located not far from Tanta; Mansoura was also home to a very active Jewish community, and had originally been home to the great Jewish philosopher, Maimonides. For the Jews of Egypt and Sudan of the nineteenth and twentieth centuries, as before, the history of Maimonides in the area was a source of pride and helped to foster their sense of rootedness in, and belonging to, the region. My ancestors of the nineteenth century would certainly have been aware of his legacy and, like my nearer ancestors, may well have visited his tomb in Haret al-Yahud in Cairo - more on this topic later.

Another famous rabbi of importance to the area was Yaakov Abuhatzeira. Whereas Maimonides connected the Egyptian Jews to their distant past, Abuhatzeira was alive at the time of my grandparents, and no doubt they would have taken a great interest in him, both because of his amazing reputation and because he, like my paternal grandmother's family, came from Morocco.

Abuhatzeira was considered a great spiritual leader; he was a kabbalist who was said to have performed many miracles in his native country, such as answering the prayers of infertile couples who desperately wanted to have children, and even healing people who had been disabled for many years. In 1879, he left Morocco and embarked on a pilgrimage to the Holy Land, but died en route in Egypt, and was buried in Darmanhour, which was near Tanta, where many of my ancestors were still living at that time. Within just a short period after his death, Abuhatzeira's burial site became a pilgrimage site, and devotees started to attend it for prayer and worship, as they still do to the present day. This important spiritual association also attracted more Jewish settlement, and quite a few families were drawn to the area by this.

People were still very interested in Abuhatzeira and his legacy when I was growing up. People often spoke about the burial-space of Abuhatzeira, and there was an annual event at the tomb when people congregated on pilgrimage. I remember visiting the site myself as a child with my family – out of curiosity and interest rather than devotion, as we were not interested in pilgrimage or in participating in religious rites at the site. Devotees of the great rabbi (who were usually Jews of Moroccan origins) believed that prayers made at his tomb were answered. My family were rather more sceptical than believing in this respect, but of course they were interested in any aspect of Jewish history, even if they were not believers in miracles. I remember very well the vast hangar-like buildings that had been constructed to accommodate travellers at night during their pilgrimage. Many of the pilgrims had come from far away, and accommodating them and providing for their needs was something of a local industry.

By the later nineteenth century, major industry in Egypt was entirely dominated by foreign businessmen, among them Jews from a variety of cultural and linguistic backgrounds.[24] Whereas my family, and many others, were only modestly successful, a number of prominent Jewish families had become extremely wealthy. The Cattaoui family, for example, had ancient Sephardic roots in Egypt, and for many generations had occupied a leadership role, not just among long-established Jews, but also with newly-arrived Jews planning to build lives and businesses in Egypt.[25] Such links between long-established and newly-arrived Jewish families must have aided the development of a sense of community and togetherness among all of the Egyptian Jews, regardless of their ethnic and linguistic background.

In Tanta, where my paternal family lived, several nationalities were represented among the Jewish community, including Italians, a few Turks, and quite a few with roots in Morocco and Libya. My own great-grandfather was originally from Italy, as I have said. Other towns had different mixtures; almost all the Jews in Mansoura, for example, had originated in Morocco.

By the end of the nineteenth century, my paternal grandfather in Tanta was involved in business on a fairly modest scale. He bought and sold men's underwear, and supplied the general stores with various items imported from Europe and obtained by him from middlemen or agents. In those days, particularly in smaller market towns, most stores were 'general stores', which meant that they did not specialize but sold a wide range of goods, including items for the house, medicines, clothing and so on. Only a very few shops specialized, and those that did typically sold specialized food items. Many Jewish families ran general stores, or supplied them, and Jewish businessmen travelled all over Egypt and Sudan bringing goods to their distribution network. This meant that they encountered businesspeople all over the territory, not just from Jewish but also from other religious and ethnic backgrounds. It also meant that they became intimately familiar with the geography and culture of the area, which fostered a profound sense of belonging and patriotism.

An interesting, if rather upsetting, historical reality is that slavery was still common in Sudan at that time, and many families still had black slaves not just then but well into the twentieth century. My grandfather, Eli, did not agree with slavery, so he bought a number of slaves, gave them their freedom, and then hired them to work as servants for a salary.

While they were typically on very friendly terms with people from different backgrounds, many Jews' everyday lives also revolved around their faith community. They ate kosher food, so they shopped in businesses that catered to their particular needs. Partly because of the requirements associated with a kosher diet, shopping could take quite a long time, and was often an occasion for housewives and others to socialize. For example, chickens were usually selected while they were still alive, and then had to be slaughtered and plucked according to the regulations. While all of this was going on, there was plenty of time to chat and exchange news. In general, Egyptian Jews held social gatherings within the community, and they attended the synagogues, which were the centre not just of spiritual life but also of the community's secular gatherings. However, they were also very well-integrated into the broader community.

Despite the ebbs and flows of economics and history, many Egyptian Jews flourished, and did so ever more as the nineteenth century progressed and they could increasingly count on support from European sources, as Europe had begun to formally discard the anti-Jewish legislation and sentiment that had prevailed for many centuries before (and, indeed, from which many Jews in history had found a safe haven in Egypt).[26]

Cairo was home to a large Jewish middle and upper class, which had become successful across a number of business sectors, and which helped to fund ambitious projects, including the building of a number of beautiful synagogues to serve the community, and the restoration of ancient sites of significance to Jewish Egyptian history.[27] Jewish influence also flourished in the intellectual and cultural realms; this was a period of considerable scholarly and artistic output.[28]

From this period onwards, French influence on Egyptian Jewish culture grew ever stronger, largely because of the profound impact of the Alliance Israélite Universelle and its mission in Egypt and the Middle East.

The AIU was founded in Paris in 1860 by a group of French Jews whose aim was to educate and liberate Jews elsewhere, with the assumption that French civilization and its various benefits would offer them a superior worldview and way of life; they felt that Jews from Arab countries, known to them at that time as 'Orientals', would benefit from exposure to, and training in, European ways of life. The AIU also dedicated itself to working against local manifestations of antisemitism.[29] It also sought to encourage the ancient Karaite community of Egypt, the indigenous Jews who largely lived in poverty and were mostly uneducated, to become less 'Arabic' and adhere more closely, instead, to the European norms lived by the majority of the Jews in Egypt.[30]

By this time, the beautiful seaside city of Alexandria was the most cosmopolitan urban centre in Egypt, with extensive trade and cultural links to Europe. Alexandrian Jews founded various organizations and professional clubs, including a branch of the AIU[31] and of the Rotary Club, an organization for businessmen.[32] The Jews of Alexandria tended to work as skilled craftsmen, in sales, and in administrative positions,[33] and to identify strongly with European cultural norms, partly because of the influence of the AIU.[34]

The influence of the AIU on the Egyptian Jews simply cannot be underestimated. People like my family, who came from a variety of backgrounds and spoke various different languages, benefitted hugely from the educational and cultural opportunities it offered and had many reasons to be grateful to it - even if the philosophy under which it was originally established was a little condescending towards the so-called 'Orientals'. Because more and more people started to send their children to schools and events set up by the AIU, French quickly became a common language spoken by Jews from a wide range of backgrounds, and speaking French became the hallmark of middle-class, upper-class, and in general socially upwardly mobile Egyptian Jews.

Other organizations were dedicated to the provision of a form of social welfare to Jews on low incomes. For example, women were expected to bring a dowry with them on getting married, and this could be a challenge for girls from low-income families. In 1863 in Alexandria, a community organization had been founded to provide Jewish girls from poor families with the dowries that they needed.[35] Similar organizations elsewhere pooled community funds and redistributed them to Jewish families living in difficult circumstances. Charitable giving, and the involvement of women in particular in charitable work, came to be a hallmark of Egyptian Jewish society and was still very important years later, when I was growing up; this was a legacy to be proud of and was a very important way in which women - who were already at the centre of Jewish households - looked beyond their immediate families and had a major influence on the broader community.

By the beginning of the second half of the nineteenth century, successful business families from both Sephardic and Karaite backgrounds increasingly left the traditionally Jewish areas of the city (there were adjacent Sephardic and Karaite neighbourhoods) and moved to affluent suburbs, where they lived among, and socialized and did business with, upper-middle class people from diverse backgrounds.[36]

Jews were also increasingly present in the print media, contributing as journalists and commentators to mainstream Egyptian newspapers, and in some cases owning Arabic-language newspapers and periodicals. At this point, the Arabic press was not seen as inherently Muslim, but identified as an outlet for writers of Muslim, Christian, and Jewish backgrounds alike;[37] nobody thought for a moment that Arabic should be the sole preserve of Muslims.

Until the nineteenth century, most Egyptian Jews still had little formal education; the majority had been given little opportunity to study. From 1840, this had started to change, especially with the foundation of Jewish schools in Cairo and Alexandria by Adolphe Crémieux, an important French-Jewish statesman and a founder of the AIU. Crémieux had been horrified to find that the only Jewish school available in Egypt appeared to be the very traditional Talmud Torah in Cairo, which offered a religious education and little else; boys learned to chant Hebrew and girls learned nothing at all.[38] The wealthy Felix de Menasce founded the Écoles Foundation de Menasce in Alexandria to provide lower-income members of the local Jewish community with a secular education (at that time, largely taught by non-Jews).[39] Later in the nineteenth century, there would be dramatic changes in the area of education that would set the scene for the rapid development of the Jewish community in terms of its success in business and in the wider world. All of this took place against a backdrop of massive immigration to Egypt generally, particularly following the opening of the Suez Canal in 1869, which heralded a period of rapid economic expansion,[40] and of the growing influence of European norms (in terms of dress, cultural behaviours, leisure activities and so on), among the Jewish community, as mentioned above.[41]

Work on the Suez had begun in 1854, when Egypt's ruler, Muhammad Said Pasha, awarded the contract to a French engineer. In the first instance, France provided about half the capital as well as engineering expertise, and Egypt provided the balance and the workers; huge numbers of Egyptian men were put to work on the project, often having been given no choice in the matter. The two governments had agreed that the company responsible for the Canal would run it for 99 years, after which it would belong to Egypt. When the work was completed in 1869, the Empress of France, Eugenie, opened it with great pomp and ceremony after riding up to the ceremonial point on a camel. She was accompanied by the Sultan of Turkey and Emperor Franz-Josef of Austro-Hungary, and witnessed by a vast crowd of onlookers, who included many illustrious visitors such as the Prince of Wales, the Crown Prince of Prussia, and the Crown Prince of the Netherlands, as well as many of the most prestigious Egyptians. To keep the Empress happy, a replica of her apartments at Tuileries had been constructed to accommodate her during her visit. With that, a new era of economic expansion and prosperity in Egypt had begun.[42] I remember my grandfather telling me that his father was present at the opening ceremony. It must have been a very grand occasion, and one can only imagine how exciting it must have been to see the fruits of many years of labour. My grandfather was a small boy when the Suez Canal opened, and I am sure that his father would have regaled him with many stories about attending the grand opening as he was growing up.

Growing numbers of immigrants, including many Jewish families, settled in places including Port Said[43] and Alexandria. The Menasce Hospital in Alexandria was constructed at this time to care for both Jewish and non-Jewish patients.[44] The Jewish population of Alexandria quickly rose from 9831 in 1897 (when the first Egyptian census to include the Jews took place)[45] to 24,858 in 1917.[46] Many of these Jews were formally citizens of a range of European nations, and they tended to retain close business and personal links with Jewish and other communities across Europe,[47] to use European given names for themselves and their children, despite what names were registered on their birth certificates, and to seek out European models for education and family relationships. The Italian Jewish community of Egypt, which largely traced its origins to the Livorno area of Italy, was strong at this time.

By 1897, there were about 60,000 Jews living in Egypt,[48] the vast majority of whom were of Sephardic or Middle Eastern origin, with only a very few Yiddish-speaking Ashkenazim, who generally hailed from Russia, Romania, and Poland, and had mostly settled in Cairo[49] - intermarriage between Jews from diverse backgrounds was increasingly the norm, helping these families to assimilate quickly. One member of such an Ashkenazi family was interviewed about their experience and described the family opting to stay in Cairo because of the work and economic opportunities it offered them:

> My father was born in Bessarabia and my mother in Sofia en route to Constantinople from Odessa. The family had left Odessa because they had sons and they didn't want them to go into the Russian army. They arrived in Alexandria by ship towards the end of the nineteenth century but decided to settle in Cairo because there were more opportunities for work.[50]

From 1882, under British colonial rule, Jews and other minorities in Egypt had been granted protections and given certain privileges, while from 1875, following a series of reforms, the Egyptian legal system was modelled after the French, and provided a more open approach to the law that was attractive to foreigners and minorities in Egypt.[51] Egyptian Jews were considered noteworthy for their entrepreneurial flair, and their ease with foreigners,[52] which derived largely from the slightly ambivalent position they held in Egyptian society; both integrated and apart. During the colonial period, they are described as being viewed, while also viewing themselves, 'as a milieu that was neither Oriental nor European.'[53]

From 1898, Britain acquired its mandate over Sudan, and governed both Sudan and Egypt. At that time, the British referred to Sudan as 'Anglo-Egyptian Sudan'. Under British government, numerous business opportunities opened up for people from all sorts of settings, some of whom were Jewish businesspeople from diverse backgrounds.

Notable Jewish business families from this period included the Mosseris, the de Menasces, and the Aghions, who had already become prosperous during the cotton boom. They now played an active role in the development of Egyptian infrastructure under the British, and in the banking sector. Many wealthy Jews also invested heavily in the railroad network and in public transport in Cairo. They were in no way partisan in their business interests, freely engaging in partnerships with Greeks and Arab Egyptians.[54] While obviously only a minority of Jews were as wealthy and successful as they were, their good fortune, and good business sense, had a trickle-down effect that impacted in a positive way on the Jewish community in general.

In 1903, there was an influx of Ashkenazi Jews from Russia, Poland, and Romania, all fleeing persecution. Most were Yiddish speakers. They arrived with nothing, or very little, and initially there was some tension between them and more established Jewish communities in Egypt because of the significant cultural differences between them. While some remained poor, by the time the second generation was born in Egypt, many had acquired an education and entered professional fields,[55] and they freely mingled and intermarried with Jews from other backgrounds.

Throughout this period, Egyptian Jewish scholarship continued to flourish, including Rabbinical scholarship in Hebrew,[56] which was not generally spoken as an everyday language, but was studied by Rabbis and those with an interest in Jewish history and theology. Jews, and especially Jews who had studied theology and history, were keenly aware of Egypt's importance to Jewish history over many centuries, and this helped to forge a sense of identity as Egyptian Jews, who were intimately bound up with the fate and well-being of the country as a whole.

The late nineteenth and early twentieth century was a period of considerable change in terms of women's role in society. Jewish women had always had more freedom in a range of areas than their Muslim counterparts, but at this time both the influx of Jews from European cultural backgrounds, and the influence of European cultural norms on the established Jewish Egyptian community, led to substantial gains in areas such as education and the general autonomy of women, who were increasingly free to make their own decisions about how to conduct their lives.[57] By the time my own parents were growing up, women occupied a stronger role in the family than ever before. As more and more women were as educated as their husbands, it was becoming easier for them to assert themselves and ensure that their views and needs were fully taken into consideration, and there were many ways for them to interact with the broader community as they attended to their domestic duties and engaged in the charitable work that was common among Jewish women of the middle and upper classes.

Increasingly, Jewish Egyptians of both sexes looked to Europe for guidelines on how their personal and family lives should be, and tended to conform increasingly to European cultural norms. Thanks to the ongoing efforts of the AIU, the standard of education among Egyptian Jews was now rising rapidly. Wealthier and more educated Jews very much embraced many aspects of European life, attending the opera and the theatre to enjoy French and Italian productions, and making frequent visits to Europe. By the late nineteenth century, educated Egyptian Jews, in particular, were in an excellent position to benefit from the various Egyptian projects funded by British and French capital, including the founding of the National Bank of Egypt in 1898[58] and the establishment of the Sugar Company of Egypt in the 1890s, which would employ as many as 20,000 by the 1920s.[59]

In the schools the AIU established in North Africa and the Middle East, Jewish children were offered the opportunity to study subjects including French language and literature, Hebrew, Jewish history, geography and history generally, maths and sciences, and - for girls - the domestic arts.[60] By 1872, there were four Jewish schools in Cairo, catering largely to poorer Jews, who could not afford to pay large school fees, while wealthier Jews often sent their children to European-run schools,[61] or hired private tutors for them. Educational standards consistently rose among Egyptian Jews in the second half of the nineteenth century, with most parents who could afford it preferring to send their children to schools that taught according to European, and in particular French, educational standards and norms (between 1850 and 1950, 150 newspapers were published in French in Egypt, illustrating just how important the language was).[62] Soon, average standards of education among Jews matched those of other foreign minorities and were considerably higher than typical educational standards among either Muslims or Copts in the region.[63] Thanks to the gains that the Egyptian Jews had made in the areas of education and commerce, Jews were now increasingly present in important positions in business and government. In 1878, for example, the secretary-general of the Ministry of Finance was a Jew called Julius Blum.[64]

In 1896, the AIU opened its first school in Cairo to cater to the Jewish community, with the hope that Jewish children would be enrolled there rather than in the Christian-led schools that most middle-class Jews then attended.[65] In 1898 and 1900, the AIU established, respectively, schools for boys and for girls in Alexandria. There was a dramatic increase in particular in the number of Jewish girls attending school in the area, predominantly girls from lower and lower-middle social classes, as wealthier families tended to send their daughters to Catholic schools, or to hire private tutors and governesses for them.

Egypt could be a challenging educational environment for the teachers; the students came from a range of cultural backgrounds, and had different mother tongues – some spoke mostly Arabic, others Spanish, French, Italian, or another European language.[66] Girls were required to wear European-style clothing to school, in contrast to their mothers, many of whom still wore traditional Ottoman Jewish clothing.[67] The issue of girls' education was central to the educational aims of the AIU; as future wives and mothers, they would have an immense influence on the next generation. By giving them a European education, the AIU hoped to turn them into agents of change.[68]

In 1902 more schools, for girls and boys, were established. The teachers provided by the AIU noted that the Jews of Egypt, unlike many Jewish communities in other areas where the AIU ran schools, were extremely well-integrated with other elements of Egyptian society, and that many Jewish families were not very religious, but considered themselves Jewish in a cultural, rather than a spiritual, sense.[69]

It should be noted that, while the primary function of these schools was to prepare Jewish children for adult life, they were also open to young people from different religious backgrounds, and in some areas (Tanta, for example, where my paternal ancestors lived) some Muslim and Christian parents also choose them for their offspring, attracted by the good standard of teaching and support.[70] This is a clear illustration of the extremely positive relationship between the Jewish and other communities at this time.

Higher levels of education among Jews, and growing levels of competence in the French language, prepared many young people for jobs in the banking and other professional sectors.[71] In 1903, business leader Maurice Cattaoui, a prominent member of the Jewish community, decided that it was time for Egypt to have its own stock market, and one was set up, initially on Maghraby Street, and employed many highly skilled Jewish professionals.

The 1907 census of Egypt reveals higher levels of literacy among Jews than among the rest of the population.[72] This was the environment in which my parents were raised - one in which parents who were ambitious for their children could ensure that they were provided with a good standard of education. My father's family, more so than my mother's, took full advantage of this opportunity. My father, Joseph, attended a convent school and was taught by nuns. Thanks to the excellent education he received, he spoke and wrote French fluently; all his life, he expressed gratitude towards those nuns for the excellent basic education he had received from them, and to the AIU, for broadening his horizons and offering him so many opportunities. My mother, Flora, grew up in a family with less progressive views on education, especially the education of girls, and received only a minimal standard of education.

My parents, Joseph and Flora, were also growing up in Egypt at a time when interest in Zionism was growing, although as young people, they could never have imagined what a big impact the philosophy and political movement would have on their lives and on the lives of the Egyptian Jews in general.

The founder of Zionism as a political ideology was the Austrian journalist, Theodor Herzl, who had argued in the late nineteenth century that Jews should migrate to the 'Promised Land' and establish a nation-state there. These views quickly gained currency among European Jewish communities, but initially attracted much less interest among Jews in the Arab world and elsewhere. In 1896, Istanbul-born Marco Barukh founded the Bar-Kohba Society, a Zionist organization, in Cairo, but it attracted very little interest among Egyptian Jews[73] who, while they shared a common faith and were typically deeply involved with the community, did not generally have a sense of nationhood, as they came from a wide variety of cultural and linguistic backgrounds.[74]

In 1897, the Zionist Organization had been founded with the explicit goal of establishing a Jewish state in what was then British-owned Palestine.[75] Most Egyptian Jews, such as my recent ancestors, were still not very aware of what was then very much a fringe organization; for many years to come, Zionism would remain a predominately European movement and concept.[76] However, this event would go on to have vast repercussions for them and for their descendants that could not have been foreseen at the time, and that are still relevant today. It is important to note that the AIU, which was clearly extremely influential in Egypt at this time, was pointedly anti-Zionist, and preferred to promote European norms among the Jews of the Middle East; clearly, this led to tension between different sectors of Egyptian Jewish society.[77]

Years after the modest beginnings of Zionism, my father, Joseph, took a great interest in Zionism and read all about it. I remember him talking to me at length, when I was still just a young boy, and explaining what he knew about Theodor Herzl and his plans for a Jewish homeland, which to many people seemed like little more than a fantasy at that time. Starting in Europe, groups of Jews had already come together to campaign and fight for the establishment of this country. The Egyptian Jews had no way of knowing, as yet, how important this movement would prove to be for them.

Judaism is everywhere both a religion and an ethnicity, and of course the same applied in Egypt. Obviously, individual Jews varied greatly in terms of how important the spiritual aspect of Judaism was to them, and while some were deeply religious, others considered themselves Jewish primarily in a cultural, rather than a spiritual, sense. However, throughout the modern history of Egypt, all Egyptian Jews had access to the pastoral care of their rabbis, who functioned as teachers and general advisors to the Jewish community, and who were so well-known for their guidance that they were sometimes consulted even by communities outside Egypt. Some families were well-known for producing rabbis and tended to dominate in this area.[78] As I have said, my own family, as far back as we can trace, was not enormously religious, but observed all the feast days and important aspects of Judaism, as well as having a strong sense of their ethnic and cultural identity. Nobody in my family ever had an interest in Orthodox Judaism, but were happy to live in a way in which they could participate fully in secular life, while respecting and cherishing the traditions that they had inherited from their distant ancestors.

Regardless of their spiritual views, most Egyptian Jews had a strong sense of cultural identity, and the desire to remain culturally intact. Jews in my ancestors' and in my parents' time continued to have a strong preference for endogamous marriage – marriage within the community – and the vast majority of Jews married other Jews, with marriage to non-Jews being very much frowned-upon. Girls were typically considered marriageable from the age of fifteen or sixteen, while men tended to get married somewhat later. Legislation was in place to prevent marriage to younger girls, and to prevent vulnerable girls from being rushed into marriages for which they were not prepared.[79]

Partly because of the work of the AIU, from the early part of the twentieth century, efforts grew to encourage Jewish girls in Egypt to have a keener sense of their cultural and religious heritage, with the introduction of a coming of age ceremony analogous to the boys' bar mitzvah, and a focus on ensuring that the girls were conversant in Hebrew.[80] This, it was thought, would help them in their roles as mothers and wives, to maintain a sense of Jewish identity in their families, and to foster a feeling of pride for who they were and where they came from.

The Egyptian Jewish community, although diverse, also had a strong sense of 'we are all in this together' and wealthier families had a sense of responsibility towards those who were less fortunate. Many of the charitable organizations that did wonderful work with the poor were still led by Jewish women. In 1911, in the provincial city of Tanah, for example, local Jewish women established a Société des Dames that supported low-income women during their pregnancies, and poor girls in the education system, as well as providing clothing to poor children celebrating important milestones and rites of passage.[81]

In 1916, some prominent members of Jewish society, including Moreno Cicurel and Isaac Banario (both members of families that had migrated to Egypt for business opportunities and that went on to become enormously wealthy) founded an organization called Oeuvre de la Goutte de Lait which, through the work of a collective of Jewish women, provided a hearty breakfast in the form of bread and hot milk to children from low-income families.[82]

The generally positive experience of being Jewish in Egypt in the nineteenth and early twentieth centuries, when my family on both sides was becoming progressively more established, was occasionally marred by the emergence of an antisemitic strand in Egyptian society that periodically appeared in the form of accusations of ritual murder and violence, among other things. While Jewish families were generally on excellent terms of cooperation and friendship with Arab and other neighbours and colleagues, these periodic accusations and the problems that arose as a result were a timely reminder that they could never relax completely.

From the 1870s, baseless accusations of ritual murder being carried out by Jews were made across the Mediterranean region, including Egypt. Most often, these accusations emanated from Greek communities, and in some cases, the authorities discovered that the children said to have been murdered were actually hidden by their families, who used the accusation as an excuse to attack local Jews.

Egypt was not immune to this frenzy of accusations. Most of them took place long before I was born, but the details of such shocking events stayed alive in storytelling and recollections, and were occasionally discussed when people got together and the topic of anti-Jewish feeling in the region arose. Just a few these examples of antisemitism serve to give a general picture of the situation:

In 1870, an elderly Jewish man from Alexandria was arrested after he was accused of kidnapping a Christian child so as to ritually slaughter him and use his blood in the preparation of Passover foods.[83]

In 1873, a Muslim boy was found in the street with an injury to his genital area. His parents initially stated that he had been bitten by a dog, but were subsequently tempted by the thought of possibly obtaining compensation, and accused the local Jewish community, in the form of Moise Salomon, the local Jewish slaughterer of domestic animals, of having stabbed him. Thankfully, following a brief investigation by the authorities, the case was dropped because of a complete lack of evidence, and the clear presence of fraud.

In 1877, a group of Jews was accused of abducting a young girl. An angry mob descended on the synagogue to search for her, and a number of Jews were assaulted. The child was found unharmed in a field outside the town a few hours later.[84]

In 1880, a Greek child fell from a balcony into the courtyard of a synagogue in Alexandria and was killed; again, the Jews were blamed.[85]

The most infamous of these scurrilous cases of false accusations was the Fornaraki affair in 1881, when the notorious antisemitic blood libel (which originated in medieval Europe and is likely to have originated in this case from among Christian, rather than Muslim, elements of the Alexandrian community[86]) prompted elements of the Egyptian press (particularly the Greek language press) to blame the Jewish community for the death of Evangeli Fornaraki, a Greek child who disappeared in Alexandria, and whose body was found shortly afterwards. A Jewish family was accused of having killed the child in a ritual murder, and both the Egyptian and European newspapers made much of the event, with some influential Greek Egyptians apparently involved in fomenting unrest against the accused family; there were dramatic scenes and riots at the funeral of the unfortunate child, who had drowned.[87] The family in question was brought to Corfu and eventually tried and acquitted of the crime, but not before they had been imprisoned and mistreated in a Corfu prison over the course of about a year.[88] Thankfully, their innocence was proven by the testimony of a number of highly-regarded Egyptian medical men.

In 1882, another manifestation of antisemitism, and of generally anti-foreigner, sentiment occurred in Alexandria with the 'Urabi' uprising. Local nationalists blamed Jews and Copts for what they saw as excessive foreign interference in Egyptian affairs, and riots broke out, which were eventually quelled by the British authorities.[89]

In 1911, the AIU continued to report periodic antisemitic incidents and repetitions of blood libel accusations,[90] although justice was generally obtained for these false accusations. The trope persisted, however.

As well as more obvious instances of antisemitism, Jews could sometimes be the subject of attempts to convert them to Christianity or, less often, Islam. For example, in 1914, the Jewish community of Cairo was aghast when twenty-two Jewish boys, attending Christian schools, appeared to have converted to Christianity under the influence of their educators, who were reported as having told the children that the Christians did 'good' things, whereas the Jews did 'evil' things. It emerged that some of the children came from low-income families, and that at least one had been offered money in exchange for stating that he desired to become Christian. Almost all of these 'converts' returned to Judaism shortly afterwards, but incidents such as these reinforced the view that it was important for Egyptian Jews to have the means to oversee their own children's education and contacts.[91] Those who did not convert remained apart from their families and were, often, mourned as though they had died.[92]

For a community increasingly at ease with European cultural norms, and with extensive business and social links with the Christian community, conversion of its members was a clear risk and experienced as a threat to the Jewish community.

Despite these occasional manifestations of anti-Jewish sentiment, for most families - certainly including mine - Egypt was a wonderful place to live, and as the twentieth century started to come of age, most Jewish Egyptian families had every reason to feel optimistic about the future, and sure that antisemitism of this sort was steadily becoming a thing of the past. The construction of the magnificent Adly Street Synagogue, which was finished in 1899, was surely a sign of a confident community, perfectly adjusted to life in Egypt, and looking forward to the future in the expectation that life would continue to be good, and that the occasional manifestations of anti Jewish prejudice would soon become a thing of the past.

Notes

1. Hanna, 2003, 7-8.
2. Landau, 1969, 135.
3. Barda, 2006, 70.
4. Lassner, 2012, 69.
5. Miccoli, 2015, 79.
6. Oppenheim, 2003, 410.
7. Laundau, 1969, 3.
8. Abdelmonem, 2016, 828.
9. Barda, 2006, 70.

10. Haag, 2004, 139.
11. Deeb, 1978, 12.
12. Barda, 2006, 11.
13. Lewis, 1984, 40.
14. Landau, 1969, 72.
15. Lane, 1836, 344-9.
16. Beinin, 1992, 14.
17. Oppenheim, 2003, 420.
18. Abdelmonem, 2016, 826.
19. Mizrahi, 1987, xiv.
20. Toledano, 1990.
21. Landau, 1969, 6.
22. Oppenheim, 2003, 411.
23. Abdulhaq, 2016, 74-5.
24. Deeb, 1978, 13.
25. Tignor, 1980, 422.
26. Lewis, 1984, 156.
27. Meital, 2017, 184.
28. Miccoli, 2016, 1-2.
29. Miccoli, 2015, 21.
30. Abecassis and Fau, 1992.
31. Shenhav, 2006, 27.
32. Landau, 1969, 32.
33. Krämer, 1989, 17.
34. Miccoli, 2011, 158.
35. Miccoli, 2015, 96.
36. Oppenheim, 2003, 415.
37. Snir, 2012, 176.
38. Miccoli, 2015, 23.
39. Haag, 2004, 139.
40. Miccoli, 2016, 3.
41. Miccoli, 2011, 151.
42. Barda, 2006, 76.
43. Landau, 1969, 34.
44. Haag, 2004, 140.
45. Landau, 1974, 109.
46. Miccoli, 2011, 149.
47. Miccoli, 2015, 4.
48. Miccoli, 2012, 165.
49. Oppenheim, 2003, 410-2.
50. Barda, 2006, 114.
51. Saleh, 2016, 982.
52. Miccoli, 2015, 1.
53. Ibid., 43.
54. Abdulhaq, 2016, 87.
55. Krämer, 1989, 19.
56. Miccoli, 2016, 4.

57. Miccoli, 2015, 102.
58. Not an entirely accurate name, as while the banks was national in function it was not state-owned, as the name might suggest. Deeb, 1976, 70.
59. Oppenheim, 2003, 420.
60. Miccoli, 2015, 22.
61. Landau, 1969, 73-4.
62. Miccoli, 2016, 4.
63. Oppenheim, 2003, 417.
64. Landau, 1969, 12.
65. Miccoli, 2015, 23.
66. Ibid., 32.
67. Sezgin, 2005, 227.
68. Ibid., 226-7.
69. Miccoli, 2015, 26; 23.
70. Ibid., 2015, 40.
71. Ibid., 2015, 27.
72. Landau, 1969, 71.
73. Miccoli, 2015, 143.
74. Tignor, 1980, 427.
75. Halamish, 2008, 120.
76. Shenhav, 2006, 26.
77. Miccoli, 2015, 30.
78. Landau, 1969, 96.
79. Ibid., 108.
80. Miccoli, 2015, 35.
81. Ibid., 39.
82. Ibid., 29.
83. Landau, 1973, 99.
84. Miccoli, 2015, 20.
85. Landau, 1974, 100.
86. Miccoli, 2011, 154.
87. Miccoli, 2015, 55.
88. Bulletin All. Isr. 1881, pp. 64-69; 1892, pp. 28-29.
89. Miccoli, 2015, 55.
90. Landau, 1969, 182-3; 198-200; 215-7.
91. Miccoli, 2015, 110.
92. Lagnado, 2007, 24.

3

An Egyptian Jewish Family in the Early Twentieth Century

In 1908, stirrings of modern Egyptian nationalism were expressed by journalists and others based in Cairo, along with the idea that Arab and Jewish nationalism were naturally fundamentally opposed, and that therefore a Jew could never be a true citizen of an Arab nation.[1] Also in 1908, Egypt's first university opened, initially as a private institution, in Cairo.[2] At this time, many Egyptians were frustrated about the way Britain had administered the country under its colonial regime; for example, education had remained relatively undeveloped, with education typically only available to those elites that the British authorities felt could be useful in positions in the administration and in bureaucracy.[3] Prior to the establishment of universities in Egypt, only the most privileged – frequently of European origins, including the members of some wealthy Jewish families – obtained third level education, generally in France, Britain, or Italy.[4] Only in retrospect is it obvious how important these early stirrings of nationalism would grow to be.

In 1914, Britain declared Egypt a protectorate, to protect the important and strategic Suez Canal. The war impacted significantly on Egypt, and on the Jewish community no less than any other. Many Jewish schools were closed for periods during the war, and fund-raising for French soldiers and Jewish prisoners of war was carried out within the community.[5] Egypt became intensely aware of its over-reliance on the cotton crop, and of the need for diversity; the war caused problems with both exports and imports that highlighted the essential vulnerability of the Egyptian economy, and the need for skilled business people (among whom the foreign population was well-represented) to improve things.[6]

The First World War had very little impact on my family, as far as I know; my father never mentioned it to me at all, and my mother discussed her memories of it with me only occasionally, and then only in the context of remembering the songs that, as a child, she heard the British soldiers in Cairo singing when the war had been won. *It's a Long Way to Tipperary* is the song that she could remember, and she sang it to me often: *It's a long way to Tipperary/It's a long way to go/It's a long way to Tipperary/To the sweetest girl I know.* That song came from the Irish battalions in the British army, and I can only imagine how homesick the boys and young men who sang it must have been by the time the war that had destroyed so many of their young comrades had come to an end. For my family, however, while I am sure that they were concerned about the war and relieved when the hostilities came to an end, by and large the period 1914-18 was simply business as usual and they just got on with their lives.

Of course, for many Jews, the First World War was far from business as usual, and in some cases their experiences intersected with Egyptian Jewish history. During the war period, over 11,000 Ashkenazi Jews expelled from Palestine, most of whom were Russian nationals, arrived in Cairo. Initially, they were housed in refugee camps, having been forced to come without any more than the clothes on their backs. Their situation was miserable; they had no clothing, shoes, or bedding. The Jewish community rallied around to help them to open small businesses to support themselves and to provide care for the young women among them, who were particularly vulnerable to exploitation.[7]

Many of these refugees had been peremptorily ejected, rounded up on the streets and sent out of Palestine with no notice. 698 arrived in Alexandria on 18 December 1914, and over the next eleven months, over 11,277 were forcibly removed from Palestine. They were housed in refugee camps that never contained more than 5,000 people; others managed to secure accommodation in Egypt, or left Egypt for elsewhere. The most vulnerable and poorest (many of whom were highly educated professionals who had been reduced to poverty) remained. They had shocking stories to tell about how they had been treated by the authorities in Jaffa. The writings of one of them, David Yudelovitz, reports on their experiences:

> We boarded boats and went to the ship, to the deportees, and found them in the depth of grief and sorrow; parents cruelly separated from their children, men separated from their wives, children seized from their mothers. Some were even practically naked and barefoot. According to their stories, the authorities in Jaffa caught people in the street, sat them in boats and rowed them out to the ship. The exiles included property owners, merchants and artisans, rabbis, teachers and students, school principals, lawyers and doctors – all of them now poverty stricken.[8]

Charitable efforts, largely led by Jewish Egyptian women, raised funds and provisions to support the refugees.[9] With the support of the AIU, schools were established to provide the refugee children with an education,[10] waiving fees for the families in question, and in some cases even providing free public transport to and from school.[11] In the case of camps too far from schools, new schools were provided for refugee children, entirely funded by the Egyptian Jewish population. Many wealthy and influential members of the Egyptian Jewish community devoted considerable funds to supporting the refugees in a wide variety of ways. It should be noted that the Egyptian state authorities also treated the Jewish refugees responsibly and kindly, supporting them in exile, and charging the countries to which they belonged for their upkeep. The government issued the refugees with identity cards and assisted them with transferring money and housing. It provided direct help, and also facilitated and supported the local Jewish community in its own efforts to support the refugees.[12]

Unfortunately, some of the newspapers published at the time erroneously claimed that the refugees were not being sufficiently supported by Egyptian Jews, leading to complaints both from the majority and from the refugee populations. Some of the Ashkenazim from Palestine complained that the education offered to their children was excessively secular and liberal, and did not place sufficient emphasis on the concept of the Jews as the Chosen People,[13] which was central to Zionist thinking. As the Jews of Egypt and Sudan were a cosmopolitan, well-integrated element of society, to them it seemed perfectly clear that they needed a well-grounded secular education in order to participate fully in professional life.

Despite the support offered to the refugees by Egyptian Jews, the relationship between the two groups was not always very easy; many of the refugees were frustrated that not all of the Egyptian Jews seemed interested in Zionism, and in a journal published for the refugees, complaints were aired. For example, one column by a Yosef Aronowitz stated: 'For twenty years now [in Egypt] the Jewish community has been stagnating spiritually, the Tora[h] is being forgotten or perhaps has already been forgotten, and the imprint of the Jewish soul is fading.'[14]

Many of this cohort of Ashkenazim returned to Palestine after the war, but some remained in Egypt and became active members of the local Jewish community,[15] often offering lessons in Hebrew and introducing many of the Cairene Jews to Zionist thinking for the first time.[16] Several of them expressed disappointment in the fact that so few Egyptian Jews were involved in the Zionist project, feeling that they simply did not understand the motivation behind the campaign to establish a Jewish state in Palestine, and accusing them of spiritual stagnation and of being excessively open to Arab cultural influences.[17]

The reality was that, at this point, most Egyptian Jews were happy in Egypt and there was nothing to suggest that anything was going to change for them there. Certainly, few of them would have seriously entertained the notion that one day they themselves, or their children and grandchildren, might also suffer the terrors and indignities of becoming refugees. I know that my family had no doubt, at that time, that their future lay in Egypt, and that it would offer them all the opportunities that they dreamed of, for themselves and for their children.

Shortly after the First World War, in 1919, the Egyptians protested about their situation and were given nominal independence, while Britain retained control of communications, defence, the protection of minorities (obviously including the Jews, most of whom were technically foreign nationals) and supervision over the territory of Sudan, which had technically been part of Egypt since it was conquered in 1821,[18] and which was home to a small but vibrant Jewish community that was effectively indistinguishable from the Egyptian Jews, as many people travelled freely between Sudan and Egypt, and the Jewish community in both areas was considered to be one and the same. Sudan's first synagogue was built in 1926. The people who attended it – many of them members of my extended family – were, in the main, devoted to their Jewish tradition and heritage, but not deeply religious.

Much of Europe had become intensely nationalist in the course of the nineteenth century. The Arab countries, however, did not develop a similar sense of nationalism until the early twentieth century. In the case of Egypt, this may have been partly because of the chronic neglect of higher education under the British regime, which feared that educational reform and greater availability of education would lead to the growth of a nationalist, anti-British elite.[19]

Ironically, in light of what would happen later, many consider Egyptian nationalism to have grown considerably as a result of the efforts of the Jewish Egyptian Yacub Sanua, who was also known as Abu Naddara. Sanua made significant contributions to Egyptian culture in the areas of literature and journalism, and he also introduced and popularised the use of vernacular Arabic in the theatre, particularly in the field of satire.[20]

As Egyptian nationalism became more pronounced, Jews reacted in various ways; on the one hand, by expressing a strong sense of belonging to the Egyptian nation, while on the other increasingly opting for a Eurocentric Jewish education for their children. Most of them, including my family, had little to no interest in politics and simply allowed it to happen around them without particularly engaging with it. Even my father, who was somewhat interested in politics, was so purely in the intellectual sense, and never showed any interest in participating in any way.

In 1917, the Zionist project took a huge leap forward with the Balfour Declaration, which had initiated as a letter from AJ Balfour to Lord Rothschild on 2 November. Balfour had been Prime Minister of England from 1902 to 1905, and at the time of the Declaration, he was serving as Foreign Secretary under Lloyd George. At this point in history, most Jews in Arab countries understood the Balfour Declaration to be of primary interest to European Jews, and not to them. It is relevant here as the point at which non-Jews in Arab countries were first encouraged, at least implicitly, to start viewing their Jewish neighbours as fundamentally 'other' and essentially foreign. In retrospect, we can see these responses to the Declaration as a major stepping-stone towards the rampant animosity targeted at Jews in Arab lands that would emerge a generation later.[21]

For obvious reasons, Jews everywhere were intrigued by the Balfour Declaration, and none less than the Jews of Egypt and Sudan - even if they could not yet understand how it would eventually impact on them. My father was fascinated by the Declaration, which was made when he was a young man in his teens. Twenty years later, when I was a little boy, he spoke of it often, to me and my siblings, and related all that he knew about Balfour and about Chaim Weizmann, a Jewish scientist whose research into making acetone had been vital to the British war effort (acetone was used to make cordite explosives). Weizmann's work had helped the British and their allies to win the First World War, and it had also given him access to senior members of the British government, to whom he spoke about his dream of a safe homeland for the Jews. Thanks to him, Zionism - which had been a fairly niche idea and interest until now - entered the mainstream of European political debate and thinking.

After the First World War, the contents of the Balfour Declaration consolidated interest among Jewish communities in a Jewish homeland, to be located in Palestine. In 1922, Winston Churchill issued a White Paper stating that Jewish immigration to Palestine would continue until there was a Jewish majority in the region,[22] but that it would be capped at 75,000 over the next five years, after which there would be no Jewish immigration without Arab permission.[23]

Despite the success enjoyed by many of the Jews of Egypt, there were still Egyptian Jews who lived in desperate poverty. A Jewish journalist, visiting Cairo, described the Jewish Quarter, the Haret al-Yahud, where the poorest Jews lived, as follows:

> Our people are crowded and clustered into houses about to collapse, in dark cellars, narrow alleys and crooked lanes choked with mud and stinking refuse, earning their meagre living in dark shops and suffocating workshops, toiling back to back, sun-scorched and sleepless. Their hard struggle for existence both inside and outside the home is rewarded by a few beans and black bread.[24]

Conversely, Jews from more recently established Sephardic, North African, and other immigrant communities tended to be wealthier, more educated, and more culturally different to the Arab majority. Like many of the immigrants to Egypt at this time, they were determined to work hard and flourish in a place that was seen as a land of opportunity. In the first decades of the twentieth century, many enterprising Jewish immigrants and their descendants from places including Italy, Corfu, southern Europe generally, and various locations in the Ottoman Empire,[25] who had arrived with very little, were succeeding in a range of areas; by around 1917, about 20 per cent of the population of Alexandria and Cairo was non-Muslim, including many Jews and their descendants.[26] Many Jews at this time were involved in business, while others worked as lawyers, doctors, and engineers,[27] and participated fully in Egyptian intellectual, creative, and artistic life. For example, Yvonne Smouha Anaf's family, originally from Baghdad, were Alexandrian Jews who enjoyed living in the cosmopolitan city, where she describes business as being dominated by Europeans, including French, British, and Swiss, most of whom spoke French among themselves.[28]

The international nature of the Jewish community at this time also meant that many languages were spoken, granting access to a wide world of business, while the many opportunities Egypt offered encouraged some Jews to identify strongly with Egypt and with the cause of Egyptian nationalism, and to participate in government alongside their Muslim and other counterparts.[29] Indigenous Jews, who were often poorer, with fewer funds and less social capital than more recent arrivals, tended now to adopt some of the behaviours and norms of Jews arriving from Europe, increasingly shaving off their beards, wearing clothing and jewellery that indicated a comfortable social status, and burying their dead in coffins rather than simply in shrouds.[30]

The situation looked good for Egyptian Jews in the 1920s, and those who worked in literary and scholarly areas were keen to focus on the various links between the Jewish people and Egypt at all stages of its political and cultural history.[31] In 1920, Bank Misr was founded by prominent Jews, including the Circurels and Cattaouis, with a view to helping Egypt to wean itself off dependence on foreign capital.[32] In 1922, Egypt was granted independence, and in 1923, a new Egyptian Constitution was promulgated,[33] granting the Egyptian monarch, King Fu'ad, vast powers and granting equal rights to all Egyptians, regardless of race, language, or religion.[34] From what I have heard, nobody on either side of my family took much interest in independence, which had little to no impact on them. They were entirely occupied with their daily lives and with attending to business, and had no reason to think, at this point, that anything would change for them. They had never had any trouble with the British authorities, and nor did they anticipate having any trouble with the Egyptian ones.

King Fu'ad and his wife, Queen Nazli, were of Turkish origin; a reminder of the Turkish dominance of the Ottoman Empire that had preceded them. They were extremely popular among the Jews. In those days, they did not have all the gossip and celebrity magazines that we have now, but a lot of people had formal photographs of them, in all their finery, hanging on their walls. Sometimes, when the subject of the monarchy came up, Mum would sing the Egyptian national anthem. The anthem used some of the music from Verdi's opera *Aida,* which had premiered in Cairo in 1871, and related a love story set in ancient Egypt.

A number of influential Jews were represented at this time in various institutions of parliament. It must have seemed to the Egyptian Jews that they were living in a golden age – and to a great extent, they were. Many of them lived comfortable, happy lives, and it was easy to overlook the undercurrent of antisemitism that still rippled along beneath the surface of everyday life. While it did not trouble them frequently, even now there were occasional moments when the Egyptian Jews were reminded that the old prejudices against them had not entirely disappeared.

In Alexandria, in 1925, a local Jesuit teacher accused the Jews of abducting Christian children for their blood; the Jewish community requested his removal from the school (which was also attended by Jewish children, as so many Jewish families had a preference for a European-style education), which eventually took place.[35] This particular situation was resolved, but in retrospect it hinted at the potential for trouble later on. My own family seems to have been completely unaffected by any problems of this sort, however, from either the Muslim majority or any of the minority groups – certainly, my father never so much as mentioned antisemitism until much later.

The establishment of the Muslim Brotherhood by Hassan al-Banna in 1928 was not immediately identified by many Jews as a threat. The Muslim Brotherhood was founded in response to a rake of cultural shifts, including the emancipation of women and the Great Depression, and it sought to re-instate the caliphate, which Turkey had abolished four years earlier.[36]

At this point, my ancestors on both sides of my family were long-established in Egypt and Sudan, and could be described as being modestly successful. They had small businesses with which they were able to provide for their families adequately. They certainly were not especially rich – their homes were quite simple, for example, being mostly apartments with no more than three or four bedrooms for what were often rather large families.

When my father, Joseph, reached manhood, his good education helped him to get a job at the bank, and he worked at the Imperial Bank in Khartoum, which I think later on became Barclays, or was taken over by Barclays. Later, his knowledge of French meant that he could work for an international firm, and he was hired to work as a junior clerk for an Italian Jewish company called 'Giulio Padova and Company', which was a big wholesaler that imported tea and other consumables and had branches in Egypt and Sudan, and was quite a large employer at the time.[37] Dad also worked in what was known as 'general merchandise', buying and selling anything from bottles and glass to shoes and underwear. In this position, he worked for a time in Cairo, and from there moved back to Sudan, which was then considered effectively a province of Egypt and was administered by Egypt.

Dad met and married my mother Flora in 1922, just as Egypt became independent. Dad was twenty-one years old at the time of his marriage and Mum was fourteen; it might seem strange now to get married so young, but this was actually quite common at the time. My mother's family had also established a business in Sudan by now; her father was involved in the export of senna pods and henna for the European market.

After getting married, Dad opened a shop on the main street on Omdurman, where he sold thread made by Coats, a British manufacturer. The thread was specially made for doing embroidery. The locals loved a bright orange thread in particular, which they referred to as 'gold' and used to embroider elaborate designs on their clothing. This shop became very successful, as everyone flocked to it to purchase the threads they needed for their embroidery. Sudanese women wore flowing garments called 'toubs' and anyone who could afford it had garments thick with detailed embroidery. At one point, Dad's name was known all across Sudan, from north to south.

Quite quickly, my parents started to have children, and soon my mother was busy with her family. From what I can gather, the first few years of the marriage were tough on Mum, who had had unrealistic views about what it would be like. Dad loved her very deeply, but he was also a very traditional man who wanted to rule the roost and he was not always very demonstrative. He had been brought up in a culture that told him not to show his wife too much love in case he 'spoiled' her. In the very early years of their marriage they lived with Dad's parents, which was difficult, as his mother was a rather stern lady who liked to have everything done her way, and Mum was still a young girl and felt very intimidated. As soon as he could, Dad got them their own house to live in and, with some breathing space, things were easier. Thankfully, as help in the house was affordable, Mum had maids to help with her domestic tasks and with her growing family.

While their ancestors had come from outside the region, my family on both sides identified very strongly with their home in Egypt and Sudan. By this stage, everyone in my father's family had left Tanta, and none of our relatives remained there; all of my family on that side now lived in Cairo and Alexandria in Egypt, and in Khartoum in Sudan. My mother still had some relatives in Baghdad, and visited them once, but did not have much interest in her Iraqi origins, and the only thing she ever really talked about in this respect was a visit she made to her aged great-grandmother, then rumoured to be a hundred and twenty-seven years old, and said to have grown a whole new set of teeth after the original ones fell out. In general, Mum often boasted of her family's extraordinary longevity and said that many of her ancestors had lived to be over a hundred. However, as birth records were not kept in those days, there is no way to prove these boasts, and it may well be that the story of the female ancestor of such an astonishing age is a bit of an exaggeration – although I was assured that it was absolutely true.

In terms of their business interests, my mother's family were quite similar to my father and his family, but Dad's family seem to always have had a greater interest in formal education, and certainly Dad's standard of education was notably higher than that of his in-laws. Mum's family was also more conservative in terms of its views on the education of women and girls. Flora – Mum – had grown up in Cairo, in what was an exciting and stimulating environment – not just because of all the city had to offer, but also because of the particularly vibrant Jewish community, in which Jews from all over Europe, the Middle East, and North Africa came together, perfectly assimilated and freely mingling and marrying one another. For them, Egypt became a melting-pot, in which Jews from all different sorts of backgrounds formed a community characterised by friendship, sharing, and cooperation. Jewish people from Polish, Russian, Turkish, Moroccan, Egyptian, and other backgrounds shared synagogues, worked together, and joined one another's families. In the matter of just a generation, all were Egyptian Jews, generally speaking French as a common language, and thinking as one on many issues. Often, the only way to understand where a family had originally come from was to look at the surname, which frequently reflected the family's place of origin.

In those days, as before – and indeed as to the present day, in many cases – the matter of marriage was considered to be of interest not just to the young couple in question, but to their whole extended families. Consequently, parents and other family members took an active role in helping people to find their spouse. In religious families in particular, marriages were often arranged, either by families or by matchmakers who specialized in the art of bringing two people together in marriage; usually the matchmaker would approach the family in question when there was an interest in a young person to be someone's potential spouse. The first steps towards making a match often started in one of the famous coffee shops of Cairo. The matchmaker would reserve a table for the prospective young couple, who would meet there for coffee and pastries while the matchmaker maintained a discreet distance and watched their body language to see if they had a good rapport. Groppi's was a Cairo institution that must have seen many thousands of young couples brought together in this way. In general, the matchmakers did an excellent job and many very happy families were formed in this way. My father was not religious, but he had traditional views when it came to marriage and family, and he had been happy to allow his family to help him to select a suitable bride, with whom he could live and raise a family. The long, happy marriage that my parents had, despite passing through some very difficult times, shows that this approach to marriage often worked out very well.

In Egypt, there was a climate of burgeoning Egyptian nationalism and the growing view that only a certain type of person had the right to consider themselves Egyptian.[38] The Ottoman legal system, which had guaranteed certain rights to Jews and other minorities, came to an end following independence.[39] In retrospect, it is clear that the tide was beginning to turn against Jews and other minorities. However, it is also worth noting that, amid calls for Egyptians to shop at 'national stores' only (rather than stores owned by foreigners), the upmarket department store Cicurel's was on the list of approved businesses; Cicurel's was owned by a very wealthy Jewish family of Italian origin, who had roots in Cairo dating to the nineteenth century.[40] Clearly, the idea that to be Jewish meant that one could not also be Egyptian had not entirely taken root in official circles. Indeed, an influential Jewish family, the Cattaouis, were well-connected with the Egyptian royal family; Joseph Cattaoui, a prominent Cairo business man, was appointed senator in 1927, and his wife, Alice Saurès, who had also been born into an important Jewish Egyptian family, was first lady-in-waiting to Fu'ad's wife, Queen Nazli.[41] Joseph Cattaoui also had a profound interest in Egyptian history and wrote on the topic in Hebrew, French, and Arabic.[42] He was given the title of 'Pasha' and known as 'Joseph Cattaoui Pasha' because of all of his achievements.

The first two decades of Fu'ad's reign have been remembered as Egypt's 'liberal age'.[43] This was a time of great progress for the country's Jewish population:

> The traces they have left behind in Cairo and Alexandria - splendid synagogues, schools, hospitals, large department stores, and comfortable residences - attest to the affluence, strength, and vitality of the Jewish community in that period. In terms of their place in society, Egyptian Jews enjoyed a position that was among the best in the Muslim world.[44]

In November 1925, Joseph Cattaoui was one of the promoters of the Cairo-based Société d'Etudes Historiques Juives d'Egypte (Society for Historical Studies of the Jews of Egypt), which published a bulletin and organized lectures on the theme.[45] Jewish Egyptians really were completely integrated into Egyptian life - and proud to be so!

Of their children already born to my parents at this point, the eldest was Albert. As the first child, and above all the first boy, from a very early age he was extremely aware of his important position in the family. As the other children came along, Albert liked to throw his weight around and impose his authority. To his frustration, his sisters and brothers did not take him very seriously. The next in the family was my older sister, Reina. She was a kind-hearted girl with striking good looks who took care of the younger ones as soon as she was old enough. After her came Leon, a lively boy who liked to throw himself into things. Then came Elie, a wonderful child. Next was Zaki, the closest boy in age to me.

Dad spent three or four months a year in Egypt the whole time he and Mum were based in Sudan. By now, the family had a full-time maid, Mastoura, who was part of the household and helped to bring up the children. Dad had bought Mastoura, who was a slave, freed her from slavery, and made her a paid member of the household; this was the norm in Sudan at the time. Mastoura still wore proof of her former status as a slave in the form of an earring that she could not remove, as it had been soldered closed. Mastoura was still with my family when I was a little boy, and I remember her fondly. She was a kind and generous person who was very loving with all the children. As well as Mastoura, Mum and Dad had a black Sudanese servant, Ahmet, who was a cook and also helped with the childcare. Ahmet was a wonderful person and a faithful Muslim; his religious views and obligations were always respected, and he was considered an integral part of the family.

Both my parents felt strongly that all of their children should have a good education, the girls as well as the boys. Their views were consistent with those of most of their peers, and my sisters' generation of girls all went to school and were at least as well-educated as their brothers. I often felt that it was a great shame that my mother had not been given more educational opportunities, as she had a remarkable mind and a photographic memory, and sometimes grew irritated when other people were not as bright and astute as she was. While she was a wonderful wife and mother, and in general happy with her life, she was sometimes frustrated by not being able to achieve all that she could have done with more formal education, and she was glad that her daughters would have more opportunities.

The broad-minded outlook held by the Egyptian Jews at this time is typified in the fact that they made very pragmatic decisions about education. Most Jews could see that the best education available in Egypt at this time was offered by various Christian orders of nuns and priests. Therefore, rather than insisting that their children be educated within the Jewish community, they were happy to send them to high-quality European schools with a Christian ethos when this was the best option locally available, where they would be well-prepared to take their place among the next generation of businessmen. In fact, some Jews from outside Egypt actually travelled there at least partly because they knew that their children could receive a high-quality education there that would prepare them to take their place in the world. This was the case for the family of Vivette Ancona, whose parents settled in Egypt between the wars largely to ensure that their family could access good schools.[46]

While embracing and supporting their Ashkenazi peers, many Egyptian Jews were also actively interested in integrating more with Arabic culture at this time; in 1917, a popular Sephardi prayer book, the *Siddur Farhi*, had been published in Arabic,[47] and, as evidenced by vintage photographs from the period between the wars, some Jewish men wore the tarboosh (also known as 'fez'), a tall hat traditionally worn by Muslim men from the region since the days of the Ottoman Empire.[48]

Actually, the question of attire in Egypt is a very interesting one. All sorts of factors lay behind people's decisions in terms of how to dress, with issues such as social class, religion, and cultural identity all playing a role. Jewish men did not routinely wear the tarboosh or fez. Therefore, when a Jewish man did decide to wear one, he was making an extremely strong statement about his identity: not just Jewish, but also Egyptian. By wearing this distinctive hat, they were indicating to everyone who saw them that they were very much part of the society in which they lived. Jewish women wore European styles – and if they could afford it, were up to date with the latest Parisian fashions.

Another indication of Jewish integration is found in the fact that they shared many of the customs and taboos common not only to Egypt but also to the broader Mediterranean region, such as a healthy respect for the evil eye and the dangers it represented. Lavish compliments were seen as tempting fate, and were to be avoided. I would say that superstitions and traditions of this sort were widespread among the Jewish community, but perhaps less deep-rooted than in some other sectors of Egyptian society, insofar as everyone was aware of them and paid lip-service to them, but at the same time did not allow these ideas to rule their lives. Among some sectors of Arab society, in contrast, the evil eye was taken very seriously, and some people were reluctant to leave the house without an amulet, in the form of a special blue bead, that was supposed to keep them safe against it.

Throughout the 1920s, drawn by the opportunities Egypt offered, and, no doubt, by the generally positive experience of being Jewish in Egypt, there was an influx of Sephardis from Salonika and Turkey, adding to the already diverse Jewish community.[49] By now, there were more than 200,000 foreigners living in Egypt, and the Jews were part of a vibrant multi-cultural society that was stimulating and outward-looking. Of course, there had been Jews in Egypt since remote antiquity, but their numbers grew dramatically during this period, with the influx of Jews from a variety of cultural and linguistic backgrounds.[50] At this stage, the indigenous Jews of Egypt had become a small minority among Jews. Most them belonged to the lower socio-economic classes, and typically were engaged in trade on a small scale, in the production of handicrafts, or even begging, and were often culturally almost indistinguishable from Arab Egyptians in terms of their lifestyle, language, and customs.[51]

Many Jews were officially stateless, and many others, like my family, were entitled to foreign passports. My father held an Italian passport, for example. This meant that he, like any other resident in Egypt with a foreign passport, had certain rights and was subject to particular laws that applied to foreigners and not to Egyptian citizens. This meant that, if he had been in trouble with the law, my father would have been tried by an international, rather than national, court. At this point, few people had started to guess the implications for the many Egyptian Jews who did not hold Egyptian citizenship or passports. After all, while the economic situation was one that offered many opportunities, and while quite a few Jews were excelling in a range of fields, most were busy with the every-day concerns of running their shops or small businesses, and caring for their families. The higher levels of business, including the finance and retail sectors, were dominated by non-Muslims, including both Jews and Europeans from a variety of linguistic and cultural backgrounds.[52] The importance of Jews in these sectors is made clear by the fact that the Stock Exchange of Egypt, as well as a large number of Jewish-owned businesses and department stores, remained closed during all major Jewish festivals.[53]

As well as holding a very prominent role in business, Jews were highly influential in the cultural sector. The Egyptian film industry was closely aligned with the Jewish minority. In 1915, for example, Joseph Mosseri founded the Josy Films Agency, which established and ran a number of cinemas all over Egypt. From 1929, he also started to import foreign films, and from 1932, his studio made films in Arabic for the viewing pleasure of the general population. Several important film directors and actors were also Jewish.[54]

As the twentieth century advanced, so too did modern medicine, and with a growing Jewish population came the view that there should be medical institutions built and administered along European lines. In 1925, the Jewish Hôpital Israélite was founded and was opened after a religious ceremony involving the Chief Rabbi of Cairo, Haim Nahum. The opening ceremony was attended by a large number of influential Jews, who had contributed generously towards the fund necessary to pay for a modern, well-equipped hospital, and also by King Fu'ad. It should be noted that, despite the Jewish founders, and the Jewish ethos of the hospital, it had not been founded to cater exclusively to the health care of Egyptian Jews; rather, the hospital was open to all members of Egyptian society, with ninety of a total of a hundred and sixty beds specifically reserved to treat the poor of all religious and cultural backgrounds.[55]

Having invested greatly in education, Jews' educational standards by this stage were, on average, considerably higher than those of the majority population,[56] and a number of Jewish families, including the Cattaouis, the Saurès and the Cicurels, were now considered to be among the Egyptian elite.[57] Wealthy and upper middle-class Jews tended to have interests that were strongly aligned with European trends, such as attending the opera and membership of a range of prestigious social clubs.[58] Younger people were members of clubs for the Jewish youth, which organized outings and provided a wholesome environment within which they could mingle.

Clearly, while moving in such cosmopolitan circles offered many opportunities, it also posed some challenges. Occasionally at this time, vulnerable young people were targeted by missionaries or others who sought to convert them to Christianity or Islam. Indeed, in 2006, there were still a few people with personal memories of having been subjected to extensive efforts to convert them, and even of having converted, to Christianity (generally temporarily) so as to gain access to education. In one case reported by Barda, a man converted at school, and returned to Judaism in his twenties for the purpose of getting married.[59]

My own family, fortunately, had no experience of any efforts to convert its members, and never experienced this as a cause for concern. In all of our interactions with Christians and Muslims, whether at school, at work, or in other ways, we never felt anything but respected. My parents were also very careful to extend the same respect to anyone they had anything to do with.

The Egyptian constitution granted all Egyptians equal rights, and the citizenship laws of 1926 and 1929 guaranteed all state citizens equal rights before the law, regardless of the religion they followed.[60] In practice, many Jews played prominent roles in Egyptian society; Yusul Cicurel, a member of the prominent Jewish family that owned Cicurel's department store, was a member of the Cairo Chamber of Commerce, while his younger brother, Salvator, captained Egypt's Olympic fencing team in 1928, proudly representing his country[61] at a time when the Egyptian authorities were increasingly inclined to view sport as a forum for the expression of a positive sense of nationalism and cultural pride.[62] Salvator Cicurel's position on the Egyptian Olympic team was rightly hailed as a great milestone, and people talked about it very proudly for years afterwards. Two decades later, or more, Salvator Cicurel was a member of the Hakoah club, as was I; the Hakoah club was an extremely highly-regarded sports club that trained young athletes for the Olympics, and also provided sports facilities to those who were less ambitious. All those years later, I can remember that people were still discussing Salvator's performance as a tremendous event that had reflected well on the Egyptian Jews and their place in society.

While many Egyptian Jews had a great deal to be happy about in the late 1920s and early 1930s, a series of events in Palestine gave some of them pause for thought. As a child, I often heard my father speak about the Arab riots in Palestine that led to a terrible massacre of Jews who were living there. The local Muslim population was angry with the Jews over issues relating to access to the Western Wall of Jerusalem. Some of them responded by attacking Jews and destroying their property. The situation escalated until serious riots broke out in August 1929, when 133 Jews were killed and many others injured; it became known as the Hebron Massacre. The British authorities countered, and there were similar levels of fatalities and injuries among the rioters. The subsequent commission into the events established that they were the first result of Arab hostility towards the Jews, and Arab anger at the prospect that more Jews might settle in the area. As you can imagine, this terrible episode was widely covered in the media, and the Egyptian Jews read all about it with great anxiety and alarm. Later on, Dad would remember this period as a sort of awakening, when he realized that the life he enjoyed in Egypt and Sudan was not necessarily as safe and secure as he had always assumed. If Jews in Palestine, which was so close to Egypt, could be attacked in this way, then how could the Egyptian Jews ever be sure that the same sort of thing could not happen to them? Dad would remind us that, if it came down to it, the Jews would have to remember that they were vulnerable and that they needed to watch out for themselves and their families. Dad had already had a degree of interest in Zionism, but I think that these events cemented his fascination with the topic.

Zionism remained a relatively obscure interest among Egyptian Jews, but it did grow somewhat during these years, particularly perhaps among people who also had an interest in communism, which was not considered to be incompatible with it, as many wanted to found a Jewish homeland that was not just a safe haven for the Jews, but also a socialist paradise in which equality would reign. Of course, communism was more popular among Egyptian Jews who were not wealthy, and therefore were not concerned by the prospect of losing their hard-earned money. Dad was always strongly anti-communist, and identified communism as a terrible threat that should not be allowed to flourish.

In 1929, the same year as the Hebron Massacre, Egypt passed the Nationality Law.[63] At the time, it was not readily apparent at first glance that this would be of great consequence to Egyptian Jews. Mum and Dad were living in Sudan at the time, and as they had never had any issues with their national status, it did not seem very important to them. However, over the decades that followed, this law would come to be used to exclude Jews (and other minorities) from the corridors of power and, ultimately, from Egypt. The law defined as Egyptians all those who had been subjects of the Ottoman Empire, and who were habitually resident in Egypt in 1914 and had also maintained their residence in Egypt until 1929, and the passing of the new law. The law did not provide for the expulsion from Egypt of those who did not hold Egyptian national status, but rather left this decision up to the Minister of the Interior. As well as describing a number of ways in which one might acquire Egyptian national status, the law referred to the issue of 'race' and to matters of religion. This would prove to be extremely problematic for Egyptian Jews. Under the law, for example, a child born to a foreign father resident in Egypt could claim Egyptian nationality if the father belonged to an Islamic nation or culture (even if they themselves were not practising Muslims). With the exception of those Jews who belonged to families that had been present in Egypt for many centuries, this rule largely excluded Jews descended from more recent arrivals from claiming national status. Furthermore, by introducing the notion of 'race' (a term that everyone thinks they understand but that can never be precisely defined in scientific terms), it made Jews more vulnerable to being understand as permanently 'other' to Arab Egyptians; people who would always be seen as foreigners, no matter their devotion and contribution to Egypt.[64] To make matters more complex, many Jews, particularly more affluent Jews, continued to hold citizenship status for a range of European nations. This tendency was especially marked among the most prominent families, who were leaders in business, in finance, and in their communities. For example, the Saurès and Mosseri families were Italian subjects, and the Cattaouis and Menasces were Austro-Hungarian subjects.[65]

Over the course of the next two decades, it would become progressively clearer that my father was right to be anxious about the potential fate of the Egyptian Jews. Without national status, and with Egyptian nationalism growing steadily through this period, they were more vulnerable than most of them realized at the time.

Under these circumstances, one might wonder why so few Jews held Egyptian citizenship, given that they were so thoroughly at home in Egypt and generally considered themselves to be Egyptians. In fact, there were very good reasons for Jews to wish to hold foreign passports. Holding foreign national status was to the advantage of all non-Muslims, as it granted them a degree of protection from a foreign power. Britain tended to grant passports only to wealthy and influential Egyptian Jews, who offered diplomatic and other services in return. French and Italian passports were easier to obtain, and many Egyptian Jews did so. Frequently, passports were obtained by means of a connection not with the 'motherland' in question, but with one of its territories – for example, Egyptian Jews might be granted the right to hold a French passport if they had a close family connection with Algeria, which was then part of the French Empire, while British passports were sometimes granted to people with connections with territories such as Gibraltar or Malta. At the time of the passing of the Nationality Law, many Jews – descended from people who had arrived in Egypt between 1848 and 1914 – were entitled to Egyptian citizenship. Certain members of the Jewish community could see that it would be to their advantage to become Egyptian citizens, and some of them – including the Chief Rabbi in Egypt at the time, Haim Nahum Effendi – called for more Jews to apply. However, as they had no way of knowing that Egyptian nationalism would shortly wreak havoc on their community, many of them did not claim it, and would become very vulnerable to the growth of nationalism (and the parallel growth in antisemitism) in the years to come. The substantial fee involved in the application process would also have been a deterrent for poorer Jews who might otherwise have sought to become citizens. Despite the fact that many Jews were successful in business and enjoyed a high quality of life, a quarter of all the Jews in Egypt at this time were still illiterate and poor, and even though their families had, in some cases, been living in Egypt for many centuries, they lacked documentary evidence of this.[66]

In 1929, however, few Jews realized how important the issue of citizenship and national status was to become with the passage of time. A United Nations report foresaw the inevitable difficulties that poorer Jews and other residents of Egypt who were increasingly not seen as suited for citizenship were likely to face in the future, and stated:

> Many of the persons concerned were simple people, or in some cases neglectful, and did not register their options within the rather short period allowed. In view of the large number of people who had not opted, further limited periods for opting were allowed in subsequent years. In spite of this, however, a considerable number of former Ottoman subjects, through neglect, ignorance or for other reasons, lost their opportunity of becoming Egyptian

nationals through option, and many of them are today still legally stateless.[67]

During the period between the wars, while there was considerable immigration into British-owned Palestine by European Jews, vanishingly few Jews from Arab countries immigrated to Palestine, while more Jews continued to arrive in Egypt. For one thing, most of the Egyptian Jews were ineligible to move to Palestine according to the laws of the time, because it was necessary for would-be immigrants to obtain a certificate that in turn depended on involvement in a Zionist organization,[68] which was rare in Arab countries, where there was still very little interest in Zionism. Those who had some awareness of it saw it as a potential solution to the difficulties facing Jews in Europe, but did not generally see it as relevant to their own lives and situations.

Despite changes to laws around nationality and citizenship, few Jews were truly aware of the growing threat to their presence in Egypt. In Egypt, there was little active involvement in Zionism save limited provision of funding from some members of the upper and middle classes for Jews who wished to move to Palestine.[69] In general, however, interest in moving to Israel was not high among Jews in Arab countries, much less Egyptian Jews. They had established themselves in Egypt, many of them were successful there and enjoyed positions of influence, and they had few incentives to leave their comfortable lives in Egypt to embrace an uncertain future in Palestine. One notable exception was Rabbi Prato, who felt strongly that Jews had a moral right to Palestine, and expounded this view to King Fu'ad, among others. Several prominent Jews threatened to resign from community organizations if he continued to do so.[70]

I was born in 1932 – obviously, blissfully unaware of the complications that were arising around me. My parents were living in Sudan at that time but, as was customary then, they came to Alexandria a few months before my mother was due to give birth, so that she would benefit from the superior healthcare available in Egypt. After a few months in Alexandria, Mum returned to Khartoum with me, and that was where I would spend the first few years of my life, at my mother's side, while my father travelled between Egypt and Sudan for work.

I was the youngest of the boys, and during my childhood I got along well with all of my siblings, although I sometimes felt a little suffocated by Zaki, who seemed to want to be with me the whole time, while I sometimes needed my space. I remember Zaki finding me frustrating at times because I did not always want to do what he said, and he liked to pull rank. Despite minor squabbles, however, because there were so many of us, we were company to one another, and kept each other entertained.

The last of my parents' children was Lily, my little sister. Lily was a beautiful child, and she would grow up to be a beautiful woman (she even won a beauty pageant as a girl). As our parents were both from big families, we all had scores of cousins to play with, and I was very friendly with several of them.

By the mid-1930s, when I was a small child, none of the Egyptian and Sudanese Jews really identified with the 'old country' that their ancestors had come from, and apart from telling stories of their origins to their children, few of them had a great deal of interest in the matter. Why would they? Most of them had wonderful lives in Egypt and Sudan; many of them travelled frequently between the two places. The climate was lovely (if rather too hot in Sudan sometimes), the food was delicious and affordable, many of them could afford to pay for domestic staff in their homes, and there was a good standard of living generally, from the schools available for children to the economic prospects awaiting those children when they grew up and graduated from school. Even those families whose success was only relatively modest – such as mine – could generally afford pleasant, but simple homes with all the modern conveniences then available, and usually also some domestic help in the house. My mother, who had a large family to take care of, was certainly very grateful for all the help she could get.

By the late 1930s, when I was increasingly aware of my place in the family as the youngest son, I was often quite resentful about my role in the family, as my brothers – and to some extent my father as well – observed a chain of authority according to age and, as the youngest boy, I was therefore the least important and was expected to do what all the others said. Still, I have to say that life was good and I had a wonderful childhood.

Always without leaving the territory of Sudan and Egypt, most Jewish families could afford to have fantastic family holidays, taking the children to the beach in Alexandria, and treating them every day to ice cream sundaes and sherbets on the promenade. Like most Egyptian and Sudanese Jews, we took our holidays in Alexandria too. Even though Dad was not a high earner, and money could be tight at times, our family holiday was considered a sacred event that could never be done without, and in fact a large proportion of Dad's fairly modest income was spent on our holidays and we cut corners and economised for the rest of the year in order to pay for them. I have many happy memories of those holidays. Mum and Dad would rent an apartment in Alexandria for two months. Those sun-drenched weeks in Alexandria were a child's dream come true.

Alexandria had several beaches, each of which was set up to cater for a different demographic. There were beaches frequented by the Egyptian upper classes, such as Agami Beach, for example – now, nobody was ever actually excluded from any particular beach, but most people simply felt more comfortable and had a better time if they went to a beach where they were likely to see their friends. Stanley Bay and San Stefano were mainly frequented by the middle classes, and Cleopatra and Sidi Gaber beach were popular among the working classes. We mostly went to a beach known as Sporting Beach, where Dad rented a beach hut for us for the duration of the holiday. Mum and Dad could entertain their friends there. The beach had everything we needed for a fantastic holiday, with ice cream vendors, falafel stands – always the Egyptian falafel made from broad beans. Falafel was considered a 'poor man's food' at the time, as it was inexpensive and widely eaten by the working classes. I can still remember its salty deliciousness as we held the hot, deep-fried balls wrapped in paper and bit into them; for us, falafel was the equivalent of fish and chips for the British, and perhaps corn dogs for the Americans. We kids liked nothing better.

In the evenings, when the sun was going down and it was getting cooler, everyone changed their bathing suits for light summer clothes and went for a long walk along the promenade, sometimes stopping for a cool drink at one of the numerous cafés, most of them owned by Greeks, that lined the seafront to cater for the holiday-makers.

It was on one of these holidays that Mum first got me involved with a youth organization that would go on to play a very big role in my life as the years passed. When I was eight, on one of these long, languorous summers in Alexandria, she enrolled me in a local organization for Jewish children. It was rather like the boy scouts in many ways – we learned how to camp and cook over an open fire and we engaged in a range of outdoor activities. A major difference between this organization and the boy scouts that people might be familiar with today was the fact that the leaders also talked to us children about Palestine, which they usually referred to as the Holy Land, and how one day this place would be a home for the Jewish people.

Egyptian Jews were very aware of how much better their standard of living was than in many other countries across the Middle East and North Africa. Even when I was a child in the 1930s and 40s, one occasionally encountered travellers from Iraq with terrible scarring all over their faces. This was because they had suffered from a disease that was transmitted by drinking contaminated water. In Egypt – or at least in modern, urban Egypt – there had been no problems with contaminated water since the nineteenth century, as almost everyone had running water and sanitation in their homes, and the overall standard of hygiene was very high. Moreover, the general atmosphere was a very positive one.

While Egyptian and Sudanese Jews had ancestors from many different places, they had all merged to become one big community. In almost all cases, they were also perfectly integrated into Egyptian and Sudanese life, mingling freely with people from all sorts of backgrounds. As an example, in the areas where my family lived, most of the doctors were Syrians or Lebanese, and we were delighted to use their services. There was never any suggestion that we should try to seek out medical care from among our own community. In fact, when I was little in the early 1930s, doctors visited their patients' homes, even for rather mild ailments, and I remember doctors visiting us quite frequently. Some of them were almost like members of the family, and my parents spoke of them not just with respect but with affection.

As a small child, I was perfectly happy and at ease in my Egyptian and Sudanese life. As soon as I was old enough, I started my studies in a school run by Italian nuns, who provided such a good education that children from many different sorts of families – Christian, Jewish, and Muslim – were sent there. Many of those children would grow up to do very well in life, thanks to the solid educational foundation they received. I remember, as a small child, feeling utterly at ease moving between Jewish, Christian, and Arab Muslim environments. I had a strong sense of my Jewish identity, but it never stopped me from playing with children from different sorts of families. Up until the end of the 1930s, I had playmates from very diverse backgrounds: Greek Christians, native black Sudanese Muslims, and more. I picked up Greek from my little friends and was able to speak it quite well. My relationships with the other children, and indeed my relationships with any of the teachers I encountered, were always characterised by a great sense of mutual respect.

While Sudan offered my family, and many others, a good standard of living, in many ways, life was quite simple there. Even in the capital of Khartoum, the streets were still unpaved in the 1930s, and great billows of dust would rise up when a car drove past. For small children, Khartoum offered a safe and free environment in which to play. I feel that I was very lucky to have had such a wonderful early childhood.

I was also lucky to have all four of my grandparents still alive, and I had a relationship with each of them. Because the tradition among the Egyptian and Sudanese Jews was to marry young, big inter-generational families were common, and many children grew up knowing not just their grandparents, but even some of their great-grandparents. In my family, the only one to die relatively young was my paternal grandfather, who was in his early sixties when he passed away. I was very fond of him; he had a charming and warm personality, and always spoke to me lovingly. His wife, my paternal grandmother, was a rather sterner figure. She had been brought up in the Victorian period, and even though many years had passed since then, she retained much of the outlook of that era. Her own appearance and behaviour were always impeccable, and she expected the same of everyone else, and expressed her displeasure when other people did not live up to her high standards. She had many admirable qualities, but we children were a little nervous of her because we were expected to maintain such a degree of discipline when we were with her and because her stern attitude sometimes came across as a lack of warmth. I was fond of my mother's parents, who were quiet and unassuming people. My grandfather was a very heavy smoker, and carried the scent of cigarettes with him everywhere. He seemed to have a cigarette hanging from his mouth almost all the time.

The sight, scent, and flavour of foods can be especially evocative when it comes to remembering childhood, and when I think about my own childhood, food often comes to mind. The produce available in Egypt and Sudan was wonderful, and we had a rich food culture in which housewives and cooks made wonderful meals from local ingredients, all the while observing Jewish dietary requirements and a range of culinary influences, because of the complex and rich cultural backgrounds of people in the Jewish community. We ate dishes made of beans and meat, cooked for hours in a clay oven. In preparation for the Sabbath, women prepared a delicious stew that simmered at a low heat for many hours overnight, and was consumed by their grateful families the following day. We loved molokhya, a bitter leaf with a texture a bit like okra, that was stewed or made into a soup with garlic, chicken, or lamb and various spices, and often served with rice. Preparing the leaves to be cooked was hard work that took a long time, and I remember my mother and other women starting the work of cutting the leaves in the morning so that they could use them to prepare the evening meal.

Looking back, I can clearly see how their shared belief system and culture gave Egyptian and Sudanese Jews a profound sense of community, in their daily life, as well as in formal and folk religious practices in locations such as synagogues and the shrine associated with Maimonides (around which the scruffy working-class Jewish neighbourhood of Haret al-Yahud was located).[71] These practices included saying special prayers there and, in the case of women suffering from infertility or issues relating to childbirth, spending the night in the shrine.[72] Lucette Lagnado recalls in her memoir being taken there as a small child when she was ill, to be anointed with oil and to spend the night together with her mother in the great man's tomb in the hope that she would be blessed with a miracle cure.[73] My own mother, Flora, had a difficult pregnancy with me, and she spent a night in the tomb before I was born to pray for a good outcome (which clearly worked). Egyptian Jew Jean Naggar, who now lives in the United States, has a similar story about his own grandmother:

> Elena and Nessim had a son, Joseph Nessim, my grandfather. When my grandfather, Joseph, was ten years old, legend has it that a holy man came to the door of his parents' house, and Elena offered him food and shelter. He told her that if she wanted more children she should sleep one night on a slab of the ancient Maimonides synagogue and should name her next son Eli, after him. Yes, this is legendary, but it is an indisputable fact that in the years that followed, great-grandmother Elena gave birth to ten more children, one a year.[74]

These stories and traditions were not just interesting in and of themselves; they also helped to provide us with a sense of connection with the remote Jewish past in Egypt that cemented our identity as proud Jews who were also proud Egyptians.

Of course, my memory of my very early childhood is not complete, but I do remember a feeling of great security and of complete embeddedness in my culture and its traditions, while knowing at the same time that I could and should feel free to play with children from all different sorts of backgrounds.

While my family was not deeply religious, of course the major Jewish festivals were important to them, as they were to all of the Jewish families that we knew. I remember in particular Yom Kippur, the fasting day, and the special Passover meal. For the event, we made sure that there was no bread in the home. We children were asked to carefully inspect our apartment home to make sure that there was absolutely no bread anywhere, and not even anything connected with bread, such as yeast. For the meal, my mother prepared matzos, special cookies, and other delicacies. The wheat that was used for the matzos was a special variety, isolated from and sold separately to the ordinary wheat that we usually used to make our bread. I have always found the Passover ceremony moving and impressive. As Passover usually fell around the same time as Easter, we were often celebrating at the same time as our Christian friends and neighbours and there was a generally festive atmosphere as everyone mingled and celebrated their respective feast days as well as observing the festivities at home.

Muslims, too, enjoyed the Passover season, even though they obviously did not participate. Local Muslim-owned grocery and other stories catered to the festival and enjoyed the positive atmosphere at this time. Jewish families typically had very friendly relationships with the Muslim owners of local greengrocers and other stores, and would ask them to set aside what they needed for the festivities. The store-owners were always warm and smiling, and offered greetings for the season. In those days, vendors generally addressed all and sundry as 'bey', which was a sign of friendship and respect. The term came from the original Turkish word 'bekh', which once meant only 'chieftain' but came to be used in Egypt as a general term of respect for males.

King Fu'ad died in April 1936; an event so important to the Egyptian Jews that I have a vague memory of it, even though I was still very small. Fu'ad had enjoyed a very positive relationship with the Jewish community, a fact evident not only in his lifetime, but at his funeral, in which a rabbi, Prato, participated.[75] Mum used to tell me that there was a period after Fu'ad's death when it was not clear who would replace him. There was a lot of anxiety among Egyptian Jews about what would happen next. Fu'ad was replaced by his decadent son, Far'uq, who was aged just sixteen at the time of his ascension to the throne.[76] As Far'uq was so young, it was not clear whether he would be a friend and supporter of the Jews, but people were hopeful that he would follow in his father's footsteps in that respect, as he had grown up in a very cosmopolitan society. The Egyptian royal family was of Turkish origins, and had mingled with all sorts of upper-class and influential people from diverse European and Middle Eastern backgrounds. At least at the start of his reign, Far'uq seemed to offer the stability that the Egyptian Jews hoped for.

In August of the same year, the Anglo-Egyptian Treaty of Alliance of August 1936 granted more independence to Egypt. From this period onwards, the Jewish experience in Egypt (and, to a lesser extent, Sudan) was played out against a backdrop of deteriorating relations between Jews and the Muslim majority population. A substantial portion of the student body in the universities of Egypt was attracted to nationalist, anti-foreigner (and by association, anti-Jewish) ideals.[77] Because of their deep-rooted links with foreign states, increasingly, the Jews were seen to epitomise 'foreignness' in general, and were progressively othered by both the government and forces operating at grassroots level. Political rallies and meetings increasingly became overtly antisemitic, and translations of antisemitic publications, such as Hitler's *Mein Kampf* and the *Protocols of the Elders of Zion* were distributed, while speakers delivered lectures that portrayed the Jews of Egypt as dangerous alien elements in Egypt who took advantage of the ordinary Egyptian people. Jewish organizations at this point tended to underestimate the threat represented by those who pushed this hateful rhetoric, and advised Egyptian Jews to keep a low profile and not to draw too much attention to themselves.[78]

It also became progressively more difficult for Egyptian Jews to formally acquire citizenship status in other countries; Britain rejected some applications on explicitly antisemitic grounds, and as Fascist ideology grew in Italy, obtaining Italian citizenship also became more difficult. (After Mussolini passed the Racial Laws in 1938, it would become impossible – and it also became increasingly clear that Italy simply was not a safe place for Jews.)

Considerable numbers of Egyptian Jews were able to claim French citizenship on the basis that they had ancestors or relatives who lived in Algeria, and were therefore entitled to it on the grounds of the French Crémieux decree of 1870, which granted French nationality to Algerian Jews.[79] Moreover, the process of obtaining foreign citizenship was much more difficult for Jews on lower incomes than for wealthier Jews, who faced discrimination on several grounds: because of their lower financial and (usually) educational status; because they were Middle Eastern; and because of antisemitism.

As a child in the 1930s and 40s, I was aware that some of the members of non-Jewish minorities could be antisemitic, but as their negative feelings were generally directed mostly towards wealthier families than mine, with extensive ownership of properties and businesses, it did not impact on me very directly, beyond adding to the general awareness that, as a Jew, I could not necessarily always assume that everyone would be welcoming and kind to me. With the passage of time, we would become increasingly concerned about antisemitism from the Arab majority, and Dad would continue to talk about the fears he had begun to experience following the Hebron Massacre of 1929.

As I continued to grow up, Egyptian nationalist sentiments were growing, and so was anti-Jewish feeling among the Muslim majority. The deteriorating situation for Egyptian Jews in the 1930s was due to a number of factors, including the rise of nationalism and of political Islam, the rise of Fascism in Europe and its influence on Egyptian political views, and the economic turmoil that was impacting on most of the world.[80] Antisemitic legends of European origin such as the blood-libel accusations that we have already discussed (in Egypt, originally springing most often from Greeks) now found fertile ground among ordinary Muslims and would become part of a more general arsenal of anti-Jewish propaganda as the years progressed.

King Far'uq, who was attracted by Fascist ideology, and who had a slender grasp on reality, dreamed grandiosely of becoming the undisputed leader of the entire Arab world,[81] and was prepared to do whatever it took to achieve his goals in the context of a society that was increasingly hostile to non-Muslims in general and to Jews in particular.

The Jewish community in Egypt was deeply concerned about the rise of Nazism and antisemitism in Europe and, from 1933, it had held a series of meetings to discuss how they should respond. The Cairo B'nai B'rith founded the League Against German Anti-Semitism[82] and decided to boycott German goods, but as their numbers were small relative to the population of Egypt overall, the impact of this boycott was negligible.[83] At this time, some Egyptian Jews became actively involved in the communist movement, in many cases more because they saw it as an important potential bulwark against Nazism, rather than because of a strong ideological attraction to its goals.[84]

The Egyptian government was not supportive of the Jewish community's efforts to facilitate the immigration of German Jews, fleeing the increasingly hostile political atmosphere of Germany as Europe marched inexorably towards war. At the same time, the German population of Egypt was involved in disseminating a campaign of anti-Jewish propaganda,[85] while in nearby Palestine, the situation was changing dramatically.

The Egyptian Jews' position within Egyptian society as a people closely associated with Europe has been identified as a factor that protected them in some ways, while making them vulnerable in others. On the one hand, many Jews held European citizenship and had extensive business and friendship connections with Europe and Europeans and could count on European support; on the other, many Egyptians could not accept the idea of Jews as also being Egyptians, in large part because of these associations – even in the case of those Jews whose ancestors had been living in Egypt since time immemorial.[86] In fact, while many Egyptian Jews held foreign citizenship because of their families' origins, a substantial proportion of indigenous Jews had also obtained foreign citizenship[87] – of countries such as France and Italy – and were therefore essentially protégés of those countries. The surge in an extremely aggressive and politicized form of nationalism in Egypt cast Jews as, by definition, non-nationals who could never experience a sense of affinity with the Arab state in which they lived.[88]

Between 1933 and 1936, 164,267 Jewish immigrants, mostly from European Ashkenazi backgrounds, arrived in Palestine, increasing between 1931 and 1935 from 18 to 29.9 per cent of the population.[89] While there was no immediate impact on the Egyptian Jews as a result of this migration, in general Arab interest in, and opposition to, the settlement of Palestine by Jews became more focused. The ongoing Jewish settlement of Palestine throughout the 1930s was also a source of consternation to many in the Arab world, and in 1937, the Pan-Arab Conference in Cairo pledged to oppose further expansion of the Jewish presence there.[90]

In response to the volatile political situation, young Egyptian Jews were increasingly politicized. A minority was interested in the growing Zionist movement, partly because of the influence of the Jewish soldiers in the Allied armies,[91] while others were intensely interested, and active, in communism.[92] Henri Cicurel, for example, the son of a prominent banker, founded the first Egyptian communist party. My parents were certainly aware of the growing interest in communism. I remember, even from when I was a child, that my father was concerned about what he could see happening politically around the world, and he briefly thought highly of Mussolini, whom he saw as a bulwark against communism. Once it became clear that Mussolini had thrown his lot in with Hitler and was an enemy of the Jews, of course he changed his mind.

Egyptian and Sudanese Jews responded in various ways to their growing anxiety about how they were seen by their majority counterparts. The 1936 Anglo Egyptian Treaty of Alliance, which limited the role of Britain in the area, and limited their presence largely to the exclusion zone around the Suez Canal,[93] was a major step towards full independence for Egypt, and nationalist views, which were inextricably linked with a politicised take on Islam, were becoming stronger.

There was growing resentment about the extensive foreign influence on Egyptian politics. Despite the fact that Egypt was more independent than before, Egyptian leaders and businessmen still had no option but to work in cooperation with foreigners and minorities in Egypt, including the Jews and the Copts. There was huge resentment about the domination of broad sectors of industry by businessmen from minority backgrounds, and about the fact that these businessmen tended to enjoy greater access to a range of financial and social resources.[94]

In 1936, the Arab Revolt in Palestine fostered anti-Jewish sentiment in Egypt, as elsewhere in the Arab world. By the late 1930s, extremist Egyptian nationalists and Islamists had begun to publish 'blacklists' of Jewish merchants.[95] In 1938, Young Egypt, which had originated in 1933 as an 'association', had become a militant political party, intensely populist, and influenced by Fascist movements abroad, notably in Germany; Young Egypt had even taken part in the Nuremburg rallies in 1936 when Young Egypt's vision was of an Egypt united by the common ties of religion, that would eject and reject all those who were different.[96] The same year, Cairo saw organized violence on university campuses; demonstrations by students who were angry about British power in Egypt had been occurring at intervals since 1935.[97] The students, who were already angry about poor facilities and employment prospects on graduation, were easy for political parties to manipulate.[98]

While these student riots were not always explicitly anti-Jewish, there must have been concern – given the broader political context – that they could easily become so. Indeed, at least some of the student protests featured demonstrators shouting 'Jews get out of Egypt and Palestine', sometimes along with demands that the Copts, too, should be expelled from Egypt.[99] Thankfully, these riots did not impinge on my family in any way, so far as I can remember, although I imagine that my father read about them in the paper and that they would have added to a general sense of growing anxiety about the direction in which the world was heading.

In this context, the Zionist movement in Egypt founded preparatory camps, known as hakhsharot, where, they envisioned, young Egyptian Jews could be trained prior to moving to Palestine. One camp was the Hehaloutz of Dessouk, a city a few kilometres from Alexandria, and another the Kiboutz Hakhsharah of Siouf, in the outskirts of Alexandria; both were located on lands owned by prominent Alexandrian Jews who were sympathetic to Zionism.[100]

Nonetheless, when the Jewish Agency visited Egypt in 1939 to explore the low levels of Zionism in the country, it reported that there was still little interest among Egyptian Jews in the Zionist project.[101] One of the reasons why so many Egyptian Jews were not, at this point, interested in Zionism was because the form it took at that time was deeply enmeshed in socialist, if not communist, principles. Zionist enthusiasts were promoting the idea of kibbutz collective living, which was portrayed as a sort of socialist Utopia. Young people were encouraged to embrace the idea of living in a very modest, self-effacing way, and of devoting themselves to collective effort. As the Egyptian Jews were, in general, a very business-minded people who combined a sense of pride in individual effort with a feeling of attachment to their community, the idea of collective living was not something that attracted them. My father was horrified by the idea of living in a kibbutz and firmly opposed to the very socialist ideals underpinning the Zionist project at this time.

By no means did all Egyptian Jews respond to growing levels of nationalism by becoming more sympathetic to Zionism. By the 1930s, growing numbers of Jews also felt strongly that the Jewish community should encourage the study of the Arabic language, to foster integration and acceptance, and from 1943, the annual reports of the Cairo Jewish Community Council were translated into Arabic.[102] Some Egyptian Jews felt deeply patriotic, and a number of leading intellectuals urged Egyptian Jews to 'strengthen their attachment to the Egyptian nation.' A society, Jam'iyyat al-Shubban al-Yahud, was founded for promoting this cause.[103] This growing interest in Arabic language and the Egyptian nation can also be attributed partly to growing fears among Jews that the burgeoning interest in nationalism was bound to start having negative repercussions for them.

The business community also did its part to attempt to quell growing nationalism by pointing out that, regardless of who the directors of a company were, all of its employees benefitted from its success. For example, in 1939, the well-regarded, and Jewish-owned, business journal *Égypte Industrielle* responded to nationalist attacks on the presence of foreign business men in Egypt on the part of both the media and the parliament by pointing out that entrepreneurs who invested so much in their business were 'one-hundred percent nationalized; the success of his enterprise, the safeguarding of his material and moral interest are tied to the prosperity, security, and progress of the country.'[104]

However, these attempts at assimilation were not enough to quell the growing tide of anti-Jewish sentiment – and soon ordinary Egyptian Jewish families were going to bear the brunt of it.

Notes

1. Sachar, 2006, 164.
2. Gorgas, 2013, 364.
3. Russell, 2001, 51.
4. Barda, 2006, 85.
5. Miccoli, 2015, 36.
6. Tignor, 1980, 420.
7. Landau, 1969, 69.

8. Govrin, 1987, 178.
9. Miccoli, 2015, 144.
10. Ibid., 34.
11. Govrin, 1987, 181.
12. Ibid., 188.
13. Ibid., 182.
14. Miccoli, 2015, 146.
15. Oppenheim, 2003, 413.
16. Landau, 1969, 70.
17. Govrin, 1987, 183-6.
18. Oppenheim, 2003, 411.
19. Gorgas, 2013, 364.
20. Landau, 1952, 15.
21. Snir, 2012, 177-9.
22. Gilbert, 2007, 34; 97.
23. Cohn-Sherbok, 1992, 149; 155.
24. Laudau, 1969, 31.
25. Oppenheim, 2003, 412.
26. Saleh, 2016, 988.
27. Krämer, 1989, 8.
28. Family history related by Yvonna Smouha Anaf, for the *Out of Egypt* celebratory booklet, printed 2019.
29. Oppenheim, 2003, 423-4.
30. Landau, 1969, 105; 109.
31. Miccoli, 2012, 166.
32. Oppenheim, 2003, 421.
33. Saleh, 2016, 984.
34. Shamir, 1987, 33.
35. Miccoli, 2014, 58.
36. Julius, 2018, location 2212 (Kindle edition).
37. Ran Oppenheim, 2003, 422.
38. Sachar, 2006, 195.
39. Miccoli, 2015, 124.
40. Beinin, 1998b, 331.
41. Miccoli, 2015, 103.
42. Behar and Benite, 2014, 46.
43. Miccoli, 2015, 2.
44. Shamir, 1987, 33.
45. Miccoli, 2012, 169.
46. Family history related by Vivette Ancona for the *Out of Egypt* celebratory booklet, printed 2019.
47. Miccoli, 2013, 199.
48. Ibid., 202.
49. Rubinstein et al, 2002, 104.
50. Krämer, 1989, 8.
51. Oppenheim, 2003, 413.
52. Saleh, 2016, 979.

53. Barda, 2006, 86.
54. Miccoli, 2015, 81.
55. Ibid., 108.
56. Krämer, 1989, 38.
57. Miccoli, 2013, 196.
58. Meital, 2017, 185.
59. Barda, 2006, 139.
60. Abdulhaq, 2016, 24.
61. Beinin, 1998b, 332.
62. Miccoli, 2015, 65.
63. Shamir, 1987, 46.
64. Ibid., 48-9.
65. Landau, 1969, 21.
66. Shamir, 1987, 52-4.
67. Ibid, 54-5.
68. Halamish, 2008, 122.
69. Miccoli, 2015, 122.
70. Ibid., 123.
71. Sion, 2015, 412.
72. Sezgin, 2005, 223.
73. Lagnado, 2006, 139.
74. Family history related by Jean Naggar for the *Out of Egypt* celebratory booklet, printed 2019.
75. Miccoli, 2015, 124.
76. Thornhill, 2010, 279.
77. Gorgas, 2013, 364.
78. Krämer, 1989, 147-9.
79. Krämer, 1983, 368.
80. Krämer, 1989, 116.
81. Gerges, 2018, 70.
82. Oppenheim, 2003, 424.
83. Krämer, 1989, 130-3.
84. Mayer, 1987, 201.
85. Oppenheim, 2003, 424.
86. Miccoli, 2015, 54.
87. Deeb, 1978, 11.
88. Shohat, 2003, 53.
89. Lemmi, 1983, 91.
90. Cohn-Sherbok, 1992, 155.
91. Oppenheim, 2003, 427.
92. Meital, 2017, 186.
93. Gerges, 2018, 54.
94. Saleh, 2016, 980.
95. Oppenheim, 2003, 425.
96. Gerges, 2018, 61.
97. Abdalla, 1985, 40.
98. Gorgas, 2013, 365.

99. Haag, 2004, 257.
100. Miccoli, 2015, 155.
101. Haag, 2004, 257.
102. Krämer, 1989, 28.
103. Shamir, 1987, 53.
104. Tignor, 1980, 439.

4

An Egyptian Jewish Family during the Second World War

I was only seven when the Second World War started, and did not realize at first its relevance to me and my family, but I do remember when it broke out, because of course all the older people in my life were worried and concerned. At first, however, it did not seem to impact on us too much. Actually, initially I mostly heard about it when I went to the movies. I loved going to the cinema. Every time I went, before the movie started, we were shown a short *Pathé* newsreel about whatever was going on in the world. While the news was often two weeks old by the time we heard about it, we were kept up to date with all that was happening. At first, I was quite annoyed by the newsreels, seeing them as a boring (or, sometimes, upsetting) interlude before the actual film started. However, as the adults around me became more concerned about the war, I started to pay the newsreels more attention. They told us what was happening in Europe, although the details of the horrors that were being unleashed by Hitler were still largely unknown. People knew that there were camps of some sort, and there were rumours of various kinds about them, but they did not understand what they were for, or what was going on in them. We still had no idea about the Nazi programme to exterminate the Jews of Europe.

By the outbreak of the Second World War in 1939, Egyptian and Sudanese Jews of all backgrounds and social classes were all keenly aware that the trend in the Egyptian government and among the majority population was increasingly towards rejecting the Jews as valid members of Egyptian society. At this point, the Egyptian government still grudgingly accepted the presence of Zionist organizations, but the political atmosphere was becoming increasingly anti-Zionist,[1] with Zionists (and by extension all Jews regardless of their political views) increasingly blamed for everything that was considered wrong and problematic in Egyptian society.[2] Arab countries were then engaged in attempting to eliminate support for the eventual founding of a Jewish state in America, which was seen as having considerable influence in this area.[3]

At different points in history, some Jewish families had felt strongly about their children marrying not only other Jews, but also Jews from the same cultural and linguistic background as them. By the 1940s, these feelings of inter-Jewish difference had largely dissipated, and most Egyptian and Sudanese Jews saw themselves as Jewish before all else,[4] and lived in a cultural, linguistic, and ethnic melting pot in which Jews from all sorts of backgrounds saw one another as peers. While they were very concerned about the possibility that Germany would win the war and take over Egypt, they did not feel that they had anything to fear from the Egyptian authorities.

Egypt's relationship with Britain was shaky, and the events of the war made the Egyptian Jews feel extremely vulnerable. The fact that so few of them had Egyptian nationality was now a more serious problem than before. Quite a few, like Dad, held Italian passports, which officially made them citizens of an enemy state, and left them vulnerable to being detained in a concentration camp for the duration of the war, as was happening to Italian citizens elsewhere, such as Britain. Anyone who had Italian nationality now tried to get rid of it as quickly as possible – but Jews could not get Egyptian nationality instead, making them very anxious about what would happen next. Some people were arrested, or fled ahead of getting into trouble. Vivette Ancona remembered how her father, after having been arrested and detained for a number of days, spent several months in a convent in Bethlehem, only returning to Egypt when it was safe for him, an Italian citizen, to do so.[5] Dad desperately wanted to get Egyptian nationality at this time, as he was concerned that our Italian connections would become deeply problematic, but because of the Nationality Law of 1929, this was now simply impossible.

Italy entered the war on the side of Germany in June 1940, and Dad's forebodings were fulfilled. Italy attempted to invade Egypt via the Libyan border, but did not make it very far, and the forces were quickly repelled by the British. There was a lot of scoffing about the ineffectual Italian forces and their general cowardice, and for a while, referring to someone as an 'Italian' was a way of saying that he was a coward. As a little boy, this was very upsetting for me, because I was used to being very proud of our family's Italian heritage. Dad repudiated his Italian nationality at the time, but still had to spend a few days in a camp enduring questioning because he had technically been an Italian citizen. In fact, all of the Italian nationals living in Sudan were gathered together in one of the local Catholic schools for questioning. While obviously this was an awkward situation for them all, none of them were mistreated in any way – in fact, they were all treated very well.

The Italian company that Dad had been working for in Sudan at the time, Giulio Padova and Company, was sequestrated. This meant that Dad was out of work, so he decided that we would move to Cairo, where there were many opportunities for anyone prepared to work hard. Because of the constant to and fro of Jewish families between Egypt and Sudan, we knew a lot of people in Cairo, and Dad was confident that he would be able to get a business up and running quite quickly. Dad was assured by the Sudanese authorities that this would be fine, and so we moved to Cairo and he set up a leather workshop there.

Aside from the changes brought by the war, I think that Dad was quite happy at the prospect of doing something new. Dad was a restless sort of a person, and liked to do different things (experimenting with the perfume industry, among others, along the way), so he was looking forward to a new career. Now my older brothers had started a leather importation business in the south Sudan, bringing in reptile skins and hides – mostly from crocodiles, lizards, and snakes – from Africa. This was an opportunity to branch out into a new field in Cairo, where there were many Jewish families working in all different sorts of business. Dad was advised that there was a big demand for well-made leather bags in Egypt, where fashion and style were considered important, and he decided that he would get into this area.

We lived in a fairly modest neighbourhood in the Cairo suburb of Heliopolis. Dad rented an apartment in a building with two storeys: a ground floor with a mechanic's workshop, and a first floor with two apartments. The mechanic, Ali – who was our landlord – and his wife, Fatima, lived in one of the apartments, and our family lived in the other.

We had had quite a lot of space in Khartoum, where real estate was inexpensive and most people could afford quite big homes and gardens, and now our apartment felt quite small for such a big family, even though my brothers Albert and Leon were now grown up and living autonomously in south Sudan. Like any sisters and brothers, we squabbled sometimes. Mum had her hands full keeping up with everything, and she no longer had the help of Mastoura, who had stayed in Sudan to take care of our house there; the house was otherwise empty, and it was Mastoura's job to keep it in good condition while we were away. Mum did, however, have help. There was a washer-woman who came once a week to do all the laundry (which was a very heavy job in the days before washing machines). Mum made a point of paying her well, as she knew how hard the work was and she was grateful that she did not have to do it herself. Ahmet, our servant, also moved to Egypt with us. Mum said that she was not prepared to move to Cairo unless Ahmet came too. This was a really wise decision on her part because Ahmet was not just a hard worker, but a much-loved member of the family. Ahmet was familiar with all of the quirks of each sibling's personality, and knew how to bring out the best in each of us. Ahmet never had a family of his own, and I think he felt as close to us as he would have felt to his own sons and daughters.

Before long, we were on excellent terms with our landlord, Ali. Because our apartments were so close, and we shared a landing, we bumped into one another often. Ali and his family were Muslims, but that made no difference to our relationship, which was excellent. During Ramadan, Ali and his family fasted all day and, in the evening, they ate sumptuous meals that Fatima had spent the whole day cooking. They often shared some of the delicious dishes with us, and I wondered how Fatima had managed to resist the temptation to sample them while she cooked. I can still remember the wonderful smell of Fatima's cooking every time I stepped onto our shared landing. She cooked wonderful dishes of rice with meat or chicken, flavoured with delicious sauces and herbs. Fatima loved to share. Sometimes, especially during Ramadan, a knock would come to the door and a plate of her food would be handed in for us to enjoy. When we celebrated our Jewish holidays, we did the same. The two families became very fond of one another.

As a young boy, I was very interested in Ali's work as a mechanic. His workshop was a very manly space that smelled delightfully of motor oil, and he was always working on at least one car. I liked to hang around and watch him work, and he always made me feel very welcome and explained what he was doing. Ali was often hired to repair vehicles that belonged to members of the British military. One of his clients was a certain General Ross, an English general whose car seemed to be forever breaking down and in need of repairs. I got to know General Ross too. I think he was quite entertained by the little Jewish boy who spent so much time in the mechanic's workshop, and he was always kind and smiling. He used to pinch my cheek and assure me that if I ever needed help, he was there.

Ali and Fatima were wonderful neighbours, and I have always remembered them with great fondness. The warm relationship we enjoyed with them was in no way unusual. In those days, the experience of the overwhelming majority of Jews living in Egypt was that they had excellent relationships with Muslim neighbours and friends, and rarely felt that they were viewed as anything but ordinary members of Egyptian society.

The buildings on our street were built rather close to one another; there was a narrow passage of just about two metres between our building and the next. To provide the apartments with light, and to ensure a cooling draft in those days before air conditioning, all the buildings had two lightwells or small inner courtyards. I enjoyed standing on the small balconies at the windows, from which I could see slices of life in our neighbours' homes, as we were all very close together. I remember curiously peering from our apartment into a neighbour's home when one of them had died. The deceased was laid out and the friends and relatives were paying their respects. I was fascinated because I had never seen a dead person before. Equally fascinating was a local couple with a very active sex life and a window through which I could clearly see from our apartment. I became a pre-adolescent peeping tom.

The balcony that looked directly onto the street also connected us with the world of local business. In those days, street vendors with a wide variety of produce and wares frequently walked up and down the streets, shouting about whatever they had to sell - succulent watermelon, delicious apricots, fresh vegetables, and all sorts of items for the household. Local home-owners got to know these vendors well, and everyone had their favourites. Rather than walking all the way downstairs to the street, we would all lower baskets carefully from our balconies for the produce, and then even more carefully pull them back up. The money to pay for the various items was sent down the same way.

One of the most well-known local storeowners was a very friendly man called Daabas. He had a shop that sold everything. As the war was on, every family was limited to rations. Housewives were given coupons every month that they could use when they went shopping to ensure that nobody was able to buy more than their allotted amount. All the local women queued outside Daabas's shop with their coupons to do their shopping. Mum was outraged at the idea of rations and coupons, and refused to let a coupon so much as enter the house.

'They are a form of begging!' she said. 'We are not going to use coupons to get our food. We have more dignity than that.'

I was ten years old at this time, and I was good at getting on with people and getting what I wanted, so I often used to do the grocery shopping for the whole family. Because I knew Daabas, he often let me skip the queue. I was usually able to get what we needed, which made us very lucky, as there were considerable shortages, and it was often very difficult to procure even the most basic foodstuffs, such as bread. I became very adept at bartering, and I also benefited a lot from my relationship with an English friend from school called Neil. Neil's dad worked with the Navy, Army, and Air Force Institutes, known as NAAFI, and was in charge of loading and unloading the provisions that were shipped over to the garrisons. He gave me John Player's cigarettes, chocolate, and other valued items, and with these I was able to procure enough food and basic household items to keep the family going, even with the rations. Daabas was generally happy to take the cigarettes for his own use. Sometimes I was also able to use them at the patisserie. Soon, I had quite an active little business. Neil's dad saw that I was streetwise, and we came to an arrangement whereby he pilfered food and other items from the British supplies and gave them to me to sell on the black market to the grocery stores that I knew. After giving him his cut, I was able to get food for the family, and even to put a small amount aside for myself in secret.

Even though I was good at finding the groceries that we needed, Mum often could not find all the ingredients she needed to make the dishes that she wanted to make, and we all had to learn how to compromise and tolerate food that we normally would have turned our noses up at, including sometimes having to flout the kosher rules, which we normally observed carefully. We ate a lot of rice and pasta with whatever sauces Mum was able to make from what was available, and often we had soup not just for lunch but as the main meal of the day. It got more and more difficult to get meat; the butcher was only allowed to sell meat twice a week. When we managed to find a chicken, Mum would cut it into many small pieces, and somehow make a meal for nine people out of it.

Reina was still living at home at this time, but she was engaged to be married and looking forward to starting adult life together with her fiancé, Nessim Gaon. At that time, Nessim - a cousin of ours who had grown up in Sudan - was a British army officer in a Cairo-based legion, and he had served some time in Italy during the British occupation. Reina had fallen for him straight away, because of his charm and good looks (everyone agreed that he was very handsome in his uniform), and they got engaged when she was eighteen. Nessim had felt the same way - Reina was a very beautiful young woman. While she was always kind and gentle, Reina may also have looked forward to having her own place, as Mum relied on her a great deal and she was kept very busy.

When Reina and Nessim got married, Mum and Dad asked Ali if we could use his workshop downstairs for the reception. After a great deal of work, the mechanic's workshop was transformed into a magical space for the celebration. We draped the walls in patterned cloths and provided tables and chairs for all the guests. It was a wonderful evening. After the wedding, Nessim wanted to leave the army so that he could spend more time with his new wife, but the army was reluctant to let him go. Ali had a word with

General Ross, and shortly afterwards, Nessim was free to go. He and Reina would be a devoted couple all their lives.

I was very close to my older brother Leon at this time. Leon was five years older than me, and a very charming young man. He never had to worry about going after girls, because he charmed the girls so much that they went after him, instead. Leon was not in a rush to get married, and nor was Albert, the eldest in the family. As my older siblings grew into adulthood, they started to work. Albert went into business, Leon got a good job for British Overseas Airways Corporation at the age of sixteen, and of course Reina was taking care of her husband.

One of the most characteristic and interesting features of everyday life in Cairo at that time was the system of lunchboxes. Men went off to work in their offices and factories, and their wives stayed at home to take care of the housework. One of the women's duties was to prepare lunch for their husbands and place it in steel 'gamel' lunchboxes with different interconnecting trays, stacked one on top of the other, for different elements of the meals. Lunchbox carriers, who specialized in particular neighbourhoods, came along late in the morning to collect the food, and bring it to the women's husbands at work. Every day around noon they could be seen, absolutely laden down with lunches. In this way, all the men got their home-cooked meal while it was still hot. I never heard of any of the deliverymen getting a delivery wrong, which is a miracle in itself. Mum was a great cook and Dad ate very well at work every day: stews of all kinds, curries, and rice. Meat, eggs, and chicken were expensive, but Mum could perform miracles with beans and vegetables – both of which were invariably excellent in Cairo – and there was always fresh fruit. The man who delivered Dad's lunchbox was a local Jewish man named Eli. We all grew very fond of him, and in fact he delivered lunches to Dad for many years.

In those days, living in Cairo as a Jew meant being extremely aware of the social class system, which was quite encoded (much the same also applied to people from other sorts of cultural and religious backgrounds). There were various strata of social class, and everyone was keenly aware of where they belonged. People did not necessarily speak about social class much, but we certainly all knew where we fitted in. Everyone knew who the upper-class Egyptian Jews were: they were people of huge wealth and considerable influence, such as Joseph Cattaoui and his family, who seemed almost to live in another world to us mere mortals. Some of the wealthiest Jews ran factories and other businesses and employed thousands of people of all denominations. They were members of extremely exclusive social and sporting clubs and mostly socialised with one another and with other, non-

Jewish members of the Cairo elite. Less well to do Jews often harboured rather ambivalent feelings towards the Jewish elite. On the one hand, they were important employers and extremely influential in both Jewish and mainstream Egyptian society. On the other, they often displayed a rather condescending attitude towards their less wealthy co-religionists, and wore a rather haughty air. The synagogues were attended by people of all social classes, but people paid rent for their seats, so obviously the wealthiest families paid the most and got the best seats, with the rest of us sitting behind them in a very vivid demonstration of where everyone belonged in the pecking order. Again, while this could be annoying for those who were less well-off, we all also knew that without the funds provided by these wealthy members of the congregation there would be no synagogue at all, as the community depended very much on private funds. At an estimate, I would say that the wealthier Jews, who represented about 5 per cent of the Jewish population, contributed 95 per cent of the construction and running costs for the synagogues and other aspects of the Jewish infrastructure, with the rest provided by humbler members of the community.

These synagogues, paid for by the wealthy Jews, were at the heart of the community in more ways than one. The local matchmakers, seated in the balcony, always had their eyes on the eligible girls and bachelors, and when they spotted a likely couple, they would make a discreet advance to the relevant families after the service on a Saturday. Families that were considered to have a good reputation, and that were generally well-liked, were also much sought-after for brides and grooms. On Yom Kippur, the men dressed all in white, with white kittels – the traditional robes worn for the ceremony – and rubber shoes, because it was forbidden to wear leather shoes on that day. Yom Kippur was a great day in Cairo, as it had been in Khartoum. Everyone fasted from four o'clock the day before, went to the synagogue still fasting, and had a wonderful feast of traditional kosher foods on the evening of the feast day. Everyone fasted – men, women, and children from the age of about eleven. Going without food was often difficult for the children, but they had a great sense of pride and achievement when they managed to stay without eating something for the requisite period of time.

At that time, I would say that we were in the lower middle-classes of Cairo. While Dad had a good education and worked hard, money was quite tight, and we were certainly not in a position of great influence. However, we were still much better off than the poorest Jews, who continued to live in very challenging circumstances. As the twentieth century progressed, there was still a substantial Jewish Egyptian minority that remained poor and marginalized, and (as in the early medieval period) largely dependent on charitable support from wealthier Jews. In the late 1930s and early 1940s, for example, a third of the adult men of the Haret al-Yahud were unemployed, and the area had high levels of illiteracy.[6]

Haret al-Yahud was divided into two parts. One area was traditionally the home of Karaite families, who often worked in the goldsmith business. Everyone in Cairo went there when they wanted jewellery for a wedding or another important event. Most of these Karaite families had shops and workshops in the area, and lived in apartments overhead. This part of the neighbourhood was wealthier than the other section, in which many of the inhabitants were unemployed or subsisted on whatever they could earn from casual labour. In both areas, the primary language was Arabic, and those who had been lucky enough to receive some education also spoke French. The goldsmiths also had a special lingo that they used for discussing their trade which incorporated some Hebrew words, even though they did not ordinarily speak Hebrew (in fact, today the Arab goldsmiths in the area continue to use this lingo, which has outlived the Jewish population there).[7]

I well remember Mum going every Friday to Haret al-Yahud, where the poorest Jews lived, to distribute food and clothing to people who had almost nothing. Because Mum had so many children, she generally had second-hand clothes to give away (she would wash and repair everything before giving it away; it was all good quality clothing). She often gave away her own clothing to those who were less fortunate than us as well, and she visited both as a member of the Jewish women's charitable organization, the Oeuvre de la Goutte de Lait, and on her own behalf. Often, Mum also baked loaves of fresh bread to be distributed to the needy in Haret al-Yahud. I remember accompanying her to the area to help her carry all the bread, which was given to the charity, and then distributed by them to all those who needed it.

I loved going with my mother on these trips to Haret al-Yahud. For me, it was one of the most fascinating places I knew. Rather like the back streets and alleys of an old southern European town, such as Naples, it had been built in a haphazard fashion over the centuries. The old buildings leaned perilously against one another, and I could peep right inside people's homes, as the doors were often left propped open to allow light and fresh air to enter. There were people of all ages, shapes, and sizes everywhere, and small shops and businesses of every sort. Outside the local synagogue, which was dedicated to Maimonides, who is said to have lived in the area when he was in Egypt, there were always beggars sitting on the ground. They wore rags and adopted a very humble posture as they kept their hands extended for alms. I used to wonder how people could claim that all the Jews were rich when it was perfectly clear that this was not the case at all. The level of poverty in Haret al-Yahud was staggering.

Although many of the people who lived in this area were desperately poor, they were very proud of their rich heritage. Nobody knew for sure exactly how long the Jews had been living in this part of Cairo, but their history dated back many centuries. In fact, families from Haret al-Yahud who had done well in business and become wealthy often preferred to continue living there, even though they could have afforded a modern apartment in an airy suburb.

Although he was not very wealthy, Dad also did what he could to support poor families living in Haret al-Yahud. Whenever possible, he would bring simple piece-work from a business that he was running at the time, and would pay them a fair wage in exchange for their labour. I remember that one of the things they did was to work with sunglasses, adjusting frames to fit new lenses. The glasses were sent to Sudan, for sale in my grandfather's shop.

Dad, like Mum, taught me to be aware of how fortunate we were in comparison to so many others. While we were far from wealthy, we had a comfortable home, and could afford to go to good schools. We could even afford help in the home, and we had a house in Khartoum, so we knew that if things got very difficult for the Jews in Egypt, we always had the option to go there. The vast majority of the people living in Haret al-Yahud considered themselves lucky if they could be sure of being able to put enough food on the table in any given week.

The poorer Jews of Cairo were extremely vulnerable to the growing levels of anger throughout Arab society. As Jews, they potentially attracted the ire of those who were angry about the presence of successful Jews in so many areas of business, but they had no wealth of their own, and no way to defend themselves against the majority population, should it decide to turn against them. At that time, 40,300 Jews were listed as Egyptians (in other words, entitled to citizenship).[8] A similar number were formally citizens of other countries, but many could have reasonably applied for citizenship. Few were aware of the impact that the Treaty of Montreux, signed in 1936, would eventually have on them.

The Treaty had abolished the privileges granted to foreign nationals, which many of the Jews notionally were, leaving them extremely vulnerable to the caprices of an increasingly nationalist governing class. After the Treaty, only those with Egyptian nationality were allowed to work in banks, or in business dealings with the government, while the state worked to ensure that it was ever more difficult for all non-Muslims, but especially Jews, to obtain citizenship.

In 1941, the Egyptian General Aziz Ali al-Mizri travelled to Beirut with the plan of defecting to the side of Germany in the war, bringing with him intelligence about the British forces. Just a month earlier, King Far'uq had communicated with Adolf Hitler through his ambassador in Tehran, stating his 'strong admiration' for Hitler, and his deep respect for the people of Germany, and describing the German forces as 'liberators'.

The Egyptian Jews, conversely, were clearly extremely concerned about what was happening. When Italy declared itself an ally of Germany, a number of Italian Jews in Egypt protested by returning their passports, and members of a Jewish anti-Fascist organization formed a picket that prevented local Jews from attending the performances of an opera company visiting from Italy.[9]

Meanwhile, some Egyptian Jews who held foreign citizenship fought with the Allies in the war, while large numbers of them gathered money for the war effort, supported the British soldiers stationed in Cairo in a range of ways, and did what they could to contribute to the end of Nazism.[10] Around this time, our cousin Shlomo died in battle in Palestine, where he was fighting with a British legion.

Quite a few Jewish women also signed up for the war effort, joining the ATS, or Auxiliary Territorial Service, which was the women's branch of the British Army. One of the Cairene women involved in a local branch would go on in future years to be a First Lady of Israel.

In June 1942, the Libyan port of Tobruk, which had been defended by Commonwealth soldiers, fell to Rommel's forces, and the region was severely threatened by Germany. The fear was that Alexandria would be seized by Germany, which would then have control of the Suez Canal. British citizens and dependents started to flock out of Cairo, and the British embassy in Egypt burned all of the secret documents in its possession. Despite this situation, the Egyptian government refused to declare war on Italy, even as Italian bombs fell.[11]

At around this time, Dad decided that he would apply for Egyptian nationality. As Italy had entered the war on the side of Germany, he had both practical and ideological reasons to reject his Italian nationality – and as his family had by now been in Egypt and Sudan for generations, he felt that it would make sense to become an Egyptian formally because he intended to make his life, and continue raising his family, in Egypt.

Part of this decision rested on Dad's horror with how Mussolini was behaving, and the direction in which Mussolini was taking Italy. In the very early years of Mussolini's government, Dad had been quite admiring of him, seeing him as a firm opponent of the threat of communism. When Mussolini made a pact with Hitler, and endorsed Hitler's anti-Jewish and racist laws, Dad felt personally betrayed, and his deep pride in his Italian heritage was damaged. However, his application to formally adopt Egyptian citizenship was summarily rejected. I remember Dad being desperately upset at this time:

'The Jewish people are finished,' Dad said. 'Mussolini will kill them in Italy, and then Hitler will win the war against the Allies, and there will not be a Jew left on the face of the earth.'

Dad said it was the Jews' destiny to fight and that we were not going to be afraid like the Jews at the Siege of Masada. He was referring to one of the final events in the first Jewish-Roman War, which took place in the years 73-4 of the Christian era, when the Jewish residents of the Masada fortress (in modern-day Israel) were said to have committed suicide en masse rather than be captured by the Romans.

'We will not be like the Jews of Masada,' Dad said firmly. 'We will not give up.'

At this point, my parents – who had been living in Cairo full-time since shortly after Italy entered the war in 1940 – decided that we would go back to Sudan until it was safe to return to Egypt. At that time, in 1942, the victory of the Allies was by no means a foregone conclusion, and from where we were in Egypt, it looked very likely that Germany might win the war. Rommel was a fierce and able commander, and the German forces were doing very well. There was huge fear that Rommel would prevail in Egypt, and that then the Germans would come for all the Jews and treat them in the same way as they had been treated in Germany and much of Europe.

I had often travelled between Egypt and Sudan, and it was a route that I was very familiar with. I had even made the journey once on my own; everyone had made a big fuss of me because I was so young. Usually, I enjoyed the journey very much. Part of it took place on a train, and part on one of the great river ferries that went up and down the Nile. Usually, we packed a delicious picnic to eat on the way, and really enjoyed the trip, looking out the window at the view, and chatting with the other passengers. However, when we left for Sudan for our own safety in 1942 – the whole family, including our servant Ahmet – we soon found out that a lot of other families had the same idea.

There were twenty people crammed into a carriage designed for ten, and we had to take turns sitting down on the long journey. The discomfort, and the general air of fear, made it a deeply unpleasant time. When we took the riverboat along the Nile, conditions were even worse. Usually, the boat trip took two nights and was a pleasant experience that we children enjoyed. The boats were well-appointed, with dining rooms and everything one needed for a comfortable stay. They dragged smaller boats with them containing cargo animals and other items for storage, but the main body of the boat was reserved for passengers. Now, because there were so many of us, we were crammed in everywhere, with people lying in rows on the decks, squished into the cargo boats, and doing their best to get some sleep despite the very uncomfortable environment and lack of adequate sanitation for such large numbers of travellers.

As we were already used to living in Khartoum and had so much family there, it was easy for us to settle back in. The younger kids were enrolled in local schools and we returned to playing with our cousins. Mum was happy, as she was back among friendly faces and could spend time with her women friends. She was especially fond of one of her cousins, Palomba, who was a similar age to herself, and a very kind and gentle woman.

Not long after we arrived, my second cousin Lola - Palomba's daughter - who had married a successful local merchant the previous year, gave birth to her first child, Lina. I knew Lola well from our various visits to and stays in Khartoum. Although she was five years older than me, we had briefly attended the same school at one point; she was in the senior class when I was just starting out. Lola had always been very kind and friendly with me. Since my family had moved to Cairo a couple of years earlier, she had blossomed into a beautiful young woman, and married a very nice man. At fifteen, she had become a mother for the first time - this was young by the standards of today, but not especially so by the standards of the time.

Mum told me to go to Lola's house to visit her and the new baby. When I got there, I dutifully admired the baby girl, called Lina, and kept to myself my thoughts on how hideous she was. At the age of ten, I did not know that new-borns are, in general, not very pretty!

Lola's grandmother was a good friend of Mum's, and when she showed me baby Lina she said: 'Isn't she a beautiful little girl? We hope that you will marry her when she grows up!'

'Certainly, you will!' Mum said firmly when I told her about this. 'No doubt about it! There's no better girl for you.'

I was horrified at the thought, and privately decided that I would marry her only if her looks improved with time. As Lola was very pretty, I was hopeful that there was a chance.

A few months later, Montgomery had won the campaign. Whereas before this, many of the senior members of government had been flirting with the idea of supporting the Germans, and King Far'uq was reported as having said that he was glad that the Germans were going to make the British leave Egypt, now the Egyptian government said that they were pleased that the Allies had won.

After we had been in Sudan for a year, Dad decided that we could return to Cairo, as peace had been restored there, and it seemed clear that the Allies were going to win the war. It was the middle of the school year, and there were no places available for me in any of the schools usually frequented by Jewish children, so Dad decided that I could be enrolled for the time being in a local madrassah Muslim school.

Attending a Muslim school was a really interesting experience for me. I was the only Jewish child in the school, and I was regarded as a rare and exotic creature and treated with tremendous respect and care by the teachers and students alike; I had the time of my life. I can still remember some of the children touching my skin curiously to see if it felt the same as theirs. As well as ordinary classes in reading and writing, the children spent about two hours a day studying the Qur'ān and singing its verses. Dad was happy about all this. He felt that, as we lived in a Muslim-majority country, it would be good for me to know a bit about Islam. I soon knew parts of the Qur'ān by heart and was used to dressing the same way as the other boys – in a robe, and with my head covered. I finished out the term there and started in St Austin's, a Catholic school, for the next school year, with nothing but happy memories of my time in the Muslim school. I am very grateful for having had the experience, especially considering how quickly things started to change for the Jews in Egypt after that.

In 1942-3, the laws changed to state that all business dealings should be carried out in Arabic. At the same time, the Zionist movement in British-owned Palestine, increasingly aware of the terrible fate that had been inflicted on so many European Jews, started to reach out more towards Jews living in Muslim-dominated countries, encouraging them to share their vision. In the spring of 1943, the Germans were routed from Africa, and the Allies were increasingly in the ascendant, especially after the resounding victory at El Alamein, after which – as Winston Churchill said – the fortunes of the allies changed resoundingly.[12]

Even before the battle, the Allies had been very aware of how crucial it was: if they had lost it, they would have lost all of Egypt, and the tide would have turned decisively against them. Thankfully, the Allies prevailed. The people of Egypt – and probably the Egyptian Jews more than any others – began to relax a little as the threat of the Nazis retreated. Marilyn Naggar Baer, who grew up in Egypt and immigrated to the United States, remembers hearing the bombs falling on Alexandria, and was told as a child that the Nazis had declared that, if they seized Egypt, they would hang the Egyptian Jews in Mohammed Ali Square.[13]

At this point, aged twelve, I was vaguely aware of the growing undercurrent of antisemitism in Egypt, but it did not yet impinge on my daily life, and I continued to enjoy my frequent interactions with friends and neighbours from all sorts of backgrounds.

In 1943-4, David Ben Gurion (at that point the de facto leader of the Jewish population in Palestine) expounded his plan for the immigration to Palestine of a million Jews from European and Muslim majority countries.[14] At the same time, in Cairo, the streets, nightclubs and cinemas were filled with British soldiers on leave, and to a great extent ordinary life continued, particularly in the affluent cosmopolitan areas frequented by Cairo's business families, who still enjoyed the fine pastries at fancy cafés such as the legendary Groppi's, as though nothing was happening at all. Behind the scenes, however, many Jews in Cairo and elsewhere in Egypt were quietly involved in a range of activities in support of the establishment of Israel.

At this time, as a youngster on the verge of adolescence, I first became involved in the junior branch of a local Zionist movement and, gradually, to become familiar with the spectrum of views in the movement. Some of the leaders were socialists, who wanted to establish Israel as a socialist or even communist paradise, with kibbutz collective communities, and no individual property at all. In the beginning, I was very attracted to socialism, which was described to us as a sort of paradise, and which seemed like a very exotic idea to me. Leaders from Palestine came to coach us not just in the principles of Zionism, but also in the basics of paramilitary skills. They were charismatic and full of enthusiasm, and in a way, I suppose you could say that they brainwashed us youngsters by telling us many stories about what life could be like in Israel, if only a Jewish state could be founded there.

While, of course, I was aware of the things happening around me, as a young adolescent boy, my main interest in life then was spending time with other kids of my age, and especially girls. Thankfully, there were plenty of sporting organizations for young people that were open to both sexes. I joined the Hakoah sports and social club; 'Hakoah' is a Hebrew word that means 'the force' or 'the strength'. We mostly played volleyball, which could be played in mixed groups and was therefore the popular option. At Hakoah, I met a boy called Robert, who was two years older than me. When we realized that we lived next door to one another, our friendship was sealed. Robert's dad, Elie, was a brilliant man who worked as a broker at the Egyptian stock market, which had been founded by Jews and which was still dominated by Jewish professionals. Elie had suffered an accident some years before, and now he was paralysed from the waist down and needed a lot of help to get around – his sons brought him to the stock market every day, where he was still able to work. Robert never complained about the responsibility he had to take for his father, but it did limit him quite a lot, particularly in terms of his education.

The organization offered young Egyptian Jews like Robert and me a venue where we could meet, play sports, and flirt with the opposite sex. It also had a strong Zionist agenda. Dad had often talked to me about Lord Balfour and the Balfour Declaration of 1917, because he took a great interest in politics in general, and was very favourably inclined towards Zionism – but I had never heard anyone else discuss it. In the Hakoah club, the leaders talked about it a lot, educating all the girls and boys about the project to settle Palestine with Jews from all over the world and to establish a Jewish homeland there. They talked to us about Chaim Weizman, whose influence had been so important in passing the Balfour Declaration, and they told us that if – or when – we moved to the Holy Land, we might be lucky enough to meet him for ourselves.

My parents were happy that I was making friends and doing sports, but as I grew more confident, I started to go out more and more on my own, which was not really the done thing at the time. Looking back, I can see that they were nervous that I might come to some harm, as the atmosphere on the streets was shifting and changing, and Egyptian Jews were increasingly aware of an undercurrent of resentment angled towards them.

'What's so great about the Hakoah club?' Mum asked. 'It's changed you. You are only a kid, but you are starting to look like a man! What have you been doing?'

I told her that I was doing nothing wrong and that I was just meeting up with my friends in the Hakoah club to play volleyball. Mum was still rather suspicious, so she went to see the club for herself. When she got there, all she saw was a bunch of kids doing sports, so she was reassured. I did not tell her that the conversations that we young people had there with our trainers, and increasingly among ourselves, were all about what we could do to help further the cause of Zionism, and how we might be able to persuade more Jewish youngsters to join our movement. I was only a boy at the time, but I was increasingly drawn to the Zionist movement, and dreaming about being able to do more for it in the future, when I was older.

Dad was not directly involved in any Zionist movement, but he suspected that I was getting quite political and, while he was supportive, he was certainly also quite concerned about my safety. After all, I was just a kid.

'Be careful,' Dad said. 'Don't take any unnecessary risks. If you are going to get involved with dangerous things, you're going to have to be very careful not to get caught.'

One November night in 1944, one of the leaders of the group I was in asked me if I could arrange for two visitors to stay in my family's apartment that night. He did not explain why they needed somewhere to stay, but he made it very clear to me that it had to be a secret and that I must never discuss it with anyone.

'I'll ask my Dad,' I said confidently. 'But I am sure it will be fine.'

'Are you sure?' he asked. 'You're very young, but I've heard you can be trusted.'

'You can count on him!' said my friend Robert.

As Robert was two years older than me, and had been in the organization for longer, his word was accepted.

I felt very good about being involved in something so important, even though I did not know what was going on. I was only twelve years old, but I felt like a man to know that I was trusted.

When Dad asked me who the visitors were, I shrugged and said that I did not know but that they were friends with one of the trainers, and he had asked for our help. Dad looked at me sharply. He did not ask more, but I am sure that he quickly realized that they must have been Zionist activists. He said that it was all right and that they could stay for the night.

Our apartment was not that big, but Dad said that the visitors could sleep on the floor, and Mum gave them a meal and some blankets. We were not told exactly why these two young men were in Cairo, but it was clear that they were somehow involved in the Zionist movement. They were polite, but rather distant, and they both looked quite pale and nervous. By the time the family had woken in the morning, they had already risen and gone out, leaving nothing behind but a tidy pile of blankets on the living room floor.

At that time, the British politician Lord Moyne, who had been involved from the start of the war in Winston Churchill's war cabinet, was serving as Deputy Resident Minister of State in Cairo to help the Allies prevail against Germany and the Axis forces. Lord Moyne was extremely unpopular with Jews everywhere. He had been opposed to the presence of Jewish army legions in the Middle East, as he was afraid that this would annoy the Arab states, and he did not believe that the Jews had the right to be considered a nation or an ethnicity in need of a homeland. He was also opposed to the proposals put forward in the Balfour Declaration, and made it clear that he was not in favour of a Jewish state in Palestine. Many people also considered him to be largely responsible for the Struma disaster in 1942, when a ship trying to take about eight hundred Jewish refugees to Palestine from Romania was torpedoed by a Soviet submarine, and almost all of the passengers and crew were killed. Moyne had been instrumental in refusing permission to land in Palestine, and was on the record as having made antisemitic remarks, and therefore many Jews held him responsible for the victims' deaths.

On 6 November 1944, two Jewish militants from the Lehi group, Eliyahu Bet-Zuri and Eliyahu Hakim, left our apartment, where they had spent what was doubtlessly a not terribly comfortable night on our living room floor. They collected weapons from a pre-arranged location, and lay in wait for Lord Moyne near his Cairo home. When he arrived in his car, they shot him, together with a number of other people in his entourage. Lord Moyne died, as did his army driver, Lance Corporal Fuller. The assassins escaped on bicycle, but did not get very far before they were apprehended. Actually, by coincidence, they were caught by a Sudanese acquaintance of my father's, Negumi. We found all this out when their photographs were published in the newspaper after their apprehension. When the paper came out, Dad called me over to him.

'Look at this!' Dad said, showing me the newspaper. 'These are the young men who stayed in our apartment! Did you have any idea? The poor things!'

I denied having had any knowledge of who they were and what they were planning to do, which was absolutely true.

'Nonetheless,' said Dad. 'We had better go to Alexandria for a while until things settle down. We don't want anyone to find out they were here – and God forbid your mother finds out who they were!'

We had a short holiday in Alexandria and, fortunately, nobody was any the wiser. Moyne's assassins were tried in Cairo, found guilty, and sentenced to death. Lehi, the organization they represented, issued a statement saying, 'We accuse Lord Moyne, and the government he represents, with murdering hundreds and thousands of our brethren; we accuse him of seizing our country and looting our possessions. We were forced to do justice and to fight.'[15] The assassins were hanged on 23 March 1945. Afterwards, we heard that they had sung the Hatikvah as they were led towards their deaths – that is the poem, composed in the nineteenth century, that would become the national anthem of Israel many years later, and that had become an anthem of defiance in those days, said to have been sung by many of the Holocaust victims in Europe as they were led to the gas chambers.

Even though we had barely met the assassins, Dad was quite upset about the whole thing, and found the detail that they had been captured by someone he knew to be particularly galling. Years later, in 1975, Bet-Zuri and Hakim's remains were repatriated to the Holy Land in exchange for the return of a number of Arab prisoners of war, and they were buried with full military honours on Mount Herzl.

Thankfully, Lord Moyne's assassins were never connected to us, and my family was not implicated for having sheltered them the night before the assassination. Although the assassination had been a rather chaotic and badly-planned affair – it seemed as though the activists had never even given much thought to how they were going to escape from the scene, as it was certainly not a good idea to try to escape on a bicycle in a city filled with cars and motorcycles – afterwards Dad told me that he was proud of me for having been trusted enough by the movement to be put forward, and of the whole family for having given them shelter.

Throughout this period, I was leaving boyhood and entering my adolescent years. I became fiercely independent and, much as Mum wanted to keep me at home as much as possible, I wanted to go around on my own whenever I could. I had been fascinated by the Haret al-Yahud neighbourhood since visiting there with my mother on her frequent trips to distribute bread and second-hand clothes, and now I liked to go there on my own and just to hang about on the bustling streets and get to know the people who lived there. Although it was scruffy, it always seemed to be full of life. I made all sorts of friends with people of different ages and types, and talked often with the local funeral director, the local matchmaker, and the tailors who made wedding clothes. Because the shops and houses were so old, and often very stuffy in the hot climate of Egypt, life and business took place primarily on the streets, and there were always people sitting around waiting for something to happen, and willing to get into conversation with a curious youngster.

Dad's leather workshop was just outside the quarter, and sometimes I went there to help him to pack sweets for transportation to Sudan, where my grandfather sold them in his shops. On those days, I often played in the street with boys of my own age who lived in that area, and sometimes I visited the synagogue of Maimonides, where he was supposed to have lived and worked during his time in Egypt all those years before. One day, an old lady who lived there offered to tell my fortune. I said that I did not believe in fortune-telling because it is not allowed in the Jewish religion, but she read my fortune anyway, and told me that I would grow up to be a courageous and generous man – basically, all the things I wanted to hear, though I hope I have done my best to live up to it. I gave her all the pennies that I had in my pocket; Dad gave me a penny for each box I packed and I was encouraged to give them to the beggars in Haret al-Yahud.

I benefited greatly from my close relationship with my paternal grandfather. He and I had always been close, and now that I was growing up, he gave me lots of advice on how to approach women and girls, and spoke to me frankly about sex and relationships, which was a topic that my father studiously avoided. To be honest, I was quite impatient to start having girlfriends and wanted to know as much as possible about girls and women so that I would know what to do.

Now that I was thirteen, I was also anxious to complete my bar mitzvah. It is customary for all Jewish boys to have their bar mitzvah when they are thirteen, and I had seen my older brothers celebrate theirs. I knew that Mum and Dad were struggling financially. When I went to Mum to ask if I would be having a bar mitzvah soon, she said, 'You know that things are tough at the moment and that Dad and I can't afford to throw you a party.'

I decided that I would organize my own bar mitzvah. As I was nearly fourteen, I was worried that if I did not take matters into my own hands, I would not get it done at the right age. I just wanted to be the same as all the other boys. I started going to the home of one of my teachers, Chaim, for lessons on the Torah (fortunately for me, he had a very pretty daughter, who was usually there when I called over). Usually, each boy had his own bar mitzvah ceremony and party, but everyone was having to compromise because the war had made things difficult for so many people, and about ten boys were going to have their ceremony together in our local synagogue. So long as I learned everything I needed to know, I could be one of them.

I studied the scrolls with Chaim and learned the verses in Hebrew so that I would be ready to read them aloud when the time came. I had squirreled away a little money from my black-market enterprises, so I bought myself a watch (I got a good price from a vendor I knew in our locality), wrapped it up, and gave it to Mum to give to me, so that I would receive a special bar mitzvah watch, as my brothers had each done in their turn.

When the war finally came to an end on 2 September 1945, Cairo erupted with happiness. Of course, nobody had televisions in those days, so we heard the news on the radio and read all about it in the newspapers. People flocked into the British garrisons and into each other's homes to celebrate together. My family did not do anything special, but we were so happy that it was over. Money was tight for a lot of people, so champagne did not flow, but there was an outpouring of absolute joy.

While everyone was happy, the reasons for the happiness varied. For the Jews and for most other minorities, the main issue was that the Allies had won and that Germany had been defeated. For most of the native Egyptians, however, the most important thing was the fact that now there would be no reason for the British to remain, and that the British forces would be leaving soon.

Notes

1. Meital, 2017, 186.
2. Mayer, 1987, 200.
3. Rickenbacher, 2010,
4. Krämer, 1989, 22.
5. Family history related by Vivette Ancona for the *Out of Egypt* celebratory booklet, printed 2019.
6. Oppenheim, 2003, 422.
7. https://www.atlasobscura.com/articles/the-secret-language-of-cairos-goldsmiths. Retrieved on 11 June 11 2020.
8. Shamir, 1987, 50.
9. Barda, 2006, 95.
10. Ibid., 97.
11. Sachar, 2006, 227-8.
12. Lugnado, 2006, 39.
13. Family history related by Marilyn Naggar Baer for the *Out of Egypt* celebratory booklet, printed 2019.
14. Halamish, 2008, 124-5.
15. Hernon, 2007, 161.

5

An Egyptian Jewish Family in the Post-War Years

On 2 and 3 November 1945, two months after the end of the Second World War, and with rumours of what had happened in the German concentration camps being confirmed, several anti-Zionist organizations held a rally in Cairo to protest British policy in Palestine, which quickly degenerated into an anti-Jewish riot. The mob entered Haret al-Yahud, attacking people in the streets, shops, and synagogues. Six people were killed, hundreds were injured, and many 'foreign' shops (including shops owned by Coptic Christians and Muslims, as well as Jews) were looted.[1] The Ashkenazi synagogue, near Haret al-Yahud, was destroyed.[2]

Increasingly, the Egyptian government pushed the view that Zionism was a direct and immediate danger to Egypt, and that it was being funded and promoted by wealthy members of the Egyptian Jewish community – although, in fact, there was no evidence of this at all, and indeed plenty to the contrary.[3]

Despite the worsening situation, some Egyptian Jews believed that, because of their position in business and public life in Egypt, they might be able to mediate between Egypt and the west and help to establish a peaceful government. They were also heavily invested in staying in Egypt, where they had become a useful and important element of the national economy. The 1946 *Stock Exchange Yearbook of Egypt* reveals a significant increase in the number of businesses with Jewish directors, including both long-established families and newer arrivals, as well as the presence of Jews who worked as directors alongside people from very different cultural backgrounds, indicating the high degree to which even more recently-arrived Jews had become integrated into the business community.[4]

Most Egyptian Jews were still underestimating the extent to which the Egyptian government had adopted both extreme nationalism and antisemitism. Traditionally under Islam, Jews (and other minorities) had been tolerated so long as they paid a special poll tax. In Egypt from the nineteenth century onwards, many Egyptian Jews had also flourished and risen to positions of influence in a business environment dominated by European cultural norms. As nationalism and political Islam grew stronger in the post-war period, the relative tolerance with which Jews had been treated in Egypt for centuries was increasingly replaced by straightforward antisemitism, and official attempts to make life as uncomfortable as possible for the Egyptian Jews.[5]

Against this backdrop, my friends and I continued to be active in the Jewish scouting movement, although now that we were older, we were increasingly aware that we were not just there to have a good time, but also to prepare for a future in which young Jews would be called to work and fight for the Holy Land. Our leaders were young, energetic, and charismatic, and they talked to us with great enthusiasm and fervour on this topic, while the youngsters all listened with respectful attention. I can remember the names of two of the leaders in my troupe: a young man called Eytan and a young woman called Grazia, who I believe was originally from Italy. Most of the leaders had actually come to Egypt from Palestine, where either they or their families had settled at some point in the 1920s or 1930s. They had a map on the wall that they used to point to, to get us used to the idea, and make us understand where they were talking about. They also showed us Hebrew books that they had brought with them, and explained that when Israel was founded, Hebrew would be the national language. They did not teach us how to speak or read Hebrew, but they did explain that it was a modern language, adapted from, but not the same as, the classical Hebrew that people had heard in their synagogues and that the boys learned how to recite when they reached the age for their bar mitzvah.

The Jewish youth organization was so much fun, it really gave me a taste for the outdoors and for collaborating with others, and over the next few years I was always ready to sign up for an adventure. Most of the young people involved were kids from similar or wealthier backgrounds to mine. There were no working-class youngsters from Haret al-Yahud or other poor neighbourhoods, for the simple reason that the poorer Jews lived on such low incomes that they just did not have the means to join an organization of the sort. Children from those families would not have had the money even for public transport, and most of them helped their families by working as soon as they were physically able to. We were certainly aware of how fortunate we were by comparison, and of the fact that, if the people of Haret al-Yahud ever needed help in the future, we, and others like us, would be morally responsible for providing it.

At this point, when I was aged fourteen, one of the trainers drew me aside one day and told me that the leaders had decided that I was now ready to take on more responsibility in the group and that I should take this very seriously. I nodded solemnly, and promised that I would do my best to help out in whatever way I could.

Our trainers took us out of town to the countryside outside Cairo, where they taught us to clear hurdles by jumping over them, how to climb a tree and remain among the branches for a long time without falling down, and to shoot the rapids in the Nile. What we did not entirely realize yet was that the skills that we were taught were not just wholesome sporting abilities, but actual paramilitary skills that the trainers and their superiors hoped at least some of us would put to good use defending the Holy Land in the years to come. Gradually, we understood more about the bigger picture of what we were doing, and one day the trainers gathered us together and said: 'I hope that one day many of you will graduate to wearing a uniform and will feel very proud of yourselves for all that you are doing for the Jewish people.'

Looking back, and having raised a family of my own, I can see that the trainers had assumed an enormous responsibility for the young people in their care, because some of the activities we were engaged in were so dangerous that it would have been very easy for a child to be seriously hurt, or even killed. At the time, I instinctively knew that Mum would not wish to know the full story of what we got up to, so I kindly refrained from telling her!

My friend Robert, who was two years older than me, introduced me to more people active in young Zionist movement, all a number of years older than me. Some of them were deeply involved and receiving direction straight from their supervisors in Palestine. I received a trickle of information about what they were doing, and found it all very enticing. It sounded like an opportunity for adventure. I also enjoyed spending time with young people who were a few years older than I was. It made me feel that I was being treated like a grown-up, which was exactly what I was looking for at the time. Gradually, I was given more responsibility.

We were all organized into little cells. The girl above me in the immediate chain of command was a young lady with a striking appearance called Marcelle Ninio, who was three years older than me. Like me, Marcelle was from Cairo and had become involved in Zionism through a sports club (she was actually an exceptionally talented basketball player on a women's team). Along with an unspecified number of other cells in Cairo and around Egypt (we were not allowed to know about each other; that way, if someone got arrested and was interrogated, they would be unable to provide much information to the authorities), we were tasked with reaching out to young people, particularly from the poorest areas, where the Jews had few options in terms of emigrating.

From 1946, shop signs were required to be written in Arabic. As many Jews operated primarily in one or more European languages, this was clearly targeted primarily at them.[6] The Company Law, passed in 1947, required that, in any company, 75 per cent of all salaried staff, 90 per cent of all employees, and 51 per cent of the owners of capital be Egyptian nationals.[7] The same year, the Egyptian director of the Passport and Nationality Office explained:

> By foreigners we mean all those who do not possess the Egyptian nationality. To hold a laissez-passer does not prove at all that the holder enjoys the Egyptian nationality. Stateless residents born in Egypt, as well as former local subjects, will be considered as foreigners.[8]

The 'stateless residents' to whom he referred included about 40,000 Jews, many of whom now had no legal homeland, and were extremely vulnerable to the growing nationalism.

Dad reacted immediately to the threat of the Company Law by liquidating his company, and working as a self-employed individual rather than as the owner of a small company. He hoped, in this way, to avoid the worst of the impact on him and his business – although, deep down, he may have feared that he was really just buying time.

A significant outbreak of the highly infectious disease, cholera, in 1947, may have been associated with business travel, although the Egyptian authorities acted decisively and quickly to close the borders to any travellers who could not show proof of having been vaccinated, in the form of the relevant WHO vaccination certificate. The fear and anxiety associated with the outbreak certainly did not help with the atmosphere in Egypt in general at that time, as movement was restricted and public meeting-places, including public meeting-places used for prayer, were closed.[9]

The health authorities knew that cholera was largely spread by contaminated water, and there was a concerted campaign to encourage people to engage in hygienic practices. I remember well the discussions in our house about the fact that soap residue adhered to the walls of our shower, and concern that this meant that the house was not adequately clean, and that the contagion would spread, as we knew that the public supply of water was not especially sanitary. We all used a special disinfectant in our bathrooms and kitchens to keep infection at bay.

In response to the epidemic, the United States and British embassies opened a number of clinics where they gave cholera vaccines for free. The Jewish and other minority communities were extremely grateful for this, and we all rushed to be vaccinated. I went on my own to receive the vaccination, although I was just fourteen at the time, and I remember the banter I exchanged with the nurse giving the injections at the United States embassy, who queried whether I was old enough to make my own medical decisions. I pulled myself up to my full height and informed her that I was a man and more than old enough to make my own decisions. She laughed.

'You look very nice,' she said, 'but are you sure you are allowed to have the vaccination? Who decided for you?'

'I decided for myself!' I told her.

'You don't have a family?' she asked.

'Sure I do, but they don't decide for me! I'm not a baby!'

'OK, you've convinced me,' she said. 'And by the way, I've just given you the injection.'

I was incredibly pleased with myself and my ability – as I saw it – to charm the pretty American nurse.

Because of the old infrastructure, the over-crowding, and the old-fashioned way in which the homes and shops were constructed in Haret al-Yahud, the cholera was particularly bad there. Many of the people who lived there were already not in great health because of their poor diet and the general poverty they lived with, so they were extremely vulnerable to an infectious disease of this sort. Other, wealthier, elements of the Jewish community quickly mobilised to help the inhabitants of the stricken quarter, clearing wards of non-urgent patients, and adding new beds in the Hôpital Israélite so that the sick could be cared for and would have the best possible chance of recovery. At the same time, the cholera vaccine was rolled out to anyone in the area who had not yet been infected. In this way, many lives were saved.

Because the minorities of Egypt were so proactive in obtaining vaccinations and caring for their more vulnerable members, the incidence of cholera was much lower among them than among the majority population – that might seem like a small thing, but in the context of the heightened emotion and growing antisemitic and general anti-foreigner sentiment, it may have contributed to the growing resentment and ire, although I was never personally aware of any concerns about this at the time.

In 1947, Britain conducted its last census of Egypt. At that time, just after the war, there were about 70,000-75,000 Jews living in Egypt, including about 6,000 Ashkenazi Jews, about 3,500 Karaites, 10,000 'indigenous' Jews, and the remainder Jews of 'Oriental' or Sephardi origins, descended from people who had arrived in the period from the latter part of the nineteenth century onwards.[10] While about 30 per cent of these Jews did have Egyptian citizenship, most did not, and the Egyptian government took steps to prevent them from acquiring it.[11] Approximately 25 per cent of Jews were formally foreign nationals, and the remaining 50 per cent were stateless, and therefore unprotected and vulnerable.[12] This was a blow to Jewish-owned businesses, particularly smaller, family-owned businesses. Most businesses, including small, family-run businesses, had to hire additional Egyptian staff, even when they could not afford to.

By 1947, leading Egyptian newspapers were claiming that all Jews were, by definition, Zionists, and that they were also a destructive element of society and posed a threat to native Egyptians. Certain elements of the population were already engaging in anti-foreigner riots, and anti-foreigner sentiment was especially venomous when it was directed against the Jews, who were often referred to as the 'puppies' of the British and Americans, which meant that they would do whatever the British and American establishments wanted them to (the term 'lapdogs' is used in the same way in English).

The majority population was extremely resentful about the power that Britain still had in Egypt, twenty-five years after the country had gained independence, and the Jews were an easy target for this resentment. The Prime Minister of the time, Mahmoud El Nokrashy Pasha – whose wife my family knew because she always bought her handbags from my father's workshop – was widely seen as too pro-western, and he was very pro-monarchy, which did not fit with the growing power of the nationalist movement. He spoke positively of the British and sought to develop a good relationship with Britain. Under him, the Egyptian government attempted to quash violence against the Jews, not always very successfully.[13]

In November 1947, when the United Nations Resolution for the Partition of Palestine was published, recommending that it be divided into Arab and Jewish states, and that Jerusalem be given international status, there were anti-Jewish riots all over the Arab world, featuring looting, burning, and repression – and even murder. People waved placards with messages such as 'Down with Balfour' and 'Expel all Jews'. I remembered the many conversations that I had had with my father about the Balfour Declaration over the years; he had never predicted anger and hatred of this sort, but he had realized from the beginning what an important step the Balfour Declaration had been. Now, many Jews were stripped of citizenship, had their property confiscated, were removed from public sector employment, and had their bank accounts frozen.[14] The statement of the Egyptian delegate to the United Nations, Mohammed Heikal Pasha, that the partition of Palestine would endanger a million Jews living in Arab countries ('If the United Nations Organization decides to partition Palestine, it is liable to bear responsibility for extremely grave events and for the massacre of a large number of Jews')[15] was – reasonably in light of recent events in Egypt, Libya, and Iraq – interpreted by many as a threat.[16]

This was a strange time to be coming of age as a Jewish boy in Egypt. I often felt torn in all directions at once. On the one hand, I had the usual preoccupations of an adolescent male; I was very attracted to women, and wanted to court women and be with them all the time. On the other, I was increasingly involved in the Zionist youth movement, and also felt a compelling attraction towards the work that they were doing, and the idea of establishing Israel as a state in which all Jews could be happy and safe.

The period following the foundation of Israel was a dramatic and traumatic one for the Middle East in general, and an exceedingly difficult time for the Jews of Egypt, whose world was turned upside-down. In 1948, the total Jewish population of Egypt is estimated to have been between 70,000 and 80,000, of whom approximately 5,000 held Egyptian nationality, 30,000 held foreign national status, and 40,000 were officially stateless, and therefore held no passports at all. As I have said, by the time Dad tried to get rid of his Italian national status and exchange it for Egyptian citizenship, he had already missed his chance. After 1948 and the foundation of Israel, the Egyptian state endeavoured not just to remove all those Jews who did not hold Egyptian citizenship, but also to remove citizenship from those who did.[17]

Israel had declared independence on 14 May 1948, under the leadership of Prime Minister Ben Gurion. Dad, who had always been interested in the Zionist movement, and who was well-informed on matters of history and current affairs, was fascinated with the whole idea of the foundation of Israel, and often talked to me at length about it. He pored over the news to see what the first Israeli president, Chaim Weizmann, had said or done. Dad, like all Jews at that time, was used to being the member of a minority. The idea that there could be a country in which Jews would be a majority was extraordinary to him. As for me, I knew that things were likely to start heating up for the Zionist youth movement in Cairo, and I felt that I was ready to do whatever was asked of me.

Israel's declaration of independence called on Israel's Arab neighbours to engage with them in a relationship of peace and coexistence,[18] and my father and mother, and indeed all the Egyptian Jews, hoped against hope that this would turn out to be the case. Unfortunately, this call was not warmly received – to say the least. There was an immediate outpouring of anger, much of it directed towards the Jews in Egypt, rather than just Israel.

Many Egyptian nationals were furious about the foundation of Israel, but also not very well-informed about it, or about the history that had led to this moment. They had heard of the Balfour Declaration, which had laid the groundwork for the foundation of the state of Israel, but they did not seem to realize that it had actually been made in 1917 – a whole generation before. Consequently, a lot of protestors made banners and posters with 'Down with Balfour!' and similar statements, and they marched around the city with them. They did not realize that Balfour himself had actually died many years before.

As for the Egyptian Jews, attitudes towards the new country and its government were mixed. On the one hand, you had people like my father, who had always had strong sympathies for the Zionist movement, and who had followed the progress towards the foundation of Israel with great interest. On the other, there was a large cohort of Jews, many of whom were Arabic-speaking Karaites, who identified very strongly as Egyptians, were not very impressed by Ben Gurion, and were very anxious that the foundation of Israel would cause them problems as Jews living in an Arab land. Unfortunately, their concerns would very soon prove to be well-founded.

From my father's stories about the Zionist project, I developed a personal interest in it. Like him, I had no interest at this time in leaving the country that I considered my home, but at the same time, I could see the attraction and importance of a homeland where Jews could flourish and raise their families safely. The history that we had all just lived through, and that we in Egypt were continuing to live through, was proof that the Jews could never completely relax and assume that they would always be welcome where they were – even if their families had been there for generations.

By 1948, the Prime Minister, Mahmoud El Nokrashy Pasha, was increasingly concerned by the power of the Muslim Brotherhood. He was worried that they would launch a coup against the government and the monarchy, and there were rumours that the Brotherhood had already been involved in a number of assassinations.

On 15 May 1948, the Arab League announced its displeasure with the foundation of Israel and its intention to enter Palestine.[19] Immediately afterwards, Egypt, together with Syria, Lebanon, Transjordan, and Iraq, invaded, and the first Arab-Israeli war had begun. The first attack on Israel came when Egyptian aircraft bombed the city of Tel Aviv, targeting the civilian population.[20] The Israelis resisted fiercely. Then, Arab armies from Lebanon, Syria, Iraq, and Egypt attacked the former Palestinian mandate, helped by Saudi Arabia. British trained forces joined in with Israel and Israeli forces, now under joint command, were able to gain the offensive.

At grassroots level, the Jews of Egypt bore the brunt of Egyptian anger about Israel's counter-attack to Arab aggressions.[21] Martial law was declared, and censorship became the norm; only the government line was allowed. Nobody was permitted to leave Egypt without applying for and obtaining an exit visa. The reason given for this strict measure was that the authorities wanted to ensure that Jews did not all rush to Israel en masse.

Zionist youth organizations, which previously the Egyptian authorities had been inclined to overlook, were made illegal. Many continued to operate underground. The bank accounts of anyone thought to have Zionist sympathies were closely monitored, and no effort was made to deal with burgeoning antisemitism among the general population. In May and June 1948, at least 1000 Egyptian Jews were arrested and held in custody in prison camps: Huckstep, near Cairo, Abu Kir, near Alexandria, and El Tur, in the southern part of the Sinai Peninsula.

Huckstep had previously been part of an American military camp, now left over after the Second World War, and used by the municipality for repairing vehicles. Located in the Cairene suburb of Heliopolis, it was pressed into use as a detention centre for Zionists and Communists – and for Jews who were in fact neither, but vulnerable to accusations that they were. The authorities had built wooden dormitories to house the detainees.

The shock of being interned merely because they were Jews, and the ill-treatment that some of the internees suffered, ignited interest in some in Zionism and in Israel, as it was by now very clear that Egypt was no longer a safe place for Jews and that the Jews of Egypt urgently needed to start making plans for their future.

One individual who was interned at this time stated of his experience in a camp:

> The guy from the secret police was there and he said: 'the Egyptians on one side and the foreigners on the other side.' I went towards the Egyptian side because that is what I thought I was. He said: 'you are not an Egyptian, you are a foreigner, you are a Jew'. Until then, I had never been impressed by the arguments of the Zionists. This is when

I realized that it was not going to help to try and integrate in Egypt because they were never going to accept us. That was the turning point for me. I started to study Zionism and Hebrew while I was in prison.[22]

Notwithstanding individual kindnesses, attitudes towards the Jews continued to harden throughout the general population. Soon, anyone practising medicine or wishing to be registered on the cotton exchange (then a major driver of the Egyptian economy) had to be a registered Egyptian national, effectively excluding most Jews from these positions.[23] Increasingly, Jews were viewed not as ordinary members of Egyptian society who happened to belong to a religious minority, but as potential enemy agents who could not be trusted.[24]

In many cases, the warm relationships that Egyptian Jews had fostered with their Muslim and other neighbours and colleagues began to sour. In general, the political atmosphere in Egypt at this time was such that minorities in general were increasingly cast as intrinsically 'other', never to truly be part of the Egyptian nation at all. Egyptian hostility to Israel resulted in particularly harsh attitudes towards the Jewish minority.

Nonetheless, in part because of the efforts of Jewish communists, at the time of the foundation of Israel, relatively few made the journey to the new state, preferring, for the moment, to remain in Egypt in the hope that the situation would improve for them,[25]and that they would be able to continue with their lives there.

For my family, up until now we had not had any significant problems in our neighbourhood, but rather had continued to enjoy the same easy friendships that we had always had with the local vendors and shopkeepers. Now there was a dramatic change. All of a sudden, people who had always been full of smiles did not want Jewish customers, and even glared at Jewish people who were just walking down the street. Sometimes people would shout things like: 'You'd better watch out, Jew! One day we'll get you; we'll get your hide!' Probably, most of this talk was idle threats, but the impact was extremely intimidatory and was highly effective at spreading fear.

Mum and Dad had decided, to their sorrow, that they had no future in Egypt, and they left for Sudan, bringing Ahmet and my younger sister, Lily, with them. I decided that I was old enough to stay in Cairo on my own and told Dad that I would keep operating the leather workshop. Dad accepted this, so I waved them goodbye. Lily was enrolled in a school in Khartoum to continue her education. My older siblings had all left home by now. Mum and Dad, and all my older siblings, felt deeply disillusioned by the Egyptian government, and while they were notionally leaving – or had already left – of their own free will, their decision to go had certainly been made in very straitened circumstances, and was a bitter one. We would all be marked by this time for the rest of our lives.

Notes

1. Beinin, 1998, 64.
2. Oppenheim, 2003, 425.
3. Mayer, 1987, 200.
4. Tignor, 1980, 433-5.
5. Roumani, 2003, 50.
6. Krämer, 1989, 206.
7. Beinin, 1998, 21; Oppenheim, 2003, 411.
8. Shamir, 1987, 59.
9. Smallman-Raynor and Cliff, 2016, 27; 33.
10. Barda, 2006, 79.
11. Meital, 2017, 190.
12. Oppenheim, 1930, 412.
13. Krämer, 1989, 209.
14. Aharoni, 2003, 54.
15. Meron, 1992, 28.
16. Shenhav, 2006, 157.
17. Shamir, 1987, 34; 60.
18. Rubin, 2012, 23.
19. Reich, 2005, 46.
20. Dershowitz, 2003, 75.
21. Krämer, 1989, 215.
22. Barda, 2006, 176.
23. Sachar, 2006, 401.
24. Abdulhaq, 2016, 25.
25. Mayer, 1987, 201.

6

An Egyptian Jew in Cairo as Zionism Grows

At this point, I was a youth of sixteen. I was still hopeful that there might be a future for me in Egypt, and I was also increasingly involved with a number of Jewish youth organizations and with the Jewish underground, as it was perfectly clear that the working-class Jews in particular were in a very vulnerable situation. As I had decided to stay in Cairo, I thought that I would try to keep Dad's leather workshop operational and to continue with my activities with the underground.

Of course, my parents were concerned about these activities, and they had warned me to be careful and not to get caught. I no longer kept any secrets from Mum about what I had been doing, and while she was supportive, I am sure that the anxiety I caused her did not help in the least with the various health problems she was suffering from at this time, including high blood pressure and rheumatism. Stress was taking a great toll on her. She had warned me to be careful and I had lied and promised that I would be. As soon as Mum and Dad left, however, it was even easier for me to become more deeply involved in activism.

One good thing about having my parents out of the picture was that I would have the apartment to myself, and I hoped that I would have more freedom to spend time with girls and women. I knew that the Jewish girls of my own age were not to be courted or touched. In those days, sex before marriage was unthinkable for Jewish girls, who were expected to get married quite young and to be virgins when they did. Most girls were very closely watched by their parents and brothers, and had few opportunities to spend time with boyfriends. Consequently, I visited a French prostitute called Maddy and, as well as studying the art of love with her, we became friends. Maddy was a like a mother, a friend, a lover, a sister, and a mentor, all at once.

One day, Maddy brought me to the upmarket hotel, Shepheard's, to meet someone whom she thought I would find interesting. To my surprise, the person she introduced me to was a young man a few years older than me, who was actually already a friend of the family, because he was a distant relative. His name was Joe Scialom, and I had known him in Sudan, when I was a child. Now, Joe was deeply involved with the Zionist movement and pleased to learn that I was also involved. That was the moment when my commitment to Zionism became even firmer, and when I decided that I was prepared to take serious risks for the cause. From then on, Joe and I were like a team. Although there were quite a few years between us, we became close friends as well as comrades in a movement that was dedicated to helping all those who wanted to move to Israel to make the journey safely. In the process, we would also take innumerable risks.

I had always stopped to talk to a local greengrocer who sold his wares from a display on the street. In Cairo, it was traditional to sample a grape to test the quality before buying a bunch – usually the greengrocers offered samples of their fruit before anyone bought them. One day, while I was waiting for my turn to make an order, I took a grape to try it before buying my bunch. The vendor glared at me, slapped my hand away, and told me that he did not wish to sell fruit and vegetables to a dirty Jew. I was absolutely stunned. I stood and stared at him for a while, and then I walked away. I never bought anything from him again.

Of all the Muslim shopkeepers and residents of the area, the only one whose attitude towards me did not change at this time was Ali, our landlord and the mechanic who had introduced me to General Ross. Not only did he continue to be kind and friendly, but he made a point of watching out for me, as I was still very young and I was on my own. I have never forgotten him for this kindness, at a time when many of his peers might have expected him to withdraw from his friendship with a Jew.

The situation was painfully difficult for Egyptian Jews, not all of whom publicly endorsed Zionist principles or had had much interest in Zionism until now. Some of them, apparently under coercion from the authorities, denounced Zionism. A very small number converted to Islam, seeing this as a way in which they could remain in Egypt and continue to pursue their communist ideals.[1] From my own experience, I believe that by this stage there was widespread support for Israel and for Zionism, but that most of it was private and unspoken outside the safety of the Jewish community. I would estimate that about 95 per cent of the Egyptian Jews did support Israel, but given what was happening in Egypt at the time, most of them were afraid to say so. Few were fully cognizant of the implications of a new state or had much understanding of what it would mean for the broader region, but they did know that they wanted to see their Promised Land become reality, even if it was not safe to say so. In fact, people were so nervous and frightened for the future at the time, that many Jews were reluctant to even say the word 'Israel' out loud, in case someone heard them and they got into trouble. With voices lowered, people would speak of 'our land' or 'the partition' or sometimes 'the Holy Land', but that was usually as far as it went. Certainly, they would never have discussed these issues with any of their Arab friends and neighbours, or even with members of other minorities, no matter how close they felt those relationships were. There was a growing sensation of not being able to trust anyone outside the community. They were right to be scared, because at this time many political opponents (both Zionists and communists) of the Egyptian government were arrested and sent to internment camps.[2]

By now, the Muslim Brotherhood had done an excellent job of disseminating the idea that Zionists were enemies of the Egyptian state. It was common, in conversation with Muslims, for them to say something along the lines of, 'I have no problems with the Jews. The Jews are wonderful people – but the Zionists are awful! The Zionists are dangerous and have to be stopped.' It is important to bear in mind that some Jews were also communists, and that the communist movement was active at times in protecting Jewish homes, businesses, and synagogues from attack.[3] Obviously, under these circumstances, hardly anyone was prepared to openly Zionist, and it is difficult for historians who rely on printed sources to accurately estimate the level of interest among Egyptian Jews in the Zionist project.

On June 20 1948, twenty people were killed in a Karaite neighbourhood in Cairo when a bomb exploded. The government attempted to blame the attack on the largely non-existent tension between the Rabbinite and the Karaite Jews; the two groups had theological differences but, in fact, had always been happy to work together, and intermarriage was relatively common. This government's attempt to smear the Jewish community for the bomb failed.

Also in June, my organization got word from contacts in the Muslim Brotherhood that an attack was planned on Cairo's Haret al-Yahud. I spoke to my friend Robert, who was more senior to me in my cell, and he spoke to other cells around the city. We took this warning very seriously, as we knew how angry people were about the Israeli bombing of Cairo, and we knew that still relatively small but escalating numbers of Jews were being killed.

The pending attack on Haret al-Yahud was a matter of great concern to me on a number of levels: firstly, since childhood I had been fascinated with this area, and was on friendly terms with many of the people who worked there; secondly, my father's leather workshop was just outside the quarter, and I had spent a lot of time growing up in that area, playing with and getting to know the locals; and thirdly, my fellow activists and I felt that we had a great moral responsibility to defend the area, where many of Cairo's poorest and most vulnerable Jews lived.

After lengthy discussions about what we could do to help the people of the area, our group and a number of others helped the locals to mount a robust defence. Organized into work teams of about fifteen, we packed rubber car wheels with cotton cloth that had been soaked in petrol, and piled them up in homes and businesses on the perimeter of the neighbourhood, which was accessed through two historic gates, one near the traditional jewellers' area, and one on the other side – usually these gates were kept open, as a matter of routine, but they still made it possible for the people inside to lock down and try to defend the area. We were granted access to two businesses adjacent to the gates, a jeweller's store, and an undertaker's, which gave us a bird's-eye view over the crowd of protestors.

The day the attack had been forecast was a Friday, and the mob gathered after attending their mosques and in particular the important al-Azhar mosque, a beautiful and impressive building and landmark in Cairo that, unfortunately, had come to be intimately associated with the Muslim Brotherhood, and with some of the most sinister elements in Egyptian society and government at that time. Some of the men in the mob were probably members of the Muslim Brotherhood, but many of them were just ordinary men who had been all fired up by the words of their imams. In fact, while the Muslim Brotherhood masterminded and coordinated many such attacks, as it was trying to represent itself as a respectable movement, it was in its interest for an unaffiliated mob to do its dirty work. The Muslim Brotherhood tended to remain in the background.

Emotions rose as they approached Haret al-Yahud, armed with clubs, chanting 'death to the Jews!', promising to kill all the Jews they found, and the like. A local Muslim businessman, who was on very friendly terms with his Jewish counterparts, rushed out in front of the mob pleading with them to see reason and saying that the Jews were their friends. Someone from the mob actually stepped forward and slit this poor man's throat, and he fell onto the ground. The hoard marched forward and tried to get into the Jewish Quarter, but the preparations that the Zionist group and the inhabitants of the area had carried out were enough to repel them: men and boys from inside the area set the fuel-laced rubber tyres on fire and threw them down onto the crowd. When they managed to get one over someone's head and around his neck, they could do terrible damage. Behind the men, the women and girls did the work of preparing the home-made weapons. Eventually, the angry mob had had enough and they went back to where they had come from.

I am sure that many young Jews from this poor Jewish neighbourhood realized then that they and their families had no future in Egypt. Many of them left shortly afterwards. I do not believe that the family of the unfortunate Muslim merchant who had tried to prevent the attack ever saw justice.

By July of the same year, Jews, Europeans, and even Arabs whom the mob thought 'looked Jewish' were being attacked in the streets. The authorities attempted to blame squabbles within the Jewish community for the violence. Even those Jews who held Egyptian citizenship were not safe; being officially Egyptian was not protection enough. Then things became even more dangerous for the Jews of Egypt. On 15 July 1948, three B-17s of the Israeli Air Force bombed a residential area of Cairo. Many homes were destroyed, and quite a few civilians were killed. I clearly remember the bombers flying over my home. I was frightened because we lived near the airport, which was an obvious target.

While things had steadily been getting worse for the Egyptian Jews for some time, the way in which the state, the Muslim Brotherhood, and large numbers of ordinary Egyptians responded to this bombing left most of us in no doubt that our days in Egypt were numbered. In retaliation for the Israeli attack (because no distinction was made between Israelis and Egyptian Jews), several Jewish-owned department stores in Cairo were bombed by members of the Muslim Brotherhood and their supporters. In September, a Rabbinate area was bombed, killing nineteen people.[4] The government claimed that it was only interested in Zionists, and that its problem was with Zionist ideology rather than with the Jews per se, but it was increasingly apparent that this was not true, and that it was motivated by a straightforward dislike of the Jews. Most of the Jews registered as living in Egypt at that time still held European, rather than Egyptian, nationality.[5] Many lived and worked alongside European nationals, and were conversant in several European languages; in the nationalist atmosphere of the time, it became ever easier for the Egyptian authorities to see them as aliens who should be ejected from Egyptian society.

The Brotherhood was declared illegal in December 1948 and many of its members were imprisoned, and had their belongings confiscated. Less than three weeks later, El Nokrashy was assassinated by a young man called Abdel Meguid Ahmed Hassan, who was a student of veterinary science and a member of the Brotherhood. When he was arrested, he said that he had

killed the Prime Minster because of his decision to crack down on
the Brotherhood. Many people were distraught about the killing of
El Nokrashy, who had been an intelligent and moderate leader. Egyptian
Jews were extremely concerned about what might happen next, as they had
seen him as a bulwark and a source of protection against an increasingly
radicalised populace.

Dad's leather workshop was still thriving under my supervision, but
this was a very clear indication that the tide in Egypt was not just turning,
but had already turned, against the Jews and – to a lesser extent – against
all other minorities. I knew that my days in Egypt were numbered.

While I remained anxious about Mum and Dad, and about the future,
I would be lying if I did not say that in some ways it was wonderful being
on my own despite it all. I was just seventeen when my parents left, and all
of a sudden, I had my own apartment. This made me extremely popular
among my circle of friends, who were mostly around my own age and a few
years older. Almost all of my friends still lived at home with their parents,
so even though they were deeply involved in Zionist activism, they were
restricted in terms of how they could conduct themselves in their social
life. As I said, bear in mind that, at the time, Jewish girls (and indeed all of
the girls from respectable Egyptian families) were expected to be virgins
when they got married. Any hint of impropriety could have a negative
impact on a girl's marriage prospects – but with all that we were going
through, and such an uncertain future, not all the girls wanted to wait until
they got married to have a boyfriend. Because I had my own place, my
friends had somewhere to meet away from the prying eyes of interfering
parents. I was busy at work and with the activism, but I still found time to
invite friends over to the apartment for beers and snacks and – without
going into too much detail – also for romance and intimacy. There was a
certain recklessness among the young Jews in Cairo at that time, a cultural
shift that had taken place in the mere year or so since I had started visiting
Maddy. Our familiar world was falling down around us. Our friends were
leaving, and our parents and their generation were making anxious
contingency plans for what to do if the worst came to the worst. In that
context, the strict social mores with which we had been brought up no
longer seemed as important as they once had. We all knew that being
attacked and killed was a real possibility for any of us, and I suppose that
no young person wants to miss out on experiencing all the good things in
life, including sex.

I blithely assumed that, because my parents were in Israel and my
siblings were in Sudan, I had nothing to worry about and could live as I

wished without any interference. I had not counted on Mum's extensive social network. Despite the difficulties involved in sending and receiving letters, one of Mum's friends somehow communicated to her that I was getting a bit of a reputation for womanising. Mum was extremely alarmed by this news. I expect that she was concerned that I would get a girl pregnant and then would have to marry her, even if she were not from a good family, or something like that. Mum arranged for my brother Leon, who was in Sudan, to come to Cairo and tell me about her new plan for me.

I was not at all pleased to see Leon, who was only too delighted to come to Cairo and start laying down the law to his little brother.

'You're coming back to Khartoum with me,' Leon said. 'Mum wants you to get married.'

'What, are you kidding?' I said. 'I am only seventeen. I won't be getting married for years.'

'You're going to do what you're told!' said Leon.

I pointed out that it was already organized for me to marry my second cousin Lola's daughter, Lina, when she was old enough, but Leon was not having any of it. He went to the father of a local girl from a family that my parents liked and tried to arrange a hasty marriage. The girl's father had a shoe-making workshop and had often bought reptile leather from our family business to make the shoes. One day I met the girl, and found that she was extremely beautiful and very friendly. I told Leon that she was just lovely, but that I thought she was more suited to him, rather than me. Leon harrumphed at this, but at least he went back to Sudan and left me alone. Leon and this lovely girl ended up getting married, and they had a long and happy life together.

I did not miss Leon at all after he left, partly because he had been hassling me about girls and women, but also because I wanted to continue with my activism uninterrupted by family matters.

El Nokrashy's murderer was hanged for his crimes, but rather than calming the waters, many of his colleagues viewed him as a martyr for the cause, and the Muslim Brotherhood only gained in strength. One small but very visible sign of the profound changes that were taking place was the fact that Egyptians stopped wearing the fez. El Nokrashy himself had always worn a fez, as had a large cohort of adult Egyptians, including quite a few Egyptian Jews. It was a style that had originally been imported from Turkey, but it had become a sign of Egyptian identity, too. With Egyptian nationalism on the upswing, it now became popular to denounce the fez as a symbol of oppression, and fewer and fewer men felt comfortable wearing one on the street.

As a result of the propaganda of the Muslim Brotherhood, anti-Jewish feeling spread and was normalized among the general population. By now, even the more respectable newspapers, such as the *Al Ahram*, attracted readers with headlines such as 'The Era of the Jews is Coming to an End' and 'Soon the Cotton Industry Will Belong to Real Egyptians'. Inevitably, constant exposure to propaganda like this influenced public sentiment towards the Jews, and even people who had never before doubted the Jews' right to be seen as Egyptians started to view them as intrinsically foreign.

When the Egyptian army was defeated in the Arab-Israeli war in 1949, the situation became increasingly untenable for Egyptian Jews.[6] The government had vastly underestimated the Israeli army, and the outcome was a national humiliation that inspired the national authorities and ordinary people to identify the Egyptian Jews as the new enemy. The agreements reached after the war involved formally-recognized armistice lines, and Israel gained some territory formerly granted to Palestinian Arabs under the United Nations resolution in 1949, while Egypt and Jordan retained control over the Gaza Strip and the West Bank, respectively.

In February 1949, Israel and Egypt reached a peace agreement,[7] which was generally referred to as a ceasefire, as everyone accepted the inevitability of fighting again. Egypt, along with the rest of the Arab countries, continued to refuse to recognise the legitimacy of Israel, and there were serious implications for the Jews of Egypt, who were now all viewed with suspicion and disdain by the government and a growing proportion of the general population. In March of that year, in a meeting in Beirut, representatives from all the Arab states agreed that if Israel refused the right of return of Arab refugees to their homes, the Arab governments would expel the Jews living in their countries.[8]

In Egypt, national anger about what was seen as a humiliation imposed on the Arabs by Jews grew, and so did discriminatory acts against Jews, who were vulnerable to being attacked in the street, to having their businesses and homes vandalized, and to being subjected to campaigns of intimidation, which could include silent or threatening phone calls to their offices or places of residence.[9]

Increasingly, Egyptian Jewish families started to pack up and leave. At this point, most (or at least most from the middle and upper classes) were still hoping that they would be able to stay, but growing numbers could see the writing on the wall and began the process of starting new lives elsewhere. Of course, starting new lives overseas was easiest for the wealthy, who often had business and family connections in various countries, but wealthier people were also more motivated to stay in Egypt, where they had invested heavily. At this time, the majority of those Jews leaving Egypt were those from the poorer social classes, particularly the residents of the Haret al-Yahud, which had already seen a number of terrorist attacks. A number of American Jewish organizations, such as the JDC (the Joint Distribution Committee, which was founded in 1917) were already working to help these people and to assist them with their departure. Many left for Israel, and others were scattered around the world. Many of them sought out destinations with similar climates to Egypt, and as a consequence quite a few working-class Egyptian Jews – about 20 per cent of all those who left at this time – relocated to Brazil, and in particular to the city of Sao Paolo. They were attracted by the tropical climate, and also by the fact that Brazil was an easier destination for immigrants, as it did not operate a quota for Jewish refugees, and was generally well-disposed towards them. One of my uncles and quite a few acquaintances of ours left Egypt for Brazil in this early wave of the second great Jewish exodus.

Quite a few people, including some friends and acquaintances of my family, moved to the United Kingdom at this time too. Many settled in the Manchester area, where there had been a large Jewish community since the eighteenth century, and where they were received with open arms by the British. One of my brothers settled in the United Kingdom and raised his family there. Despite the kindness with which the Egyptian Jews were treated in Britain, it was very difficult for them to leave the wonderful climate of Egypt, with its rich fruits and vegetables, to start a new life under the grey skies of grim post-war England, but they did it, nonetheless.

King Far'uq, already a weak and dissolute ruler who was easy to manipulate, felt personally humiliated by the Egyptian defeat and this impacted on his attitude towards Egyptian Jews. Gamel Abdel Nasser, then an officer in the army, stated that the 'greatest jihad [holy war] is in Egypt' rather than elsewhere, and that he and others like him should 'save the homeland' from people whom he compared to 'wolves' – the Egyptian Jews.[10]

Because of the work that I was doing in my father's leather workshop, and because of the fact that I had contacts all over the city, I heard a lot of news and gossip about some of the most influential people in Cairo. I was very friendly with a photographer who lived near and had access to the royal court, and he often gave me titbits of information about what the king and his family were doing, and what their views were. I heard a lot about King Far'uq's capricious nature. It was clear that he was not half the man that his father was, and that he was no real ally to the Jews at all and could not be trusted to represent the interests of Egypt's minority populations.

There was a mosque right in front of the workshop, and the Muslim Brotherhood held protests outside it on a regular basis, sometimes even escalating to breaking windows in the shop fronts of the area. Honestly, I was quite nervous at this point, and I worried about how to keep me and the business safe. The Muslim Brotherhood maintained that a fundamentalist interpretation of Islam should underpin every aspect of life. For its members (who included the Muslim men who worked in the leather workshop Dad had left me in charge of), the nationalist movement in Egypt was secondary to their aim of establishing these Islamic principles, which did not admit the possibility of a multi-cultural and religiously diverse society, and which certainly would not be welcoming of a substantial Jewish minority. I was lucky to have a connection who provided me with information from time to time about what the organization was planning. His name was Ismael, and he was one of the providers of materials to the leather workshop; he sold us accessories. Ismael was a decent person and a very devout Muslim. He was always very honest in business. It clearly troubled him that I was Jewish – we had an excellent professional relationship and he could see for himself that the terrible things that he had heard about the Jews were not true for me.

'You're an honest man,' Ismael would urge me. 'Why don't you convert to Islam? Islam is the true religion, and I think you would be a lot happier if you were Muslim, like me. Allah will always accept any genuine convert.'

I told him that I had a lot of respect for Islam. This was actually true – the Islam that I had studied years earlier as a little boy in the Madrassah school was not at all like the violent interpretation being promoted by the Muslim Brotherhood. I was able to speak knowledgeably with Ismael about the Qur'ān, and even to quote some verses from it, as I still remembered what I had been taught at the Madrassah.

Ismael looked at me in surprise: 'How do you know the Qur'ān?' he asked. I was able to show him my class photograph from the term I spent at the Madrassah, in which he could clearly see that I had not just studied with the other boys, but also dressed the same way as they did, in traditional Egyptian robes.

'Come on,' I said. 'We are both honest people here. Let's try to help one another.'

'What do you want me to do?' he asked.

I told Ismael all about the vandalism that we had been dealing with at the leather workshop. The plate glass windows had been broken several times and I wanted to avoid this happening again, and also to avoid the shop being looted – looting of Jewish and, to some extent, other 'foreign' businesses was by now a serious problem.

'Can you do anything about it?' I asked Ismael. 'I can't afford to go on like this.'

'Leave it to me,' he said.

Ismael went and talked to his colleagues in the Muslim Brotherhood, and I never had any problems with vandalism again. When he came back, he recommended that I get a bodyguard, and said that it would not be a good idea for this bodyguard to be Muslim. This was his way of telling me that, even with his intervention, there was only so much he could do to keep me and the business safe. Things were going to continue getting even more difficult for the Jews of Egypt.

Following this exchange with Ismael, I went to Haret al-Yahud, and hired a man called Juri, who was a huge, dark-skinned man with a very Arab appearance. I paid Juri a salary and he followed me everywhere like a shadow, keeping me safe. From then on, every time I saw Ismael, I also gave him a little money, just to make sure that things stayed good between us.

While at first glance, many Jews were continuing to work in their businesses as normal, there were many signs of the rapidly deteriorating circumstances they were living in. One clear sign of the fact that large, and growing, numbers of Egyptians did not see a future in Egypt for the Jews is represented by the fact that, in 1949, very few Jews were accepted to study at either of the national universities.[11]

Now operating underground, the Jewish Zionist movement started preparing to transfer Jews from Egypt to Israel,[12] with an emphasis on the poorer Jews who did not have the resources to emigrate elsewhere, and who were particularly vulnerable to the populist violence that was spreading. As an activist, my job was to get in touch with young people in their late teens and early twenties, and encourage them to start thinking about leaving Egypt and going to Israel, which was crying out for young Jews who were strong and motivated and could work hard. I had met lots of young people like myself in the Zionist group I was in and in the sports clubs that I was a member of. I had no doubt that I was doing the right thing when I talked to them about how Israel could really flourish and become a viable, and even thriving, homeland for a Jewish population.

All of the young Jews who became interested in moving to Israel were invited to take part in paramilitary training in an area near the Delta Barrage called El Qanater El Khayreya, which was a large dam that had been built in the nineteenth century about five kilometres outside Cairo. There was no public transport to the area, so we were all crammed into the back of a truck and brought together. Many of the youngsters who trained here would go on to serve in the Israeli army. Girls and boys alike were trained, because the Israeli vision was for a Jewish homeland in which both sexes would play a part in protecting its people. Obviously, if the authorities had known that we were engaging in paramilitary training, we would all have been arrested. Therefore, we would pack for a picnic, and represented our activities as normal boy scout/girl guide type outings. We wore no uniform and there was nothing obvious to show rank among the group, so to the casual onlooker there was really nothing to distinguish us from any other group of young people having a picnic and a nice time under the Egyptian sun. The police and other authorities never had any idea what was going on, or how grand were the plans that we and our leaders were working towards. Even if they had started to suspect us and decided to investigate, they would never have found us doing anything illegal or inappropriate. Our leaders had found the perfect way to train us for a future Israel, by hiding us in plain sight.

Some of the strains and tensions present in Israel at that time were also represented in our trainers, who were a diverse group. While they had all come to Egypt from Palestine, some of them were Europeans who had survived or escaped the Holocaust, and others were of European descent, but had been born and raised in Palestine by Jewish parents who had settled there before Israel was founded. Some of them subscribed to extremely socialist ideals, which actually verged on communism. Their group was known as Shomer al-Zahir, which means 'the young guardians'. Others, instead, were right-wing and would go on in the future to form the Likud, a right-wing political party that was founded in Israel in 1973. A third group, known as Mizrahi, was much more focused on the religious aspects of Judaism, and its members talked a lot about the Holy Land in the Biblical sense of a country that had been literally promised to the Jews by God, and to which one day the Messiah would come.

I was much more attracted to the secular and (at this point) the socialist side of the movement, as my family had never been deeply religious, and I was not really very interested in praying to and talking about God. I heard all about the socialist ideals on which many believed the new Holy Land should be founded. The trainers talked about collective money, which was an utterly alien concept to me, as an Egyptian Jew from a very business-minded family. Most Egyptian Jews were in business, so the idea of money that was collectively owned was exceedingly strange. They also talked about collectively-owned land, and about farming, both of which were also very strange ideas to me. Egyptian and Sudanese Jews of all social classes were almost exclusively an urban people, who lived and worked in cities and towns. We did not know anything at all about farming or working the land,

and while Jews either owned their own houses, apartments, and businesses, or aspired to do so, I had never heard of Jews being owners of large tracts of land, either individually or collectively. I tried and failed to imagine people like my relatives working on the land and engaging in tasks such as counting or milking cows. It seemed almost absurd. It was also exceedingly difficult to imagine a situation or a country in which Jewish people would be in a majority and would form the government, the police force, and the army. Being part of a minority seemed to be an integral aspect of Jewishness as, at that time, it was all we knew.

Somehow, despite their philosophical differences, all three groups managed to work together in training young Jews from Cairo, and getting them ready to leave Egypt and start new lives in Israel. It was exciting and motivating to hear them talk; they were fervent and excited about Israel and all that it could offer, and they spoke in extremely emotive terms, referring to Israel as 'the Promised Land.' While we Egyptian Jews mostly spoke French with one another, our eastern European trainers did not all speak French, and English was the common language for much of our instruction, which meant that most people present at our meetings were communicating in what was their third, or even their fourth, language. Since the arrival of the British troops during the war, English had become much more widely spoken in Cairo in general.

While, as a younger adolescent, I had been quite attracted to the socialist ideals preached by many of the Zionist trainers, now that I was running my father's leather workshop and acquiring business experience, I had begun to feel that socialism was not the way forward, after all. Even at this young age, I could see that hard work and entrepreneurship should be rewarded. While I retained a great interest in the success of Israel as a state and as a Jewish homeland, I became quite unconvinced about the idea that socialism was the system to apply in the new country.

While I was largely alone at this time, once in a while a family member travelled from Sudan, and we would meet and exchange news. When my maternal grandfather became seriously ill with pneumonia on a trip to Cairo, I was the only one of the family left, and I was with him during the last months and weeks of his life. I am grateful to have had the opportunity to have helped him on his final journey; I arranged for his stay in hospital, where I had some contacts, and where he received the care that he needed as he died. I can still remember visiting him in hospital during his final days.

In some ways, it was good that my maternal grandfather did not live to see what was to become of the community in which he had grown up.

Shortly after his death, more than a thousand Egyptian Jews were arrested on suspicion of Zionism, the assets of many Jewish businesses were peremptorily seized, and Jews were forbidden from holding meetings. One Jewish Egyptian remembered:

> We found ourselves stateless from one day to the next. I started to feel I did not belong, and we were not welcome. Around 1949, the government sequestrated everything we owned and that is when we discovered we were blacklisted because my father had properties and money. We were kicked out of our apartment. We then became determined to get out of Egypt.[13]

Many Jewish homes and businesses were bombed, including a number of prominent Cairene stores and landmarks that were owned by Jews and were significant employers of Jews, Muslims, and others in the city.[14] My connections in the Muslim Brotherhood heard that there was a plan to bomb Cicurel's, Cairo's most famous department store, because of its Jewish ownership. They told me about it, and I took this information to the Director of the department store, who was a distant relative of mine – the brother of my uncle by marriage. When I told him what was going to happen, he just laughed at me and told me to go away. He could not believe that anyone would be so daring as to bomb such an important Cairo institution.

'Young man,' he said, 'stop playing children's games with me. I am a Director here, and I have given you a meeting because we are relatives, that's all. I don't know where you got this information, but it's clearly false.' He smiled at me reassuringly. 'Try not to worry,' he said. 'Everything is going to be OK.' Before I left, he gave me a bag of chocolates. I felt very insulted to be treated like a child who did not know what he was talking about. A week later, Cicurel's department store was bombed, along with a number of other Jewish-owned premises on King Fu'ad Street, which was the premier shopping street in Cairo at the time. The bombing was probably carried out by supporters of the Muslim Brotherhood.[15]

A new law authorised the Egyptian authorities to place under state supervision the property of anyone who had been either under surveillance or interned; many of the Jewish-owned department stores fell into these categories.[16] From August of 1949, Jewish-owned homes, businesses, and other property had to be disposed of at a reduced rate of value, and in most cases these assets were reverted to the Egyptian state.[17] The new laws were ruthless, and their impact was devastating:

Bank accounts were blocked, private and commercial property was confiscated, business firms were liquidated, and Jewish employees were discharged. Jewish department stores, banks and other businesses were confiscated and taken over, as were the Jewish schools, youth centers, old age homes, welfare institutions, hospitals, and synagogues. Jewish judges and lawyers were expelled from the bar, and Jewish engineers, doctors, and teachers were denied the right to practice. The Egyptian Medical Association instructed the population not to consult Jewish physicians and surgeons...[18]

Even though Egypt no longer wanted to have a Jewish minority, it also did not want Egyptian Jews to move to Israel. Consequently, it was exceedingly difficult for those planning to leave to obtain the papers they needed, which were known as an exit visa. This meant that many people, and particularly those with little capital and therefore without the ability to bribe government officials, had no choice but to leave illegally.

Between 1949 and 1950, 16,514 Egyptian Jews left Egypt for Israel (generally illegally, with the support of the Mossad Le-Aliya Bet, the Institute for Immigration, a branch of the Haganah that had operated since prior to the foundation of Israel to facilitate Jewish immigration to Palestine and, later, Israel, and discreet financial support from Jewish community leaders),[19] and about 6,000 left for other destinations.[20] Considerable numbers of on-the-ground activists were also involved in helping Jews to leave at this point, of whom I was one. This work was organized through the youth groups to which we belonged.

Given how desperate things had become for so many Jewish people in Egypt, it was not very difficult to find young people who were prepared to take a gamble on the future of the Holy Land. What was more complicated was the issue of how to get them there. Jews were currently in a terribly difficult situation. Life was getting progressively more difficult in an increasingly hostile Egypt, but as many Jews were officially stateless, it was not always very easy getting the paperwork necessary to leave – and Egypt, like all the other Arab countries, was extremely hostile to the idea of a Jewish state. Therefore, it was illegal for young would-be settlers to leave Egypt for Sinai, and it was also illegal for anyone else to try to help them to leave. We needed to find a way to get large numbers of young people to the coast and onto boats without the authorities realizing what was going on. As we were just a bunch of kids, that meant that we would definitely need help.

I remembered General Ross, whom I had got to know on his frequent visits to the mechanic's shop on the ground floor in the building in which

I lived; I had known him for several years now, and he had always been very friendly. I knew that General Ross was based in a British garrison conveniently located beside the Suez Canal. If we could persuade General Ross to help, then maybe there would be a way to smuggle them out through the garrison.

General Ross had always been very kind to me when I met him in Ali's mechanic's workshop. He also knew one of my relatives; my distant cousin Joe Scialom, who managed the bar in the well-known Shepheard's Hotel, where all the English officers liked to drink gin and tonic and try to pick up girls (Joe was famous, among other things, for having invented a popular cocktail known as the 'Suffering Bastard'; he had been working at Shepheard's for years, and was well-known to all of the British officers). I asked Joe to let me know when General Ross was likely to be at the bar, and intercepted him there.

General Ross remembered me well, although he had not seen me for a couple of years:

'Look at you,' he said. 'You're all grown up.'

I explained to General Ross that I was looking for a way to get young Jews out of Egypt by bringing them through the British Garrison. He was immediately inclined to be helpful, and became even more so when I made it clear that we were prepared to offer him a backhander and that Joe would open a bar tab for him that he would never be expected to pay – all the Suffering Bastards that he and his friends could drink, for as long as they wanted.

The British garrisons were enormous. They were practically towns in their own right, with living quarters, streets with shops, concession stands and cafés, and of course all of the infrastructure that the army needed. A large Egyptian staff came in and out of the garrisons all the time providing a wide range of services. General Ross and I agreed that I would be allowed to open a concession stand, registered not to me but under a friend's name, selling handbags from our leather workshop, and, further, that he would issue a large number of official passes to young Jews to enter the garrison under the guise of being construction workers brought in to repair the potholed roads. Once they were there, it would be possible for us to smuggle them onto boats and ferries, which would bring them to Sinai and the waiting Palmach members, who had been alerted as to what was happening, and who would tell them what to do next, and start them on their journey towards becoming Israeli citizens.

As the situation continued to become more difficult in Egypt, there were quite a few young people from all over Egypt, predominately from low-income, Arabic-speaking Jewish families, who wanted to take this trip – there were multiple cells of activists like mine, scattered around the parts of the country where the Jewish community lived, talking to young Jews and getting them ready to settle in the Holy Land. Most of the young people who were now prepared to take the trip were slightly older than me – typically, they were aged between eighteen and twenty-one and usually from very religious backgrounds and deeply invested in the Jewish Promised Land. They and their parents felt that there was no future for them in Egypt, and so they packed a few small items wrapped in a cloth and tied into a bundle with a piece of string – typically a prayer book, a few changes of underwear, and a hand-knitted jumper lovingly made by a proud but tearful mother who did not know when (or even if) she would see her beloved son or daughter again.

At this point, I was arrested and brought to the local Chief of Police Intelligence. Fortunately for me, he knew my father very well, and liked him.

'You naughty boy,' he said when I sat in front of him for my interrogation. 'What have you been doing? This is not good work for you – you're not a Zionist!'

'No, no,' I said. 'Of course I am not a Zionist.'

I had no idea how much he knew about what I had been doing, and of course I understood that it was not in my interest to let him know.

'Well, I have been given instructions to have you locked up,' he said. 'What do you have to say about that? You've put me in a very awkward situation. On the one hand, I don't want to lock you up because I know your father, and on the other I have to, because if I don't, I will get into trouble!'

I just sat there and waited to hear my fate.

'Here's what we are going to do,' he said. 'You are going to go to Huckstep without protest, and as soon as I can, I will sign an order to have you released. At that point, I strongly suggest that you think very carefully about what you want to do next.'

I agreed to do whatever he said and was sent to sit on a hard wooden bench outside his office, where I remained for about four hours before being brought to the camp.

'Don't worry,' the Chief of Police Intelligence said. 'It's not that bad in the camp. You will be with other Jewish boys like yourself.'

I ended up staying in Huckstep for just five days, and I was not frightened at all, but actually rather enjoyed myself. Life had been quite difficult and stressful over the previous few years, and at times I had forgotten what it was like to just be young. A friend of mine, Joe Dabbah, and his brother, Bondi, were among the young Jews detained in Huckstep, and the other detainees considered them to be leaders of the group. The conditions were not bad at all – in fact, we were treated very well. We were allowed to bring food in from outside the camp (we actually ate like kings while some of the people on the streets of Cairo found it difficult to feed their families), and Joe and Bondi organized games to keep us all entertained. Although we were all facing a very uncertain future, we were still able to enjoy ourselves.

Vivette Ancona, who immigrated to the United States, has a similar account of her uncle's detention at this time, saying that he and many of his friends were arrested together, and that their mothers brought home-cooked food for all the detainees and their guards.[21] Lawrence Lewitinn, another immigrant to the US, also has a similar account. His grandfather, together with many others, was confined in Huckstep. Seeing that the guards were badly-paid and poorly treated, the Jewish prisoners started up a vegetable garden for them, and their wives brought cakes for the guards' families. Later on, when some internees who were members of the Muslim Brotherhood rioted and threatened to kill the Jewish prisoners, the guards remembered these kindnesses and intervened firmly on their behalf.[22]

In some ways, it was less frightening being in Huckstep than being outside the camp, as murders and attempted murders of Jews were becoming more common, and we were all keenly aware of how vulnerable we were. I think that we were all experiencing complex emotions at this time. It was really difficult to reconcile the anger so many Egyptians were now directing towards the Jews when, for most of our lives, we had known the Egyptian people to be warm, friendly, and loving. The Egyptian culture was predicated around family values, hospitality, music and dance, and friendship. Even now, on an individual level, many of the Egyptians we met – including some of the guards at the camp – were as kind as ever. At the same time, it was becoming increasingly clear that a mob mentality was taking over, and that one should never underestimate the viciousness of a mob, and the capacity of the mob mentality to transform even the kindest person into a thug.

While conditions in some of the camps (and particularly in El Tur, which was greatly feared) were poor, not all the guards mistreated the inmates; anti-Jewish sentiment was not universal, and some of the guards treated the prisoners not just with humanity, but with kindness.[23] This is indicative of the positive relationship most Jews had enjoyed, until very recently, with the Egyptian majority. But now things were changing quickly, and with each change, the situation grew worse.

I was arrested again one day as I left Shepheard's Hotel after another meeting with my cousin, Joe Scialom, who was still acting as a facilitator between the organization I was in and the British officers who were helping us to get young Jewish migrants out of Egypt and across the Suez Canal. This time, I was in serious trouble. A police swoop into our activities meant that a large number of Jewish activists were arrested at the same time. After the first arrest, of an optician called Lichaa – who was a Karaite and an agent for Mossad, the Israeli intelligence organization – they were given the names of everyone in the group. I am sure that Lichaa was tortured and forced to reveal all that he knew. I can still remember the moment the police approached me and I realized that I had finally been caught.

The police were strangely matter-of-fact and even friendly, in a way, as they took me to the prison.

'You need to be careful,' one of them said. 'You're a good-looking kid, and there's a problem in prisons with a certain type of man who likes young boys.'

The officer gave me some tips on how to keep myself safe, and I had the impression that he was genuinely concerned for my welfare. I reassured him, saying that I knew how to take care of myself.

At the police station where I was processed, I was told to strip so that they could make sure that I was not carrying any weapons or other forbidden items about my person. My clothes were replaced by a striped uniform in a thick, heavy material that was unsuited to the Egyptian climate.

One the way to the prison, another of the officers felt sorry for me, because I was so young.

'Look here, young man,' he said. 'I am going to give you something that will keep you safe.'

He handed me a ruler which was really a switchblade, with the knife perfectly hidden inside.

'You'll be able to bring this into the prison because we've already inspected you and confirmed that you do not have any weapons,' he said. 'But I'm warning you – only use it if you are in danger, and be careful, because if the prison guards catch you with a weapon, you'll be in trouble.'

Gratefully, I took the knife and hid it in my pocket.

At this time, the penalty for those found guilty of Zionism was execution, and even though I was still only seventeen, I knew that others, just as young as me, had been executed before. There was considerable evidence against me.

The police had searched my apartment and found papers with incriminating evidence, and they also had the testimony obtained from Lichaa, so I was condemned to death by a small tribunal that had been formed specifically for the purpose of trying Jews who had been accused of Zionism. However, I was given the right to appeal the sentence, which was a glimmer of hope in an otherwise very bleak situation.

While I waited to see what would become of me, I was held in Abu Zaabal, a prison about an hour away from Cairo on the way to Port Said. There was a special area for foreigners to which I was sent, as Jews were now automatically considered to be foreigners, even if they had never lived outside Egypt. The prison was swelteringly hot, because it was located in an arid area with little to no wind. There was almost nothing around the prison, just land that was only of agricultural use during the rainy season, when shepherds brought their flocks there to eat the grass that was only able to grow when it rained. The rest of the year, the ground in that area is barren and scorched, and it reflects the daytime heat like an oven. It got so hot in the prison, it sometimes felt as though we could hardly breathe.

On the outside, my friends were trying to help me, but there was not much they could do. The state appointed an individual to represent me. He informed me - not unkindly but rather in a matter-of-fact way - that it would be hard to persuade the authorities to drop the charges, and that I was facing the very real prospect of being hanged in the public square, where I would serve as an example to anyone else who might be tempted to get involved in Zionist activism; Lichaa had already been hanged in this manner.

While obviously this was an extremely frightening prospect, on some level I accepted it as inevitable. I entered a strange state of mind in which I was numb and unresponsive to the thought of what was likely to happen. The one thing that helped me at this time was the fact that nobody in my family knew that I was in prison and in danger of being executed.

The state representative who had been appointed to me asked if there was anyone outside who could vouch for me, and I thought immediately of Ali. Ali had been my family's landlord for years now, and he and his family had always been good friends of ours. He was well-known in the area for his successful mechanic's business, he was a very respectable individual - and he was a Muslim.

I asked my state representative to let Ali know what was going on. He agreed to do this and, thankfully, he did. Without a moment's hesitation, Ali told him that I was like a son to him, and that he would never denounce me. He offered the state representative a considerable sum of money, and a newly refurbished car, as a bribe in exchange for my freedom. A week later, I was told that I would be moved to Al-Shalal prison, and shortly after that, I was allowed to leave, on condition that I depart Egypt immediately. My paperwork was sorted out, and I went straight to Sudan.

I never told my family about the time I had spent in prison and took a few months to decide what I was going to do next. Soon, I had decided to move to West Africa, and that I would try my luck as a businessman there. I wanted to be independent from my family, and to build my own life without their help, which I often experienced as interference.

Meanwhile, even though my parents were safe (for now) in Sudan, Dad had come to the decision that he and Mum should move to Israel. He had always been very interested in the Zionist project, and considering how the family had been treated in Egypt, he felt that it made sense for him to throw his lot in with the new Jewish state. Dad hoped that, in middle age, he and Mum would be able to make a happy home for themselves there. Their children were grown up and, like many Egyptian Jewish families, we had scattered far and wide. While several of their children would go on to support Israel in various ways, none of us were attracted to moving there at that time.

In 1950, the Egyptian nationality laws were revisited, and changes were made that were intended to achieve 'national homogeneity' by decreeing that, henceforth, only those resident on Egyptian territory before 1 January 1900,, who had maintained their residence until the current decree, and who were not citizens of another state, were Egyptians.[24] This meant that all Jews who had been granted Egyptian national status after 1 January 1900 were rendered stateless while, in theory, those who had been naturalized between that date and 1932, and who were not Zionists, could still remain in Egypt. However, the very next day, all Jews were declared enemies of the state and therefore subject to immediate expulsion. This was a signal to many people on the street that the authorities would probably look the other way if they engaged in aggressions against Jews. It became increasingly common for Jews to be attacked in the streets and for vandals and looters to damage Jewish businesses and steal items from Jewish-owned shops.

Young couples rushed in huge numbers to the synagogues so that they could travel out of Egypt together; they knew that their families would all be leaving for different destinations, and that if they were separated now, they might never see one another again. Many of them hugged and kissed their parents goodbye almost straight after the wedding, and boarded transport to their various destinations.[25]

One Jewish individual with Egyptian citizenship remembered what had happened to his family: 'The factory was nationalised, the house sequestered. All the furniture was rated. We had nothing to sell. We left the house with just a few suitcases with our clothes.'[26]

Relieved that they had left Egypt before things got even worse (although they had lost the business Dad had built up, and were much worse off than they had been) Dad converted most of his capital into gold, which he stored carefully in a suitcase, and he and Mum went to Israel in 1950 on a direct flight from Khartoum, leaving Lily in the care of our older sister Reina for now, because she was happy in school and needed to complete her education.

When Mum and Dad arrived in Israel, Dad declared the gold to the customs authorities, who promptly confiscated it, as the policy in Israel – which had been determined by President Ben Gurion – was that all gold should be treated as property of the state, as private individuals were not allowed to import gold into Israel. Dad was told that he would receive Israeli money in return for the gold, but not straight away.

Reeling from this loss, Mum and Dad went to the accommodations that they were offered, which were a series of shacks stuffed with 'Oriental' Jews from Arab countries. These were the so-called ma'abarot absorption camps for immigrants and refugees that had been hastily constructed by the Israelis, and which were largely occupied by Jews from the Middle East, while most incoming European Jews were being given houses. Many of those arriving from European locations were housed in hotels until permanent housing became available to them, which the Israeli state treated as a matter of priority.

The ma'abarot were roughly built on the ground, and the earth inside and all around the shacks quickly turned to mud as too many people were crammed into this unsuitable accommodation. It was impossible for anyone to stay clean under these conditions, and there were high levels of disease, including malaria and a range of gastro-intestinal disorders. Sometimes children were even separated from their parents, who were only allowed to visit them occasionally. The camps were also located on the outskirts of the towns and cities, which made the people who lived in them feel that they were seen as illegal immigrants, who had no right to be there.

There was not enough water for everyone in the ma'abarot and it was hard to sleep or even to relax. Knowing that European Jews were being treated very differently was galling. Sometimes the frustration that everyone was feeling spilled over into arguments between people from different cultural backgrounds.

Mum and Dad were extremely uncomfortable and unhappy in the ma'abarot and felt that they would never get a fair chance so long as Israel was dominated by European Jews. Egyptian Jews found it very difficult to get work suitable for their skills. Even those who were highly educated and/or very skilled in business were often offered only quite menial work. The best one could hope for was a low-level entry job in a bank, while a lot of people who had formerly worked in the professions were now expected to labour in the fields, even though they had no agricultural experience.

Some of Mum's siblings had managed to move into private housing and were doing modestly well in Israel (my maternal grandmother, who moved there with one of her children in her later years, would die in Israel in 1971 at a very advanced age), but there was no obvious route for Mum and Dad to take into a similar situation.

At the same time as having to deal with the same issues as all the other so-called 'Oriental' Jews, Mum and Dad were having their own problems: her health had been badly impacted by all the stress that she had suffered in recent years, and the trial of living in the camp made everything worse. Dad, who had been a convinced Zionist for many years, was deeply disillusioned by his experience of Israel. He had never imagined that large numbers of immigrating Jews would be treated like second-class citizens simply because of where they came from, or invited to feel ashamed of the Arab-influenced aspects of their culture and heritage; people were told that they were wrong to sing Arabic folk songs, for example. While the intentions of the European Jews were, I believe, nothing but honourable, they had a condescending attitude towards the Jews from Arab countries that was very frustrating for people like my parents.

At this point, the postal system between the newly-established Israel and Arab countries was not very well established and it was difficult for Mum and Dad to stay in touch. Their letters arrived infrequently, and I think that many of them were lost in the post. The same applied to the letters we sent to them, whether from Sudan or from West Africa. Their growing sense of disillusionment was ever more apparent with each letter that arrived. Dad had harboured such high hopes of Israel, and it was terribly disappointing for him to realize that, even here, not all Jews were considered to be equals. Of course, I was very concerned about them – especially about Mum, because of her health problems, and because I was sure that she was missing her children very much. It was hard not to be in contact, as I had always felt very close to my parents and particularly my mother. Even though we had been apart in recent years, at least when they were in Sudan it had been easier to stay in touch, and there had always been some people coming and going.

Having started to establish myself as a businessman in Egypt, and realizing that a life of entrepreneurship was what I wanted for myself, I was not impressed by the socialist philosophy that dominated Israel at this time. My parents' experience of trying to move to Israel and establish new lives for themselves there convinced me that Israel was not the place for me – or at least, not for now. I was glad it was there, and I would do anything to support it, but until Israel would accept me – an Egyptian Jew – as a person entirely as worthy of respect as a European Jew, I would continue to build my life elsewhere.

Mum and Dad stayed in Israel for three years. That is how long it took the Israeli government to recompense Dad for the gold that he had brought with him from Sudan. As soon as they could, they returned to Khartoum.

By 1951, 30 per cent of the population of Israel was comprised of Jews from Arab countries, the Egyptian Jews among them.[27] For many of them, moving there had been absolutely heart-breaking. Ada Aharoni, a child at the time, remembered twenty-five years later her little school friend coming to say her farewells:

> The last time I saw you was in 1949, when you came to bid me farewell before we left for France. My father, Jewish and a French national, had his business permit withdrawn. You whispered wistfully – I can almost hear your tremulous voice – 'Why are you leaving Egypt? You were born here, this is your country!'
>
> I couldn't explain then what I shall try to do tonight, twenty-five years later, that for me, unlike you, Egypt was not my country. The first powerful impact of that stark fact hit me full in the face when I was only seven years old. This is a part of my childhood that I don't like to remember, as it has left a sore spot in my mind even after all this while…[28]

The exodus of Jews from Egypt continued. After the first Arab-Israeli war, about 50,000 Jews had remained in Egypt, hoping to stay there. Jews' property, as well as the property of English and French nationals, was confiscated.[29] Many Karaite Jews strove to remain, and even to demonstrate loyalty to the Egyptian government.[30] Others could see the writing on the wall and made plans to leave. Sephardi Jews, who tended to be wealthier, more educated, and to have more financial incentive to remain in Egypt, were less likely to leave at this time, as many hoped that the situation would improve and that they would be able to keep their businesses. Poorer Jews, and poorer Ashkenazi Jews in particular, frequently had connections in Israel and fewer financial reasons to stay in Egypt. Large numbers of them had already left – many with the help of my organization. Large numbers of them continued to leave in a short period of time, often with the help of Jewish activists who were able to use their resources and their connections with the Egyptian army to secure the release of Jews who were in captivity, and to assist them on their journey. The names of most of these activists remain unknown except to themselves and their close associates.[31]

On 26 January 1952, what started as an apparently spontaneous protest against the British degenerated into an anti-Jewish riot that would be remembered as 'Black Saturday' or the 'Cairo Fire', leaving 500 Jewish businesses badly damaged, many Jews maimed, and some dead.[32] The famous café, Groppi's, was one of the businesses damaged by flames. I was already long gone by then, but of course I heard about it. It was just another indication that Jews were simply not safe in Egypt. Thankfully, none of the staff of Groppi's were harmed, but everyone in the area talked for days about how the whole neighbourhood had been filled by the odour of burning sugar, and those of us who were used to seeing Groppi's as a symbol of Cairene sophistication were horrified. Shepheard's Hotel was also set ablaze;[33] Joe Scialom, who had worked there for a long time as the head waiter, had also spent some time in prison and had been expelled from Egypt, taking his vast knowledge of cocktails with him.

The Jewish community lived in even more fear after the terrible events of that day. One witness later remembered:

> I witnessed many demonstrations and riots because we lived in the centre of Cairo. The one that is the most vivid in my mind is when they burned Cairo down in 1952. They were burning people alive. We could see the Shell building from the back of our flat and we could see the people being torched alive as they were trying to get out of the building. I was terrified.[34]

Also in 1952, the Egyptian monarchy was overthrown and Far'uq and his family went into exile overseas, abandoning their lavish palaces, many cars, and the jet-set lifestyle that they had enjoyed. The newspapers showed photographs of the royal family in tears and quoted the king's mother, Queen Nazli (who had been living in California since 1946), as saying that she bid farewell to the country that she loved. Far'uq went on to live a playboy lifestyle in Monaco. Even though King Far'uq, unlike his father

Fu'ad, had never been a good friend to the Egyptian Jews, without him things were worse, because now the nationalist movement in Egypt, which was deeply anti-foreigner and anti-Jewish, was in the ascendant.

The leader of the new regime, General Muhammad Naguib (who was originally from Sudan), stated that all religions were equal in Egypt, and that the Egyptian Jews would be respected, pledging that he would pursue a positive relationship with the Jews of Egypt.[35] The Egyptian Jews mostly viewed Naguib as a good man, but held out little hope that he would actually be able to help them. While Naguib was the titular leader of Egypt at this time, real leadership came from Gamal Abd Nasser. With Far'uq out of the way, an ambitious programme of social change was rolled out. The army was sent out to patrol the streets and ensure that the populace accepted everything that was going on. There were heavily armed soldiers everywhere. Everyone knew that, even if Naguib was notionally in charge, they were actually taking their orders from Nasser.

In June 1953, Egypt was declared a republic. Nasser led a delegation demanding that the British withdraw from the Suez Canal. While anti-semitism had already flourished under Naguib, his effective loss of power was a significant blow to the Jews of Egypt. Nasser's brand of nationalism was distinctly anti-Jewish, and extremely ambitious; he envisioned Egypt becoming a leading nation in a pan-Arabist movement against the west and supported the confiscation of property from Jewish business owners. He was especially interested in larger and more profitable businesses, so at least at the beginning, smaller businesses were able to go under the radar. The Minister of National Guidance, Salah Salim, stated that Egypt would never make peace with Israel, even if all of the General Assembly resolutions and partitions and refugees were respected.[36] The same year, following a growth in nationalism in Sudan that paralleled that which had occurred in Egypt, Sudan was given the right to self-government.

In 1954, a number of young Egyptian Jews were arrested and convicted of being spies for Israel; the so-called Lavon Affair. One of them was my old friend Marcelle Ninio, who had been higher up in the chain of command in the young group I had been involved with some years before. Actually, I knew several of the people involved in the incident, and more than one of them told me later on that they had always regretted being so stupid.

Marcelle had been recruited to act as a liaison for an Israel spy cell in 1951, and she had done her work fearlessly. Her cell had been quiet until 1954, when it was told to activate the plan, which was to plant explosives in British, American, and Egyptian-owned premises, in the hope that

Britain would assume that they had been placed by the Muslim Brotherhood, would become alarmed, and would feel obliged to occupy Egypt again.[37] Marcelle was arrested when one of the cell members' devices, which was no more powerful than an ordinary firework, exploded prematurely in an ashtray at a cinema. She went on to serve a lengthy sentence in prison. My whole family had left Egypt by the time of the Lavon Affair, so we learned from the newspapers that two of the arrested agents were hanged, one died of suicide, and the rest were imprisoned.[38] (Marcelle would eventually be released in 1968, after which she moved to Israel, where she married and settled down.)

The poorly thought-out Lavon Affair further hardened Egyptian attitudes towards Egyptian Jews, even though there was no evidence of substantial support among them for these activities, which had clearly served only to heighten the dangerous situation the Egyptian Jews were already in. While the Lavon Affair was an exercise in bungling on the part of the Israeli authorities, for many Egyptians in positions of power, it was a welcome excuse to continue to harden their attitudes towards the Jews in general.

For the Egyptian Jews, it was devastating to live through this time – so much so that many people, even now, could hardly believe that it was happening. It was very difficult to understand how neighbours, friends, and colleagues with whom the Jews had lived and enjoyed their lives side by side for generations now seemed to hate them, and even to wish them dead.

The military regime in Egypt further eroded the rights and safety of minorities in Egypt, particularly the rights and safety of Egypt's Jews, while Israeli military activity, including attacks on Egyptian military headquarters in Gaza, continued to harden Egypt's attitude not just towards Israel, but towards the Jews in general. Egypt continued to amass impressive arms and military equipment, much of which was provided by the Soviet bloc, which had a vested interest in helping Egypt to maintain a strong position against the west.[39]

In 1955, schools were informed that they must now teach according to Arab norms, including the provision of classes on topics such as history and geography through the medium of Arabic. As most Jewish children attended schools teaching a European curriculum, this was widely seen as a strike against the Jews.[40] Many Jewish children, not accustomed to speaking Arabic at home, found themselves failing at school. Lucette Lagnado remembered the crisis that ensued when her teacher informed her parents that she was failing at Arabic in school, and how this language difficulty seemed to seal her fate as a foreign child:

In Egypt, I was called a foreigner because of my inability to speak Arabic.

In France, where we'd briefly sojourn, and where I was completely fluent in the language, I was a foreigner, because I was from Egypt.[41]

In the years to come, the situation in Egypt continued to deteriorate for the Egyptian Jews.

Notes

1. Miccoli, 2015, 112.
2. Beinin, 1998, 67.
3. Mayer, 1987, 201.
4. Beinin, 1998, 68-9.
5. Sachar, 2006, 401.
6. Oppenheim, 2003, 411.
7. Reich, 2005, 52.
8. Shenhav, 2006, 157.
9. Julius, 2018, location 291 (Kindle edition).
10. Gerges, 2018, 70.
11. Laskier, 1999, 143-4.
12. Oppenheim, 2003, 427.
13. Barda, 2006, 172.
14. Oppenheim, 2003, 428.
15. Beinin, 1998b, 332.
16. Beinin, 1998, 67.
17. Sachar, 2006, 401.
18. Aharoni, 2003, 57.
19. Oppenheim, 2003, 427.
20. Beinin, 1998, 70.
21. Family history related by Vivette Ancona for the *Out of Egypt* celebratory booklet, printed 2019.
22. Family history related by Lawrence Lewitinn for the *Out of Egypt* celebratory booklet, printed 2019.
23. Miccoli, 2015, 158.
24. Laskier, 1995, 582-3.
25. Lagnado, 2006, 94-5.
26. Barda, 2006, 182.
27. Aharoni, 2003, 54.
28. Aharoni, 2008/9.
29. Beinin, 1998, 18-19.
30. Beinin, 1998, 72.
31. Hastings, 21 July 2019.
32. Levick, 15 January 2020.

33. Lagnado, 2006, 63-5.
34. Barda, unpublished manuscript, 12.
35. De Aranjo, 2013, 205.
36. Sachar, 2006, 472-5.
37. Sachar, 2006, 480.
38. Oppenheim, 2003, 428. Shmu'el Azhar and Moshe Marzuq, were executed, Me'ir Meyuhas and Me'ir Za'fran were sentenced to seven years and Robert Dassa, Victor Levy, Philip Natanson and Marcelle Ninio were ultimately released in the prisoner exchange following the Six-Day War in 1967.
39. Sachar, 2005, 481-2.
40. Abecassis, 1994, 521-7.
41. Lagnado, 2006, 148.

7

The Suez Crisis and Ongoing Exodus

In 1956, Nasser – who had been returned as President in June of that year and now had absolute authority – nationalized the Suez Canal and other British and French properties in Egypt, following which Israeli, French, and British forces attacked Egypt to protect their interests.[1] Access to the Suez Canal was particularly important for Israel, which was trying to build a viable economy. It was, however, also important to other economies, including the British and the French.

At this time, I was living in Nigeria, where I had developed a business around hunting crocodiles and exporting crocodile hides to France and elsewhere for the fashion industry. In this role, I took many risks, both in business and with my personal safety. Possibly I felt that, as I had already faced my demons in Egypt, and had even had the threat of execution hanging over my head for a few weeks, nothing further could harm me. I had a sense of reckless invulnerability that allowed me to do all sorts of dangerous things that I shudder to think about now.

I was so wrapped up in my business, and in my life as a single young man, that I did not think much about Egypt on a daily basis anymore. To tell the truth, when I did allow myself to think about it, I often started to feel upset, so would repress both the feelings and my memories of an Egyptian boyhood. It still hurt to know that I had been rejected by Egypt purely because I was Jewish, while at the same time I knew that many families very much like mine were still living there, in an environment that was becoming progressively more hostile all the time. Nonetheless, I could clearly see that Nasser's actions were inevitably going to lead to an even worse situation for the remaining Jews of Egypt.

Britain's Prime Minister Anthony Eden considered Nasser's actions to be illegal, and in contravention of the Convention of 1888, which had guaranteed free use of the canal for all time. Eden also considered Nasser a communist, and Nasser's government a threat.[2] At the same time, there was widespread support in France for a strike against Nasser, whom the media often compared to Hitler. Nasser's power had been growing steadily, but his move to nationalise the Suez made it grow exponentially.

In late 1956, on 29 October, in an attempt to regain western control of the Suez Canal and to remove President Nasser, Israel invaded Egypt, followed by Britain and France, who were Israel's allies. Following pressure from the United States, the Soviet Union, and the United Nations, the invading countries withdrew, leading to humiliation on the international stage for Britain and France, and the strengthening of Nasser's position. Anthony Eden resigned; historians have recognised the Crisis as a major blow to Britain's position as a world power.

The Suez Crisis and the subsequent consolidation of Nasser's power prompted great concern on the part of the remaining Egyptian Jews as to their future in the country. European citizens, particularly from France, were also anxious about what the Crisis would mean for them, and steps were taken to safely remove them from Egypt.

However, while many Jews held European, including French, citizenship, they were not always regarded in the same light as other people with European passports. Egypt responded to the hostilities by expelling the staff of French schools, choosing to view these schools as symbols of French colonialism and presence in Egypt. British schools and congregational schools specifically run for the Jewish community were also closed.[3]

Following the Suez Crisis, the situation continued to deteriorate for the Jews of Egypt. The remaining Jews in Egypt were targeted not just by angry mobs, but by government policies aimed firmly towards removing them from Egypt. Many of the leaders of the Jewish communities in Egypt were arrested and led through the streets of Cairo and Alexandria; some were stoned. Jewish families with long histories in Egypt, but without citizenship, were evicted. A government order was read in the mosques instructing the congregants that Jews were to be seen as enemies.[4]

While many Jews had already left, nearly 1,000 of those who remained were imprisoned or tortured,[5] with some only released and allowed to emigrate following the intervention of representatives of nations such as Spain.[6] Following a government directive, hundreds of Jews were blacklisted and many families lost their property, with about 460 Jewish enterprises confiscated at that time, while, in late October 1956, thousands of Jews with Egyptian and European nationalities were arrested or expelled. The Ministry of the Interior established a Department of Jewish Affairs to oversee what had become a sustained attack.

By November 1956 new, extremely restrictive, criteria were applied to Egyptian nationality. Anyone who had ever been accused of Zionist activity was excluded – and as the accusations did not have to be proven, this effectively excluded all Jews, including those who were legal citizens of Egypt, or had the legal right to apply for citizenship, based on the length of time their families had lived in Egypt or the Ottoman Empire.[7] The process of applying for an exit visa, which was necessary for anyone who left Egypt, also involved the renunciation of one's Egyptian citizenship. In general, the process of obtaining the necessary paperwork even to leave the country was mired with harassment and petty point-scoring on the part of many of the officials involved, who seemed to enjoy making things as difficult as possible for the Jews, whose situation was growing ever more untenable.[8]

Also in 1956, a military order was issued, giving the Director General of 'absentees' property' the right to manage and even to sell the property of people who were in prison as political prisoners – and therefore absentees through no fault of their own. Clearly, there was now a substantial incentive to arrest Jews and imprison them, as this made their property available to others.

Unsurprisingly, some of the wealthiest and most respected members of the Jewish community were arrested at this time. Large numbers of Jews were issued with instructions to leave the country within a few days. They were allowed to bring no more than thirty Egyptian pounds and jewels worth up to 140 Egyptian pounds. Between November and March 1957, 14,012 were expelled from Egypt, and another 7,000 were expelled in September of the same year.[9]

The expulsion of one member of a family, generally the father and the breadwinner, meant that the whole family had to leave, as they were dependent on him for their sustenance. It also meant that all of his Jewish staff members, if he were a business-owner, were now out of work, as businesses closed or were taken over by others, who would not have Jews on the workforce. Consequently, the expulsion of each Jewish business-owner had far-reaching repercussions that went way beyond his immediate family. These repercussions impacted on the broader Egyptian economy, and on the incomes and well-being of countless Egyptian families from all sorts of backgrounds.

Even though many Jewish families had been on very friendly terms with Muslim Egyptians, now their relationship with the majority population became ever more strained. Broad-ranging propaganda efforts, including sermons preached in mosques, convinced large segments of the Egyptian population that the Jews were to blame for all the problems facing Egypt. This propaganda was supported by the government, which used it as an arm of their general policy of harassment of the Egyptian Jews. The experience of the expulsions, and living in Egypt during this period, was inevitably experienced as deeply traumatic, leaving intensely painful memories that would scar those who lived through it for the rest of their lives. One individual remembered the terrible impact on her at the time:

> As a British subject, my mother was expelled, her shop seized, and she had to leave within three days with only £10. I was also expelled and was supposed to leave without my family but was saved by the Dutch Consulate who gave me a false passport declaring I was Dutch since my marriage. It was a very difficult time. We were living in fear of our servants who were brainwashed every day, during their prayers at the mosque or by loudspeakers in the streets. They were coming back to work with hate in their eyes. I remember walking along the streets and hearing some Arabs yelling 'we will cut your throat'.[10]

The great Jewish Egyptian poet Edmond Jabès, who wrote in French, was successful in the fields of both poetry and stock-broking in Egypt. In his role at the Stock Exchange Commission, he had been influential in stabilizing the Egyptian stock market. Yet despite the many services he rendered to the Egyptian state, once the government had formulated the policy of getting rid of all the Jews, he was allowed to stay in Cairo only for long enough to train those who would replace him. The same went for other individuals with important roles in the finance, education, and business sectors. Those who resisted faced intimidation, threats, and the risk of public humiliation. In the case of Jabès, government officials taunted him by preventing him from going to work, and sometimes confining him in his apartment, even though he was doing important work for the Egyptian government.[11]

In the 1950s, most private and foreign schools were taken over by the government, and British, French, and other foreign teachers were expelled. By 1960, the numbers of students studying in these schools had dropped by half. Despite this, because of reduced teacher numbers, the schools were now overcrowded. They were also under-funded by Nasser's government, and the quality of education available dropped significantly.[12]

While resentment towards those Jews who had become wealthy in Egypt was often expressed, little thought was given to the fact that the wealthy Jews had also provided employment, and had engaged in philanthropic work that had benefited everyone, not just their own community. Still less thought was given to the fact that a substantial minority of the Jews – up to a third – was very far from wealthy. Among this cohort was a large number of people with no or poor literacy skills, no formal citizenship of any nation, and very little social capital on which to rely should they need to leave the only homeland they had ever known.

Of course, the events in Egypt were not occurring in a vacuum, but in the context of great unrest, growing nationalism, and burgeoning anti-semitism across the entire Middle Eastern region. Large numbers migrated and emigrated, frequently involuntarily. Among them, the large numbers of Jews, about 800,000, who were forced to leave Arab nations and settle in Israel or elsewhere. The Egyptian Jews were part of this broader trend; 40 per cent of the Egyptian Jews moved to Israel, with the remainder spreading all over the world, to countries including France, the US, the UK, Australia, and Brazil (we will discuss the diaspora in more detail in the next chapter).[13]

Newspaper reports of the time often characterized Arab Palestinians as 'refugees' while describing Jewish migrants differently, even though many of the Jews would have preferred to stay where they were, where they had established businesses and networks, rather than start a new life somewhere else.[14] The source of the reluctance to acknowledge that Jews, too, were refugees was more complex than it might first appear; anti-Jewish feeling was high, and growing, in Arab countries, but the Israeli authorities were often reluctant to acknowledge that some of the Jews who came to live in Israel had come under duress, and would have preferred to remain in their homes in Egypt or elsewhere, had they been given the opportunity to do so. The Israeli government was keen to promote the idea that Jews were proactively choosing Israel as their home, and was reluctant to accept that some came only as a last resort.

After 1956, most of the remaining Jews of Egypt left, either voluntarily or when they were forced to do so. Small numbers of Jews and other minorities were, however, sequestered and forced to train their Egyptian replacements in their profession or industry before themselves being expelled after a period of months or even years. From 1956-7, over 500 Jewish businesses were seized, and their bank accounts frozen, while a further 800 were blacklisted and their accounts were also frozen. All were instructed to fire their Jewish employees.[15]

Between 1956 and 1957, unsurprisingly, the figures for immigration to Israel show a massive upswing, with a total of about 125,000 new arrivals, about 25,000 of whom were from Egypt. Some fled directly into Israel, while others fled initially to Europe, and were then transported to Israel by the Jewish Agency, where they tended to settle in coastal towns, generally having left everything they owned behind.[16] Other Jews settled elsewhere around the world.

One of the great ironies of Egyptian policy towards the Jews in the middle part of the twentieth century is that it effectively forced large numbers of Jews who had been perfectly happy in Egypt to move to Israel. Rendered stateless, and denied the opportunity to apply for citizenship, increasingly they had no option left other than to move to Israel. It is no exaggeration to say that Egypt's harsh treatment of its Jewish minority helped to swell Israel's population considerably and contributed to Israel's success as a new nation.

Amid the horrors unfolding in Egypt and in other Arab countries, the United Nations was grappling with the issue of refugees in general. How could refugees be defined? What supports and protections were they entitled to? In 1951, the Geneva Convention attempted to define the term 'refugee' within rather narrow geographical and temporal parameters, as follows:

> The term 'refugee' shall apply to any person who... as a result of events occurring before 1 January 1951 and owing to well-founded fear of being persecuted for reasons of race, religion, nationality, membership of a particular social group, or political opinion, is outside the country of his nationality, and is unable to or, owing to such fear, is unwilling to avail himself of the protection of that country; or who, not having a nationality and being outside the country of his former habitual residence as a result of such events, is unable or, owing to such fear, is unwilling to return to it.[17]

Under this narrow definition, only those Jews from Egypt who were formally stateless could be considered refugees and be entitled to the various supports available to them. As many of the Egyptian Jews were formally citizens of various European countries (even though, in some cases, they had never even visited them) this did not apply to them. Those campaigning for the rights of Jewish refugees have identified the role of the United Nations as "'pernicious and prejudicial"... by systematically excluding the narrative of Jewish refugees or by exclusively identifying only Palestinian refugee rights...'[18]

The French authorities associated the expulsion of Jews with the foundation of Israel, while the British linked it with British retreat from the area of the Suez Canal, and Nasser's control over it. Jewish Egyptian refugees in both Britain and France were not considered to be covered by the Geneva Convention, but rather viewed as non-nationals of Egypt who had been expelled. Consequently, despite the fact that many of them had lost all, or almost all, of their assets, and faced the same sort of problems as other refugees, they were not considered to be entitled to similar supports. In France, they were referred to as 'repatriés' as if they were returning 'home', even though most of them had lived in Egypt all their lives.[19]

In the late 1950s, a further series of laws made it even more difficult for Jews to remain in Egypt. Egyptian nationals were forced to apply for permits to work with 'foreigners' and import-export companies had to register with the authorities, which did not provide Jews with work cards.[20] In 1958, Nasser banned the use of the fez, although fewer and fewer people had felt comfortable wearing it for a number of years. It was a further sign of the ongoing rejection of anything interpreted as 'foreign'.

The already greatly diminished population of Jewish Egypt shrank yet further. The few Jewish-owned businesses that remained did not resist for much longer. Cicurel's department store was placed under sequestration, the family ceded their majority to a new, Muslim-dominated group, and the last of the Egyptian Cicurels left the country.[21]

In 1958, after a number of adventurous years in West Africa, I felt ready to settle down, and decided that I would return to my family in Sudan, and then move from there to Geneva. Mum had written to me to let me know that the baby I had been informally affianced to all those years before, when I was just ten years old, was now a beautiful young woman. She had attended school in Britain, but now she was back in Sudan. I packed up my business in Nigeria, and returned to Sudan. Mum was right: the 'baby' was stunningly beautiful, and when I got to know her, I realized that she was also sweet, intelligent, gentle, and kind. Lina, the love of my life, and I were married in the synagogue in Khartoum, and shortly after that, we moved to Geneva, Switzerland, where we have lived ever since. My parents and some other members of the family had already settled there.

Not long after our marriage, my wife Lina and I had the opportunity to meet David Ben Gurion. He asked us to consider moving to Israel, telling us that the country was crying out for young couples like us and that we could have a very bright future there, and raise our future children in a Jewish homeland. While I was still very much a supporter of Israel – as I have remained to the present day – I remembered the terrible experience my parents had when they tried moving to Israel, and felt that I did not want to raise a family in a country that considered some citizens to be more equal than others. Moreover, I had started to become a successful businessman, and was loath to move to a country with socialist ideals that would hamper my ambitions.

By 1961, following ongoing intense anti-Israeli and anti-Jewish propaganda, the Jewish population of Egypt numbered only about 7,000, of whom about 2,000 were Karaites, with the majority relatively unskilled and not very highly educated.[22] All of them were extremely vulnerable to false accusations of treachery and espionage, and to summary arrests and imprisonment.[23]

When what would become known as the Six-Day War broke out on 5 June 1967, 350 of the remaining Egyptian Jews were incarcerated in the notorious Abu Zaabal Prison, where they were terribly mistreated.[24] Some were detained for as long as three years[25] and were released only after foreign governments and agencies had made numerous representations on their behalf. One such was the Organization of Casualties of Antisemitic Persecution in Egypt, which wrote to the then Prime Minister of Israel, Levi Eshkol, reminding him that Egyptian prisons contained not just Israeli soldiers who had been captured, but also Egyptian Jews who had been arrested on suspicion of acting for the state of Israel.

Ultimately, when many of these Egyptian Jewish prisoners were eventually released, it was in the context of a prisoner exchange between Egypt and Israel,[26] which took place only after considerable effort on the part of the Hebrew Immigrant Aid Society, with the help of the Spanish Embassy in Cairo.[27] All those who were released were simultaneously expelled from Egypt, never to return again. Indeed, they were only allowed to leave so long as they agreed to renounce their Egyptian nationality, leave all of their possessions behind them, and promise that they would never return to Egypt again.

Watching the events unfurl from Israel, I once more felt obliged to do what I could do support the Jewish homeland. In Switzerland, a large number of Jews gathered to show their solidarity and requested support from the Swiss government. Ten thousand people – among them Lina and I – marched together to the United Nations building to make our point.

Yet more Egyptian Jews left the country, mostly for Europe or Israel, while life became ever more difficult for the few who remained. 'Zionism' was now a criminal offence, but no official definition of Zionism was offered, making all Jews extremely vulnerable to being accused of it. There was a resurgence of violence against the Egyptian Jews, whose numbers, at approximately 2,500, were now vastly depleted. Jewish Egyptian males over the age of sixteen were held in internment camps or tortured.

In the 1970s, in response to international pressure, remaining Egyptian Jews were allowed to leave the country. It was estimated at this time that the Jews of Egypt, some of whom had been among the wealthiest members of the business community, had lost $500 million in personal property, $300 million in communal religious property, and $200 million in religious artefacts.[28]

For the tiny numbers of Jews who remained in Egypt, their situation was precarious. Legally, they were defined as 'local subjects', but they were not granted citizenship and therefore could not fully participate in Egyptian society.[29] That they managed to survive in Egypt at all is testimony to their attachment to a country that had rejected them so thoroughly. The struggles of the small number of Jews who remained in Egypt were also considerable. Some, such as the Marxist Chehata Haroun, saw the issues in Egypt through a political lens, and remained for ideological reasons. While some communist Egyptian Jews converted to Islam (at least notionally) to make it easier to remain in Egypt and continue to fight for Marxism, Haroun resisted all efforts to make him give up his Jewishness, and persisted in being both Jewish and Marxist, as well as well as proudly Egyptian.[30]

By the 1980s, there were only about 300 Jews left in all of Egypt,[31] after several decades during which their numbers were steadily and systematically depleted. Also by that stage, a new generation had been born, and had grown up, in the scattered communities around the world of Egyptian Jewish descent.

Notes

1. Reich, 2005, 65.
2. Eden, 1960, 474-5.
3. De Aranjo, 2013, 213.
4. Aharoni, 2003, 57.
5. Levick, 15 January 2020.
6. Rubinstein et al, 2002, 104.
7. Miccoli, 2015, 167-8; Shamir, 1987, 60.
8. Beinin, 1998, 73.
9. Roumani, 2003, 62.
10. Quoted in Barda, unpublished manuscript, 13.
11. Israel Pelletier, 2008, 804.
12. Cochran, 1986, 45.
13. Miccoli, 2015, 166.
14. Negrine, 2013, 451.
15. Laskier, 1995, 581.
16. Sachar, 2006, 515.
17. UN General Assembly, Convention Relating to the Status of Refugees, 28 July 1951, United Nations, Treaty Series, vol. 189, pp.137-84. Accessed at: http://www.unhcr.org/refworld/docid/3be01b964.html
18. Julius, 2018, location 3802 (Kindle edition).

19. De Aranjo, 2013, 14.
20. Oppenheim, 2003, 429.
21. Beinin, 1998b, 332.
22. Laskier, 1999, 287.
23. Lagnado, 2006, 148.
24. Meital, 2017, 190.
25. Roumani, 2003, 62.
26. Rabalo, 2019, 333.
27. Barda, 2006, 18.
28. Levick, 15 January 2020.
29. Beinin, 1998, 62.
30. Meital, 2017, 187-8.
31. Krämer, 1989, 221.

8

Egyptian Jews as Refugees, in Israel and the Diaspora

During the 1940s and 50s, large numbers of people were displaced in many different contexts all over the world. Among them, of course, were the Jews of Egypt and of other Arab lands. Of these displaced Jews, some went to Israel and others to destinations all over the world, including France and Britain, and the United States, Brazil, Argentina, and Australia.

My own family was completely typical in this regard: by the late 1940s, after briefly facing the very real prospect of execution in Egypt, I had decided to try my luck in West Africa. By then, my parents had moved to Israel, where they would spend three unhappy years before returning to Sudan, my siblings were in Sudan (which they would soon leave), and my extended family was scattered all over the world. By the late 1950s, not one single member of my Jewish social circle – whether friend, relative, or acquaintance – was left in Egypt, and I had largely lost contact with most of the aunts, uncles, and cousins who had played such a big role in my childhood. For example, an uncle I had been very fond of settled in Brazil; in those days, when we relied on an often rather inefficient postal system to stay in touch, inevitably often there was little to no contact.

At the time, as a young man in West Africa, my main concern was finding my own path, building a business, and enjoying life. In some ways, I regret that the huge extended family that provided us all with such a sense of closeness, warmth, and security was cast in all directions such that it could never be put back together again. On the other hand, if I had the opportunity to live my life all over again, I am sure that I would make all the same decisions, because the years I spent in West Africa on my own were a wonderful time and provided me with a learning experience and the foundation on which I have built everything that I have achieved subsequently. However, I believe that for most of the Egyptian Jews, the loss of their family and friendship networks was a terrible blow, from which many never fully recovered, and despite my positive experience in West

Africa, when I look back over my life, I can see how trauma has affected every aspect of it.

While clearly the Egyptian Jews came from various socio-economic backgrounds, after the events of the 1940s and 50s, they generally shared not just the experience of having left Egypt, often under duress, but also of having lost property, businesses, and/or savings. Many had been forced to leave with no more than what they were able to carry – frequently just a suitcase with a few humble possessions and a paltry amount of money, along with passports stamped with the words 'Never again to return to Egypt.'[1] Frequently all of the property was nationalized by the state; in other cases, property was taken over by an Arab Egyptian neighbour or colleague.[2] Either way, Jews had been forced to relinquish their rights, their properties, and their possessions.

Following the Suez Crisis, when remaining French, British, and Jewish residents of Egypt were expelled, typically police officers came to the workplace or home of those who were being expelled and ordered them to leave Egypt within two to seven days. Their assets were frozen and seized by the Egyptian government as they were forced to sign papers stating that they agreed to leave everything behind. They were allowed to bring nothing with them beyond what they could carry in a suitcase weighing no more than twenty kilos, and twenty Egyptian pounds, then of a similar value to twenty English pounds.[3] To ensure that those leaving were obeying these rules, many were subjected to intrusive body-searches to ensure that they had not hidden any of their valuables about their persons. One individual who lived through this time remembered:

> We had to pack in six days. We were putting boxes after boxes in the basement for my uncle to take care of. The porter saw what was happening and although we had given him money to appease him, he denounced my mother to the authorities, saying that she was putting diamonds in the suitcases. The day that we left, we just closed the house as if we were coming back. Our ship was delayed because we were all bodily searched. They didn't find anything and finally they let us aboard.[4]

Women were not even allowed to bring their engagement rings with them, in many cases. As they knew that all of their funds would be confiscated, Jews planning their departure attempted to spend as much as they could on clothes and other items that they hoped they would be able to bring with them; Lucette Lagnado's family initially planned to bring some valuable items, such as jewellery, with them by having them sealed inside jars of preserves, only to change their mind when they heard how strict the customs officers were when it came to inspecting the Jews' belongings before they left. Of one of their friends, they heard the following tale:

> One woman, a seamstress, had hidden her engagement ring in a small iron she used to press hems. Then, in a touch of ingenuity, she had taken gold coins, covered them with cloth so that they looked like ordinary buttons, and affixed them to a dress. As she prepared to leave, an inspector had examined the iron and found the hidden ring. Minutes later, he had stripped the phoney buttons off the dress. He proceeded to tear through nearly every item of clothing, even ripping the shoulder pads off her husband's fine, hand-tailored suits, in search of hidden jewels. Miraculously, she had still been allowed to leave, albeit with none of her valuables.[5]

While not only Jews were expelled from Egypt at this time, Jews were particularly vulnerable, as they did not always have citizenship status elsewhere, and even when they did, they were often not seen as 'full' or 'real' citizens of the European nations in question. Although, clearly, the expelled had no choice in the matter, this form of expulsion was referred to as 'voluntary'. Clearly, this designation is laughable; the only alternative they faced was house arrest or the loss of liberty, the loss of all personal and business property, and the prospect of expulsion. It is very evident that the emigration of the Jews of Egypt was forced in all but name, and that the overwhelming majority of Jews who left Egypt at this time did so as refugees.

According to some estimates, lost Jewish property in Arab countries could amount to $150 billion,[6] incorporating a substantial amount of property that belonged to Egyptian Jews, who had to leave homes, businesses, and other possessions behind. The consequences of these confiscations were far-reaching, and had both a practical and an emotional impact. Those who had come from the middle and upper classes lived with first- and second-hand memories of the comfortable lives that they had once enjoyed in Egypt. Many men, who were accustomed to working hard and providing for their families, found the situation deeply painful and humiliating, as they had to start from scratch in a new country. In the case of those in Israel, they were often expected to do very different work to what they had been used to in Egypt. Many, who had been born into affluent and educated families and had grown up with the reasonable expectation of a certain standard of living, found that they had suddenly been reduced by their circumstances to the working classes and the necessity of competing with others for jobs that they had never imagined doing.[7]

Many Jews fleeing Egypt were given official documentation by the United Nations recognising their status,[8] but Jews who left Arab lands for destinations other than Israel did not necessarily consider themselves refugees in the first instance. They were soon reminded that, in fact, this is what they were. For example, Jews who left Egypt for France often found that their first experience of a land that many of them had assumed would seem familiar, because of their proficiency in the French language, was a cold, uncomfortable refugee camp. The sorrow that many Jews in Arab countries felt on being compelled to leave was a serious ideological challenge that they were often reluctant to accept for reasons that they did not always fully understand. They left their countries of origin, Shohat says, 'with mingled excitement and terror... buffeted by manipulated confusion, misunderstandings, and projections'.[9]

Since the foundation of Israel, many elements of the media and other commentaries have tended to characterize Arabs displaced by Israel as 'refugees' and Jews displaced by Arab states as 'settlers'[10] - including the large numbers of Jews who had no wish to leave. The reasons for the reluctance to recognise Jews from Arab countries as refugees are complex and nuanced. The Arab states did not wish to characterize the Jews as refugees, because of the implication that they are entitled to compensation for the property that was seized, and elements in the Israeli government did not wish to see them as refugees either, as they felt this challenged the idea of Israel as a Jewish homeland.

Historical matters also add to the complex picture. Throughout history, many Jews - such as the Sephardim in 1492 - had come to Egypt to escape difficult living conditions and persecution elsewhere. Similarly, many Jews also came to Egypt in later centuries to escape difficulties and pressures of various kinds in their countries of origin. Many of these Jews, who initially came to Egypt essentially as refugees, or at least as migrants fleeing trouble elsewhere, went on to thrive in business and commerce. With the rise of nationalism in Egypt, the descendants of these people were increasingly cast as foreigners who could never really be nationals, and they were accused of exploiting the generosity of their Egyptian hosts. Having established this nationalist interpretation of history, and designated the Egyptian Jews as ungrateful *arrivistes*, there was certainly Arab reluctance to accept the fact that their forced removal from Arab lands that had long been their home classified them as people seeking refuge,[11] and entitled to particular protection and compensation from the culture ejecting them. It is also a fact that those Jews who moved from Arab lands to Israel in particular were often leaving a situation in which they had never fully been accepted as citizens and were now about to have all the rights of Israeli citizenship.[12]

Egyptian Jews settled all over the world, forming a widely-dispersed diaspora that has maintained a sense of its Egyptian identity to this day. Whereas the poorer Jews most often went to Israel, many from the middle and upper socio-economic classes had cultural and other connections with Europe. Large numbers moved to Italy, France, Switzerland, Britain, and other European countries, and from there, some moved further afield, to the Americas or to Australia. While most families did their very best to maintain contact and stay in touch, inevitably – as happened with my own extended family – many drifted apart and lost their connections to one another and to their former Egyptian homeland.

My parents and siblings had always looked on Sudan as a safe place to go when things got difficult in Egypt. When my family left Cairo, my brothers founded a chemical company in Sudan, and this provided an income for the family. But soon things became difficult for the Jews in Sudan too. In 1953, Egypt and the United Kingdom signed an agreement supposed to show the way towards Sudanese independence, and the first parliament was inaugurated in 1954. My parents had moved to Geneva in 1953, and the events in Sudan confirmed the wisdom of their decision. Civil war broke out in 1955, and the Premier of Sudan, Ismail al-Azhari, declared independence on January 19. Sudanese independence was formally recognised by Britain and Egypt, and shortly afterwards by the United States. In 1958, Chief of Staff Major General Ibrahim Abboud overthrew the parliamentary regime in a bloodless coup d'état. This was the year of my marriage, and the coup was the reason why my parents chose to remain in Geneva rather than attend the ceremony in Khartoum, and are in none of our wedding photographs.

Abboud was greatly influenced by Nasser, and the nationalist policies of Egypt infiltrated the Sudanese government and both official and popular attitudes towards the minorities there. Sudan had been a refuge for Egyptian Jews like my family, but the safety they enjoyed there did not last for long, and as hostility towards Jews in Sudan also grew, the Jewish community of Sudan also scattered.

For writers of various kinds, the traumas experienced by the Egyptian Jews were explored in a range of forms, including memoirs, biographies, biographical novels, and poetry. In these works, a number of themes quickly become evident, including happy memories of their lives in Egypt before the events that interrupted them so brutally, the trauma of the events that led up to their departure, and the departure itself. Evident also is a type of survivor guilt relating to the knowledge that, much as they had suffered, the Jews murdered in the Holocaust of Europe had suffered much more, and a sense of stasis and silencing relating to the fact that, for so many years, it felt as though Egyptian Jews were simply not supposed to discuss their feelings with respect to what they had endured. These works contain themes dealing with 'memory, dislocation and loss, the inevitable consequences of any forced emigration and the loss of and search for an identity'.[13]

Despite the horrors of the Holocaust, and the extremely difficult situation now facing Jews in Arab countries (and indeed elsewhere), many countries were reluctant to accept Jews from Arab lands as refugees, and/or were keen to shift responsibility for them to other nations. Many European countries had a long history of limiting Jewish immigration. For example, following a wave of Jewish immigration to Britain of Jews escaping pogroms in Russia and Eastern Europe, in 1903, the British Royal Commission on Alien Immigration published a report that described Jews as 'undesirable'.[14] Further British legislation, including the Aliens Act of 1914, the Aliens Restriction Act of 1919, and the Aliens Order of 1925, had the result of expelling Jews, as well as other minorities, as well as further hardening public opinion against them. Even during the war, as the horrors that were experienced by the Jews under the Nazis become increasingly apparent, government policy in Britain was to grant asylum only to those European Jews who were not likely to require any financial support from the government, with a preference for child refugees, who could be anglicized more readily than adults. After the Second World War, Britain was extremely reluctant to accept refugees from Egypt unless they already had family members settled in the United Kingdom. In government, and at popular level, there was little support for this cohort of refugees, whom many British considered to be the responsibility of the French because of the cultural links they had with France.[15] Because the Jewish refugees of the mid- and late 1950s reminded the British of their failure in the Suez campaign, there was little public interest in them, and their presence was experienced as a political liability at a time when growing numbers of colonies were agitating for freedom.

Also mitigating against the Egyptian Jewish refugees was the fact that both Britain and France were much more positive towards refugees from working-class and less educated backgrounds (such as many of the

Hungarian refugees in Britain, and Algerians in France), who could be used as cheap labour in the redevelopment of their infrastructure following the war.[16] The Jewish refugees from Egypt who sought to travel to European countries were generally educated, middle-class people (albeit now reduced to penury by the confiscations of the Egyptian state) whose aspirations were to find work in the professions for which they had been trained, or in business. This was still a time when antisemitism was common among the monied classes, and there were concerted efforts to keep Jews out of privileged positions in law and other elite professions.

In the post-war period, countries such as Britain and France were also invested in limiting immigration (except where it was seen to be convenient) from colonial countries, from which large numbers of people wished to migrate in search of greater opportunities elsewhere. At this point, Egyptian Jews were not welcome, both on grounds of their Jewishness and because they were associated with other countries that were seen as culturally inferior. Only Egyptian Jews with close family connections to British territories such as Gibraltar, Malta, and Cyprus were considered to have grounds to apply for British citizenship.[17]

Even when Egyptian Jewish refugees were allowed to stay, the situation was not always very easy for them. At this time, an influential thinker in France on the matter of immigration was Georges Mauco, an antisemite whose argument that the Jews were too different to the so-called French race to be successfully assimilated was influential in France's development of an immigration policy that favoured immigrants from European backgrounds, and mitigated against the arrival of large numbers of Jewish refugees from Egypt, among other Arab countries.[18] France granted the right to remain to 10,000 Egyptian Jews. However, they were often made to feel unwelcome, and even for those who held French passports, their right to citizenship was often questioned; they were referred to as 'Français de Code Civil' and efforts were made to limit their numbers,[19] including limiting the right to remain in France to those who were in a position to support themselves; clearly, at least in the short term, a problem for people whose property and other assets had been seized by the Egyptian government.

All this occurred against a backdrop of official silence about the treatment of French Jews during the war, including the issue of the deportation of Jews who were killed in the Nazis' death camps; official reluctance to acknowledge some of the terrible things that happened, and the fact that some French people, and French authorities, colluded or, at minimum, turned a blind eye, did nothing to help the cause of the Jewish refugees from Egypt.

By and large, France accepted Jewish Egyptians as refugees only on the basis of a very limited number of criteria, with priority given to those who were French nationals, and excluding even those who had received a French education, habitually spoke French, and lived according to French cultural norms, as was the case for many Egyptian Jews who did not hold the all-important citizenship. Nonetheless, France was the preferred destination (over Israel) for Egyptian Jews who spoke French and had been to French schools. Between November 1956 and March 1957, 80 per cent of the Egyptian refugees arriving in France were Jewish. Those who had no contacts in France to help them were met by the Red Cross and dispersed to repurposed sports centres and budget hotels which served as temporary accommodation, often with two families to a room, without cooking facilities. Some covertly cooked on improvised devices in their bedrooms, while others attended soup kitchens.[20] Many were sent to live in isolated rural areas, hampering their ability to integrate and build new lives. As most of the refugees were essentially penniless on arrival in France, they received a small payment from the state for their essential needs. Because of the extremely restrictive definition of refugees under the Geneva Convention, France could have withdrawn support from them at any moment; a situation of which the Egyptian Jews were certainly painfully aware. Even those with French passports were often seen as a 'problem' that needed to be addressed by local Jewish communities, which were urged to take responsibility of their various needs. Clearly, then, even in the post-war period, Jews were seen as something less than authentically French, even in the case of local Jewish populations.[21]

The French authorities were helpful to those refugees from Egypt who wished to relocate to Israel; they numbered approximately 25 per cent of all those who came to France. They were often less helpful to those who wished to remain in France. There were considerable barriers to employment for Jewish refugees from Egypt, who were often refused positions suited to their qualifications and experience on the grounds that they were not accustomed to French technology. Often, they were offered menial manual work for which they were over-qualified, and in which they had no relevant experience. Most experienced a dramatic reduction in social status and income, generally experienced as humiliating as well as distressing. While most of the Egyptian Jews who settled in France spoke French fluently, and had received a French-style education, they spoke with a particular accent that made them easy to identify. The indigenous French often considered them a type of Arab, which – in the context of widespread

anti-Arab, and especially anti-Algerian, sentiment in France at the time –
did not help them to assimilate or find suitable employment.[22]

While some Jewish Egyptian families integrated into French society
relatively quickly, for others it was a long journey. Some dealt with their
difficult situation by living in close proximity with one another, in clusters
of housing in which they endeavoured to recreate their familiar Egyptian
lifestyle. In some cases, this led to resentment from local populations.
Nonetheless, fairly large numbers of Egyptian Jews settled in France, and
especially in the southern parts of France, such as Marseille and Nice, where
they found the climate agreeable.

It was often very difficult for Jewish Egyptian refugees to manage the
profoundly conflicting emotions they experienced around how they had
been treated in Egypt, and their struggles in forging a new life in France.
Somehow, they had to balance the anger and betrayal they experienced,
and the loss of their possessions and standing in society, with profound
feelings of homesickness and longing for their former home. Often, they
were also disappointed by how they were received in France; having been
brought up to speak French and admire French culture greatly, it was
painful to be rejected as people who could never truly be French at all.

A smaller, but still significant, portion of the Egyptian Jews held British
citizenship (and had therefore suffered in Egypt from anti-English
sentiment around the Suez crisis, as well as the antisemitism that had
become rife), and many of these went to Britain when their situation in
Egypt became untenable. About 4,000 arrived in late 1956, and were housed
in hostel accommodation around the country that was often very distant
from potential centres of employment and opportunities to integrate to
local communities. Many did not speak English fluently, which was clearly
a further barrier to rapid assimilation.

Like the French, the initial British response was to grant asylum in the
first instance only to those who already had a close family connection with
the country, and not to treat them any differently to other refugees, even if
they held British passports. This was consistent with the long-established
British policy of keeping Jewish immigration to a minimum.[23] Antisemitism
remained relatively widespread in Britain; during the War, not long before,
one of the reasons given for limiting admission of Jewish refugees to those
from Germany was the risk that antisemitism would rise, effectively
blaming the Jews for the discriminatory feelings and actions of others.

By contrast, the British government was more welcoming to refugees
from Hungary, who were not British subjects, but who were viewed in a
more favourable light than the Egyptian Jews with British citizenship. The

British also struggled to understand or appreciate that many of the Jews from Egypt were highly educated people who had enjoyed considerable social standing in their home country; British views of people from 'the colonies', as many still saw Egypt, did not allow for the possibility that many of these people were upper-middle and upper-class in their education and tastes. Distressed by the circumstances in which they found themselves, some of the refugees resorted to hunger strikes in a desperate attempt to draw attention to their plight.²⁴

A relatively small number of Egyptian Jews travelled to Australia, including a number of girls with whom I had been friendly in Cairo. Again, some found that they were treated less favourably than Jewish refugees from European backgrounds, even in some cases by Ashkenazi-dominated Jewish philanthropic organizations as well as the Australian government, which operated an explicitly racist and Anglo-centric immigration policy at that time. Until 1939, less than twenty years earlier, the Australian authorities had enforced specifically anti-Jewish immigration legislation. In 1946, the Minister for Immigration restricted the number of Jewish travellers on ships heading towards Australia to 25 per cent of the total, and the authorities were told not to offer permanent residency to anyone who was not European in origin. While most of the Egyptian Jews were, in fact, European in origin, this was often interpreted to exclude Jews in general.²⁵ While attitudes towards the Jews had mellowed somewhat as a result of the atrocities of the Second World War, the Egyptian Jewish refugees who settled in Australia were certainly not coming to a land that welcomed them with open arms. The fact that most of the Egyptian Jews who moved to Australia were highly educated helped, as well as the extensive lobbying on the part of established Jewish communities. In fact, the Australian government also made it clear that it considered the accommodation and welfare of Egyptian Jewish refugees to be the responsibility of established Jewish communities.²⁶ Over time, many of those who went to Australia thrived and prospered, thanks to their own grit and determination.

Quite a few Jews left for Brazil, particularly people from the lower and lower-middle classes. Brazil was a welcoming environment. The government did not demand quotas and there were no great barriers placed in the way of integration. Today, there is a thriving Jewish community in Sao Paolo, largely descended from Egyptian Jews who moved there in the first wave of the great twentieth-century exodus of Jews from Egypt.

Jews in general, and perhaps the Egyptian Jews in particular, have long been noted for their pragmatic ability to settle down, work, and form communities anywhere. In part, this is due to the long history of anti-Jewish discrimination, and the simple necessity of developing the practical and emotional skills required to build a new life periodically, in response to anti-Jewish legislation and persecution. The strong social and familial ties in Jewish families have also played a role. However, the apparent ease with which so many Jews have been able to re-establish themselves in new environments should not be read as an indication that they have been left unscarred by their experiences as refugees. The difficulties Egyptian Jewish refugees faced in the examples provided, as in other destinations, added to the already considerable trauma they experienced in association with their expulsion from Egypt and the loss of their worldly goods. The many psychological impacts on refugees around the world are very well-known. They include such disorders as anxiety, depression, eating disorders, loss of a sense of self, and much more. Clearly, the Egyptian Jews who were forced to leave their homes were in no way immune to any of these negative impacts, which in many cases persisted for years – and even generations – after the initial trauma took place.

After our marriage in 1958, Lina and I had decided to settle in Geneva, Switzerland. As well as having my parents and various other members of the family nearby, I liked the pro-business attitude of the government, the clean and efficient cities, and the beautiful landscapes, as well as the fact that much of Switzerland is French-speaking, which meant that it would be easy for us to build a life there. In fact, I chose to move to Switzerland without even having visited.

The Jewish community in Geneva was not very large. There was already a small and well-established Jewish population of about two hundred families composed of Ashkenazi people of Turkish origins, as well as those who had managed to escape the European Holocaust by fleeing to neutral Switzerland. When the Sephardi Egyptian families, including my parents, and two of my maternal aunts and their families, started to arrive, the established Jewish community of Geneva was quite ambivalent about them. The Egyptian Jews were not immediately welcomed by them as we had hoped we would be. Unfortunately, some of the Ashkenazim in Geneva shared the view, widely held at the time, that the Jews from Arab countries were not culturally or educationally at the same level as European Jews, and I think that they were anxious that their institutions and traditions would be overwhelmed and taken over by the growing number of Sephardim who were arriving. There was also a certain amount of snobbishness and distancing on the part of the Ashkenazi and Turkish Jewish people towards their Sephardi brothers and sisters. The Turkish community had previously been considered the poorer class among the Jews, and I think that elements among the Turkish community were quite pleased to have a new group to look down on and consider socially inferior. There were also some significant cultural differences that could sometimes lead to misunderstandings and feelings of hurt.

Initially, the Egyptian Jews' attitude was that, if they were not going to be fully accepted as equals, then they would establish their own community and worship and socialise separately. Bear in mind that those who had left Egypt were still struggling with the competing emotions of nostalgia and sorrow – familiar to all those who have had the refugee experience – and with the aftershock of trauma relating to the experiences they had endured. At the time, most of the Egyptian Jews in Geneva had lost so much that their main concern was to find a way to make a living. At first, most of them were only just managing to get by. Dad was working as an agent for my brothers' chemical company. Most Egyptian Jewish refugees went into entrepreneurship of one kind or another, and had to work extremely hard to get established, especially because banks were often reluctant to lend to people who arrived as refugees and who were an unknown quantity.

As often happens, social barriers started to break down initially through the women. When Lina and I started to have children, she got to know other young mothers. She was a devoted mother and became deeply involved in the children's education. In this way, she was able to make friends and establish herself relatively quickly. Fortunately, the social barriers did not take too many years to break down, and by the early 1960s, we were a fully integrated community – so much so that I was even voted President of the Jewish community in Geneva, and was honoured to hold this position for quite a number of years. By this stage, I was an established member of the business community, and life was going well.

Of the Egyptian Jews who settled all over the world, the vast majority of them integrated quite quickly and with relative ease. Most of them were self-sufficient within a short period of time, and quite a number of them went on to become hugely successful in business. Despite all that they had lost, they still had a number of advantages: many of them were highly educated according to European norms and standards (often thanks to the work of the Alliance Israélite Universelle); they had grown up and were used to working in the cosmopolitan and multi-lingual environment of early twentieth-century Egypt, and therefore generally spoke several languages fluently and found it relatively easy to adapt to a new business climate; and they had been trained since childhood to think and work in an entrepreneurial way, accepting risk and seeing opportunity.

While Jews who held foreign nationality and who managed to immigrate to Europe, the Americas, and the Antipodes, generally found their feet and were thriving after a number of years, the experience of the poorest Egyptian Jews was very different – and in many ways, much more difficult. The many Jews who were left without any nationality often had no option but to relocate to Israel, whether or not this was in their interest, and whether or not they actually had a desire to do so. While Egypt now wanted to be rid of all its Jews, it did not accept the existence of Israel, and made it very difficult for the remaining Jews to leave. A highly organized grassroots, underground movement, together with its supporters, helped these stateless Jews to move by providing them with funds, and with the means to do so, alongside the efforts of activists on the ground. For example, the Setton Travel Agency in Cairo arranged visas and arranged for transportation, which had to take place in secret, so as not to alert the Egyptian authorities.[27] The Egyptian Jewish refugees who went to Israel arrived with nothing, and were generally housed in camps in the short term, before being dispersed by the Israeli authorities to various locations around the land of Israel.

Israel had adopted a free immigration policy towards all Jews, ruling that Jews from anywhere in the world were welcome to settle there. This policy would see the Israeli authorities struggle to accommodate the massive influx of people, resulting in the doubling of the population of the Israeli state within the first four years of its existence (a rate of immigration unparalleled anywhere in the world, at any point in history)[28] despite the support the new state received from Jews and allies from all over the world:

> ...the accumulated burden of absorbing the mass immigration was devastating Israel's economic, health, welfare and education systems. There were not enough housing facilities, jobs, schools or medical infrastructure, and at a certain point even food supplies ran short in spite of the austerity regime imposed on the entire population. The shortage of economic means and lack of infrastructure reached the point where there were not even enough tents to shelter the newcomers.[29]

New arrivals, such as my parents, during their brief and unhappy sojourn in Israel, were often housed in camps that quickly reached full capacity and more, and the emerging state struggled to provide them with even the most basic facilities, mobilizing the Israeli Defence Force to care for a population that was often ill-equipped at first for the demands of settler life.[30] In her memoir, Lucette Lagnado remembered what became of her family members who, having no other option, moved to Israel: 'Some were placed in rugged settlements in the middle of the desert or in remote agricultural areas where home was a tent, an army-like barrack, or a flimsy structure made of aluminium.' They were also disconcerted to have to eat simple, primitive meals rather than the luscious dishes they had been accustomed to enjoying in Egypt.[31]

Despite the many challenges facing them, the Jewish Agency Executive did not consider the situation of the Egyptian Jews to be as urgent as that of the European Jews, and passed a number of restrictions on who could enter, stating that 80 per cent of the immigrants had to be aged thirty-five or under, that they should be members of youth or other organizations, and that they should be found physically healthy on inspection by a Jewish physician.[32] Nonetheless, in 1951, an Israeli intelligence officer, Avram Dar, arrived in Cairo under a British alias to help a local organization that was involved in assisting Egyptian Jews who wished to emigrate to Israel.[33]

Some elements in the Israeli government and cultural elite were also reluctant to accept the refugee status of Jews from Arab lands, including Egypt, because they were heavily invested in the Zionist ideal of a vast diaspora of Jews longing for a place in an Israeli homeland. According to this schema, all Jews moving to Israel from elsewhere were to be seen as 'returning' to their historic homeland, and it represented their departure from Arab lands and arrival in Israel as the fulfilment of their destiny, and therefore not only right but also inevitable, and even preordained by God.[34]

The stateless Jews of Egypt, most of whom had lost everything, and all of whom were dealing with trauma to varying degrees, often faced considerable difficulty in adapting to their new homeland of Israel. Contrary to what the propaganda in the Israeli press maintained, most of the Jews who left Egypt at this time did so for economic reasons and because of their distress at the violent situation. Most, if not all, had a profound sense of belonging to Egypt. Poorer Jews sometimes went to Israel because they had no other option; without a passport, it was impossible for them to get a visa to travel elsewhere. While Israel welcomed them and found a place for them, they were certainly refugees in all but name.

After the first Israeli election, which was held in 1949, the overwhelming majority of candidates returned were from Eastern Europe or Russia.[35] Since even before the foundation of Israel as an independent nation-state, prominent positions had come to be filled by Ashkenazim from Eastern Europe, when Palestine was still under British rule.[36] European and North American social norms dominated, and some of the traditions of Jews from Arab countries were frowned upon, or even suppressed.[37] In this context, it was often difficult for Jews from Arab countries to feel at home. Many had come with nothing and had to rebuild their lives from scratch, often coming up against the emerging reality of a new elite largely composed of Jews of European extraction and tacitly excluded from the higher echelons of Israeli business and government.[38]

It should, however, be noted that absorbing such a large population of refugees, in a newly-founded nation state that was still finding its feet, was an enormous undertaking and a huge challenge.[39] Egyptian Jews, like all Jews from the Middle East, were required to spend a number of months in transit camps before accommodation was made available to them.[40] According to one historian of the era, migrants were not always treated very well:

> The vulnerable new immigrants were ordered around by arrogant officials, who called them 'human dust,' and crowded into ma'abarot (transient camps), hastily constructed out of corrugated tin.[41]

Homes were constructed in an impressively short period of time to accommodate refugees from Arab lands. These were often in more remote parts of Israel, some distance from major urban centres. For Jews of Egyptian origin, who were predominately an urban people, this was difficult to cope with.[42]

Since early adolescence, I had been convinced of the need for a Jewish homeland in Palestine, and I have remained convinced of this all my life. However, in the early years, I was bitterly disappointed by how Egyptian Jews, and Jews from Arab lands in general, were treated by some of the Israeli authorities. It was upsetting to see that many European Israelis, having themselves suffered so much at the hands of the Nazis and their supporters, and being descended from people who had suffered literally centuries of discrimination and persecution in Europe, could now turn around and suggest that some Jews were more equal than others. Surely, I felt, the very concept of a homeland for the Jews demanded equal treatment for all of them. Clearly, the Jews from Arab lands were given a safe home in Israel – but their treatment was anything but fair, and for people who had lost so much, it was galling not be to accepted on an equal footing, but rather to be seen as second-class citizens.

For Jews who had long felt very much at home living in Arab countries, and who had even identified with the Arab majority in many respects, being looked down upon by members of an Ashkenazi elite was a double blow;

they had been effectively turned out of the land that they had considered home, and now they were looked down upon as social inferiors, despite comprising a large and growing percentage of the population.[43] The assumption was often made that Jews from Arab countries were all socially and culturally inferior to Jews of European origin, even though, in the case of the Egyptian Jews particularly, they often identified as Europeans, spoke European languages, and often even held European citizenship.

In the early 1950s, Israeli scholar Yosef Gross stated that Jews from Arab lands had a mentality that could be compared to that of 'the primitive expression of children, the retarded, or the mentally disturbed'. Languages and dialects spoken by many Arab Jews, such as Ladino, were neglected, and seen as second-rate in comparison to Yiddish, and the long history of the Jews of Arab lands was generally overlooked in any discussion of the history of the Jewish people of the Middle East.[44] As Shohat says:

> The cultural affinity that Arab Jews shared with Arab Muslims – in many respects stronger than that which they shared with European Jews – threatened the Zionist conception of a homogeneous nation modeled on the European nationalist definition of the nation-state.[45]

Even in the late 1960s, by which stage they had been in Israel for many years, Israelis of European extraction often looked down on their Middle Eastern counterparts, and even described them as having a lower level of civilization.[46] Immigrants from some Arab lands were dismissed as 'primitives' (and were sometimes explicitly described as such, for example, in an otherwise respectable printed source as late as 1970).[47] Inevitably, these views were often experienced as hurtful, and were in fact a barrier to assimilation, evidenced by the fact that religious Jews often preferred to worship at synagogues associated with their specific ethnic community.[48]

While a new life in Israel was a wonderful dream come true for some, for many Jews who had come under duress as refugees, including most of the Egyptian Jews, adjusting to their new circumstances was not always easy or quick. The Jews from Arab countries were painfully aware of the fact that many of the Israelis of European origin looked down on them and even saw them as a problem that had to be dealt with. They advocated for themselves. For example, Yitzhah Cohen, the chairman and founder of the Organization of North African and Francophone Immigrants, protested directly to president Ben Gurion about an article by journalist Arie Gelblum in *Ha'aretz*, the major Israeli newspaper, stating that it defamed, gossiped about, and committed libel against Jewish immigrants from Arab lands.[49]

Even after their release from the camps, Jewish immigrants from Arab lands then had to adjust to a new society that was geographically close to Egypt, but that tended to be dominated by European Jews, politically and culturally.[50] The situation has been described as one in which 'The rigid ethno-class structure that arose was characterized by ethnic separation, in which Ashkenazi institutions, culture, and rabbinical leadership were regarded as more "advanced" and of higher quality than their Mizrahi counterparts.'[51] In general, Jews from Arab lands were often expected to gladly cast off many aspects of their cultural behaviour – even elements of traditional culture such as folk music – to become more similar to the Jews of European origin.[52] In some cases, Jews from Arab lands were even expected to change their given names to names considered more appropriate for Israeli Jews.[53] The general view held at higher levels of government in Israel was that it was both desirable and inevitable that the Jews from Arab lands should assimilate to the cultural and linguistic norms of the European Jews, with almost all of the compromises being made by one side; little consideration was given to the fact that Jews from Arab countries also had much to offer Israel, if only they were given the opportunity.[54]

While Egyptian Jews tended to be more educated, to have been more affluent (very affluent, in some cases) and more European in their outlook than Jews from elsewhere in the Arab world, these prejudices inevitably impacted on them to varying degrees. As a primarily urban people, it could also be difficult for Egyptian Jews to adapt to a state that placed huge emphasis on rural settlement and work, and that expected many immigrants to work in the fields, even if they had no skills or aptitude in this area.[55] Particularly for people from more modest circumstances, integration and finding a path to success took time although, gradually, integration did take place and the number of marriages between Jews of Middle Eastern and of European origins grew.[56]

Because of their less powerful position in modern Israeli society, and also their somewhat ambivalent situation in terms of the experience of the Jews from Arab lands, the experience of the Egyptian Jews has often been relegated to the margins of discussions and understandings of the Israeli experience. For many Jews of Egyptian origins, it had become difficult to talk about their experiences of growing up and living in Egypt. The terrible things that had happened in the middle of the twentieth century seemed to sully happy memories of the past.

By the mid-1970s, there was more willingness in Israel to speak openly about the fact that many Jews from Arab countries came only under duress, which meant that their situation was directly analogous to that of displaced Arabs. Certainly, they fulfilled the criteria to be understood as refugees:

> The essential quality of the refugee [is] that he has left his country of regular residence... as a result of political events in that country which render his continued residence impossible or intolerable and has taken refuge in another country... In general, the refugee cannot return to his country of abode without danger to his life or liberty.[57]

In 1975, Mordechai Ben Porat, a prominent Israeli politician, stated:

> We want to ground it in documentation, how the Jews who arrived in Israel as refugees... how they lived in transit camps, huts... it was not only the Arab refugees who lived in camps, as they describe it, but that our Jews suffered greatly [too].[58]

After the 1978 peace agreement between Israel and Egypt, during which normal trade relations, including the sale of oil, were established,[59] things eased somewhat and a number of Egyptian Jews, now living in Israel and elsewhere, published memoirs and other books that spoke of their positive associations with Egypt.[60] Only now did Egyptian Jews start to talk more openly about their history and identity, and their shared past in Egypt. In 1979 the French Association Pour la Sauvegarde du Patrimoine Culturel des Juifs d'Egypte was founded to protect and cherish Egyptian Jewish heritage.[61]

Gradually, it became clearer that, for many Jews, leaving Egypt – where their families had been living for countless generations, where their ancestors were buried, and where their children had been born – had been a source of tremendous sorrow. They were Jews, yes, but they were also Egyptians, and they loved the land that they called home. The lack of recognition for the sorrow experienced by so many of the Egyptian Jews can be attributed in part to the strong, and growing, anti-Jewish sentiment among Arab nations at that time, but also to the narrative stressed by some of the settlers of Israel that moving there was, by definition, a joyful event for any Jew. For many, it was experienced as a tragedy and an injustice. Their property had been seized by the Egyptian state, years of hard work had been transformed into nothing, and they had been forced to leave the land that they had considered home to live in another country where they were not always immediately accepted as equals.

While it may have been less difficult for Egyptian Jews to integrate than for some others,[62] even today, although the social and economic gap between Jews of Middle Eastern and of European origins has closed considerably, those of Middle Eastern origins remain under-represented in positions of power and authority, including in academia.[63] At the same time, while the voices of Jews from Arab lands have grown in influence over the years, often these voices do not include those of the Egyptian Jews, precisely because of the more European nature of their linguistic and cultural profile. For Egyptian Jews, who had deep links with European culture and commerce, adapting to Israeli culture was often easier than for Jews from other Arab lands – but nonetheless, their struggles to adapt and accept all that they had lost, while also dealing with a degree of discrimination, should not be underestimated.

In 1975, the World Organization of Jews from Arab Countries (WOJAC) was founded to represent the interests of these people, who were now a vast diaspora, with members in many countries. My brother Leon, who lived in the United Kingdom, was the co-chair, along with Mordechai Ben Porat. Scholars and other interested parties engaged in vigorous debate about the migration of the Jews of Arab lands to Israel, and sought to '[insert] the Mizrahi memory on the map of the Zionist-Israeli national collective memory.' Some maintained that their choice to come to live in Israel was born of Zionist idealism and the fulfilment of two millennia of dreams, hopes, and aspirations. If one accepted this point of view, the Jews from Arab lands could not be seen as refugees. Others argued that they came as refugees from their countries of birth. They pointed out that yearning for Israel did not negate their status at the time of departure from these Arab countries, and that an interest in Zionism did not mean an absence of love for their original homeland. WOJAC campaigned for compensation for the property confiscated from Jews in Arab countries, but sought for the recovered funds to be given to the state of Israel, rather than to the individuals concerned and their families.[64]

At this time, the Israeli government was under pressure to provide compensation to displaced Arabs, and was keen to emphasise that many Jews had lost a great deal in their countries of origin, and that they had never been compensated. Sabri Jiryis, a member of the Palestinian National Council, stated that the Jews of Arab lands had been 'driven out of their ancient homes... shamefully deported after their property had been commandeered or taken over at the lowest possible valuation.'[65]

In 1977, the UN Security Council issued its Resolution 242, which stated that the refugee problem in the Middle East needed to be settled. Shortly afterwards, while reiterating the UN resolution in a press conference, then US president Jimmy Carter stressed the fact that the refugees in question included both Jews and Arabs, stating clearly that Jewish refugees must be recognised as having the same rights as others.[66] In 1979, then Prime Minister Menachem Begin said:

> The problem of the Jewish property that was plundered in the Arab states, not just in one country, has been and will be raised…When the day comes, we shall submit our claim for the return of the illegally taken property.[67]

In 1980, my brother Leon founded the World Movement for a United Israel to address the lingering problems in Israel among the various ethnic groups. He felt strongly – as do I – that all Jews must be accepted as equals, and that there is no place in the Jewish community to consider some people as 'naturally' superior or more important than others. Leon knew for himself how difficult things had been for the Egyptian Jews, and he wanted to do what he could to ensure that new immigrants to Israel would be treated with respect and care. I am sure that he was thinking of the treatment experienced by our parents, as well as many other of the so-called mizrahim.

Since the foundation of Israel, much international attention and effort has been given to the issue of compensation for Arab refugees from Palestine. Since 1949, the United Nations has supported Palestinian refugees to the tune of many billions of dollars. Despite the efforts of a small number of organizations, such as WOJAC, there has been no such outpouring of support for Jewish refugees from Arab countries,[68] many of whom, of course, are now deceased.

The issue of refugee status is a complex one. During a crisis, when a population is forced to flee, it is clearly essential that their refugee status be recognised, and that the global community provide them with all of the supports that they need. However, I think that the respective experiences of the Palestinian and the Jewish refugees show that being officially recognised as a refugee in the long term – throughout generations – can be a poisoned chalice that causes more problems than it solves.

At the time of the establishment of Israel, there was a massive displacement of people all over the Middle East and North Africa. While each person's experience is, of course, unique, we can look back now and see that the refugee experience of the Palestinians and the Jews from Arab lands was very similar for a time. Both groups were cast out of their homes, many lost their possessions, and many were deeply traumatised by all that they experienced. Yet, in the long term, the experiences have been very different. The United Nations extended huge supports to the Palestinians that may have been helpful in the short-term, but that in the long-term have prevented millions of people from reaching their potential. By granting refugee status not just to the first generation of displaced Palestinians, but also to all of their descendants, an entire culture has been condemned to live in the past, yearning for the return to a status quo that is never going to happen. Conversely, the displaced Jews who also suffered the refugee experience did not receive the same degree of international support (and in many cases, would have refused support even if it had been offered to them) – but they were able to accept that what happened, happened, and that now they have no choice but to integrate into their new setting. The result has been that the descendants of the Jewish Egyptian refugees (and the Jewish refugees from other Arab lands) have largely integrated well and succeeded all over the world, while many promising Palestinian lives are blighted by the false hope of a return to the past.

While all of the refugees of the 1940s and 50s needed and deserved international support then, I do not believe that it is helpful to young Palestinians today to be taught that they are, and will always be, victims, because of what their grandparents experienced. I wish that the Arab countries that confiscated land, property, and so much more from their Jewish minorities would see that today they have a moral responsibility to offer citizenship to the Palestinians, and free them from the burden of perpetual victimhood. If they had done so at the time of the foundation of Israel – when the Jews of Arab lands started to find their neighbours and their governments turning against them and forcing them to flee – the descendants of the original Palestinian refugees would not today be living in such difficult circumstances. They are all the unwitting victims of the anti-Jewish and anti-Israel policies of the Arab countries of that time and subsequently.

In Egypt, the infrastructure once associated with the Jewish minority, including synagogues and even the shrine and synagogue of Maimonides, crumbled and became derelict.[69] Official views in Egypt towards Jews continued to harden, particularly in the context of ongoing conflicts between Israel and the Arab world. Government figures, journalists, and others increasingly blamed Jews for all the problems in the world. The Muslim Brotherhood, in particular, frequently engaged in diatribes against the Jews in general, and Israel in particular, as well as bragging about having taken part in vandalism and other acts of violence against Jewish people and Jewish-owned property. Long-established antisemitic tropes, such as the idea that Jews controlled the media, were frequently aired. Even the fact that many Egyptian Jews had gone to great lengths to assimilate into Egyptian culture was interpreted as an attempt to gain power and influence, and discussed in the most negative terms,[70] rather than understood as an indication of the deep affection and sense of belonging most Egyptian Jews felt for their country. All Jews, including those who were directly descended from Jewish communities indigenous to Egypt, were increasingly described as guests who had outstayed their welcome. The fact that some of the Egyptian Jews were the descendants of communities that had been in Egypt since the period before Islam was completely overlooked.[71] Certainly, for the few Jews who remained, the atmosphere in Egypt was anything but welcoming.

In Israel, however, there was a resurgence of interest and pride in the heritage of the Jews who originated in Arab countries, and a growing sense of wanting their contributions to both Arab and Jewish culture to be recognised and respected.[72] There was also interest in the issue of the property that had been confiscated from Jews in Arab countries.

One Egyptian Jew, who left in 1967, could see that Jewish heritage in Egypt was threatened, so he tried to save it by arranging to have as many families as possible take with them a Torah scroll from one of the synagogues. In this way, and because the customs authorities were prepared to look the other way, many of the scrolls from the Cairo synagogues were saved. Today, it is impossible to take the scrolls out because the Egyptian government considers them to be 'Egyptian Relics', while at the same time not recognising the fact that the Egyptian Jews are also part of the country's great heritage.[73]

In 1967, I decided that I wanted to do what I could to help Jews in difficult situations around the world, and I became involved with the Jewish Joint Distribution Committee. At this time, I was the vice-president of the High Commission of Refugees and had a certain amount of influence. The JDC had a base in Switzerland, and I was very impressed by the work they did. Through my work with the JDC, I actually had the opportunity to be reunited with some of the people from Haret al-Yahud whom I had helped to flee through the British garrison. The JDC, and other organizations such as the Hebrew Immigrant Aid Society had helped many of them to build new lives outside Egypt. They would go on, over the years, to work with Jews in other terrible situations – notably Romanian Jews under the horrifying regime of Nicolae Ceausescu. I still feel that my experiences in Egypt helped me to understand the suffering of others in similar circumstances, and that I have a moral obligation to do, and give, what I can. I started to learn this lesson as a small child when I helped my mother to bring bread and clothing to the poor people of Cairo's Haret al-Yahud.

I remember returning to Egypt for the first time, on a business trip in 1981. I was so excited on the day I left for the trip that Lina told me I was like a little child on the day of his birthday. I was so thrilled at the prospect of seeing my old neighbourhood, and at the thought of being able to eat some delicious falafel, straight from the vendor. How strange it was to walk the streets where I had lived as a child, knowing that all the families I had once been so familiar with were now long gone. Within a day or two, I had remembered the Egyptian Arabic that I had once spoken fluently, and I surprised the people I met with my Cairene accent. While many elements of Jewish material culture had been destroyed and built over, many others still remained, including the landmark department stories and luxurious homes of the wealthier Jews, at the top of the social heap. It was clear to me that, even if I wanted to, I could never return.

In the 1980s, a very small number of Egyptian Jews who had been living in Israel attempted to return to their Egyptian homes and resume their lives there, but according to the Egyptian constitution, any citizen who takes Israel citizenship is automatically stripped of their right to Egyptian citizenship, and so their applications for permission to return were automatically denied.[74]

In 1987, a tribunal was held in Washington at which WOJAC presented evidence as to the plight of the Jews who had been forced to flee Arab lands. After hearing all the evidence, the tribunal recommended that the Arab states which had forced Jews to leave and seized their property should acknowledge their responsibility for what had happened and supply appropriate compensation; that they should be supported by the international community, which had already supported Arab Palestinian refugees in a variety of ways; and that a claims committee for the settlement of compensation claims of both Arab and Jewish refugees should be established.[75] None of this happened, and unfortunately following the death of my brother Leon, WOJAC gradually lost its effectiveness, largely because it received very little support from the government. This was a serious missed opportunity, as WOJAC had been a powerful voice.

As the years passed, Egyptian Jews in Israel and elsewhere gradually felt more empowered to discuss their shared past. For most of them, it had been easier to integrate into their new homes than it was for Jews from other Arab lands. However, many Egyptian Jews regretted the fact that, with the passage of time, their Egyptian Jewish heritage began to fade. Concern grew that the new generations would be completely assimilated into their families' new homes, and would know nothing about who they were and where they came from. While many Egyptian Jews were descended from families who had come to Egypt only in the nineteenth century, or even later, most had a profound sense of identification with the long history of the Jews in Egypt, and even saw themselves as the spiritual – if not the literal – descendants of the great Egyptian Jews of old, such as the scholar and man of God, Maimonides.[76] Reflecting this feeling, numerous memoirs and novels based on the Egyptian Jewish experience were published and, in 1983, the first World Congress of Jews from Egypt was held.[77]

For the Egyptian Jewish diaspora, the popularization of the Internet from the 1990s provided a new medium in which they could discuss their shared past, and a number of websites, based in America, Europe, and Israel, provided a forum in which they could talk about their past and preserve a sense of shared history.[78] From this period onwards, there was also growing interest among academics in exploring and studying the contributions of Jews to Egyptian society and culture.[79]

Today, Egyptians and Jews alike are still assessing history and endeavouring to understand the impact of the past on the present. For many Jews of Egyptian origin, the memory of all that their families lost in the middle part of the twentieth century continues to rankle. There is a sense of profound loss at all that is lost, including matters of cultural and religious heritage. Speaking for myself, I still have a very deep sense of affinity with Egypt and consider myself to be culturally Egyptian in many respects. Many of my favourite foods are the same dishes that I ate as a child in Sudan and Egypt, and while I do not exactly support Egypt in the World Cup, I always feel sad when they are eliminated. I love the Egyptian people and I want them to thrive and be happy. At the same time, I am very proud of Israel, of the small part I played in helping it, and of what Israel has become. I own a property in Israel, am involved in various philanthropic endeavours there, and will always feel a profound sense of attachment to it. Today, Israel is one of the most pro-business, progressive countries in the world. It is not perfect, as nowhere is, but it has brought Jews together from all over the world and, notwithstanding the considerable cultural, linguistic, and other differences between them, it has made them into a nation. Israel has become a world power, and even if it has few friends on the global stage there are many who respect it.

By 2001, there were about thirty-six Jews in Egypt, most of whom depended on the Jewish Joint Distribution Committee for support.[80] By 2017, according to *The Economist*, only about twenty Jews remained in Egypt, mostly very elderly people, many of them in care homes for the aged. By 2019, the number of Jews living in Egypt may have numbered just five, while at the same time, approximately half of all Israeli Jews claimed descent from Jews from Arab lands.[81] *The Economist* reported on the new incarnation of the Oeuvre de la Goutte de Lait, which once fed the poor Jews of Egypt and is now dedicated to preserving the heritage of the Jews of Egypt. Many of the members of the organization are descended from Jewish fathers and grandfathers who converted to Islam to avoid expulsion under Nasser.[82] There are so few practising Jews that it is impossible for them to bring together a *minyan*, or a quorum of ten male Jews, which is the smallest number required to conduct a traditional religious service in a synagogue.[83]

Today, there are at last some tentative signs of a more positive relationship between Egypt and the Jewish world. It has become a little easier for Jewish pilgrims to visit holy sites in Egypt, such as the tomb of Rabbi Abuhatzeira, near the area where my ancestors first made their home in Egypt. Starting in recent years, the Egyptian government has sponsored the renovation of a number of sites of great historic and spiritual importance to the Egyptian Jews, and there is renewed interest in Egypt in culture and literature from Jewish sources.[84] In January 2020, Eliyahu Hanavi Synagogue, the oldest synagogue in Egypt, was reopened in Alexandria after extensive, and expensive, renovations paid for and overseen by the Egyptian government. The Embassy of Israel, and representatives of the tiny community of Jews that remains in Israel, hailed this as a positive step. Yet, the fact remains that there are too few Jews living in Egypt today to enable worship to take place here.

These modest signs of a more positive relationship between Egypt and the Jewish aspects of its heritage are certainly very welcome, but true healing simply cannot take place until the Egyptian state assumes responsibility for how the Egyptian Jews were treated in the middle part of the twentieth century, and makes tangible reparations to the survivors and/or their descendants, in recognition of how much was unjustly seized from them. Throughout the period 1948-78 Israel and Egypt had been in a state of war. Despite this, Israel had managed to absorb as many as 600,000 Jewish refugees from Arab countries and, increasingly, to integrate them into every element of society. Even after the peace treaty was signed, no help from the United Nations was forthcoming for the Jews who had left

Egypt as refugees, while even though the agreement specified that Egypt and Israel would make a mutual settlement of financial claims, Egypt has never made any moves to actually do so.[85]

Understanding the past should not be about blaming the people of today for the deeds of their ancestors, but it can involve taking steps to right those wrongs by giving a voice – even after death – to the displaced, the homeless, and the refugee, by acknowledging the things that happened that should not, and by doing whatever is possible to right historic wrongs.

As Ada Aharoni wrote with respect to ongoing efforts to establish peace in the Middle East:

> The various efforts for peace between Israelis and Palestinians have overlooked an important factor in the Arab–Israeli conflict: the displacement of Jews from Arab countries, the loss of all their assets and property, and the hardships accompanying their emigration to Israel. As almost half of the Jewish citizens of Israel, together with their descendants, are from Arab countries, peace research and future peace efforts should take this into account.
>
> To reach a peaceful solution between Israelis and Palestinians, this neglected part of history must be addressed. The Jews uprooted from Arab countries who now reside in Israel feel that the displacement of Palestinians is well documented and relatively well known, but that their own forced migration from Arab countries has been overlooked. This makes them rather intransigent toward a solution to the conflict that does not take account of their own heritage and history. Taking into account the forced migration of Jews from Arab countries – as part of the tragedies incurred during this long and painful conflict – would give peace a better chance.

In the words of Ben Porat, one of the founders of WOJAC:

> [T]he Jews arrived in Israel as refugees... the Jews who arrived in Israel... lived in transit camps... it was not only the Arab refugees who lived in camps, as they describe it, but... our Jews [also] suffered greatly.[86]

This is absolutely the case with the Jews of Egypt, who are still waiting, many years on, for both the recognition and the reparation that they deserve.

Notes

1. Tignor, 1980, 417.
2. Roumani, 2003, 55.
3. Laskier, 1995, 581
4. As reported in Barda, unpublished manuscript, 18.
5. Lagnado, 2006, 157.
6. Lavie, 2019.
7. Miccoli, 2015, 175.
8. Miccoli, 2015, 174-5.
9. Shohat, 2003, 57.
10. Fischbach, 2008, 7.
11. Shamir, 1987, 40.
12. Roumani, 2003, 41.
13. Barda, 2006, 45.
14. Layton-Henry, 1992, 6-7.
15. De Aranjo, 2013, 11.
16. De Aranjo, 2013, 17.
17. De Aranjo, 2013, 202; 208.
18. Weil, 1995, 80.
19. De Aranjo, 2013, 207.
20. De Aranjo, 2013, 228 ; 237-8.
21. De Aranjo, 2013, 231-2; 238.
22. De Aranjo, 2013, 241-2; 250-4.
23. De Aranjo, 2013, 269-70.
24. De Aranjo, 2013, 281-4 ; 313.
25. Barda, 2006, 31; 35; 191-2.
26. Barda, 2006, 134-5; 197; 221.
27. Barda (unpublished text, no date given) Http://www.nebidaniel.org/documents/ Whence _ Hence by R.Barda.doc
28. Halamish, 2008, 119; 127.
29. Halamish, 2008, 127.
30. Gat, 2002, 197-8.
31. Lagnado, 2006, 116.
32. Halamish, 2008, 129.
33. Sachar, 2006, 480.
34. Shohat, 2013, 49; 56.
35. Shindler, 2008, 67.
36. Cohen, 2011, 329.
37. Picard, 2017, 3.
38. Ginat, 2014, 593.
39. Roumani, 2003, 68.
40. Miccoli, 2016, 322.
41. Shohat, 1988, 12.
42. Roumani, 2003, 69.
43. Behar, 2009, 750.
44. Shohat, 2003, 5; 8; 64.

45. Shohat, 2003, 62.
46. Sachar, 2006, 540.
47. Brilliant, 1970, 115.
48. Shokeid, 1984, 248; 256.
49. Kabalo, 2019, 328-9.
50. Behar and Benite, 2014, 48.
51. Nissim, 2014, 28-9.
52. Sachar, 2006, 116; Picard, 2017, 3.
53. Miccoli, 2015, 174.
54. Behar and Benite, 2014, 54.
55. Shapira, 2014, 231-2.
56. Goldberg, 2008, 181.
57. Roumani, 2003, 48, citing Justice Yaakov Zemah, lecture delivered on behalf of WOJAC before the World Conference of Jewish Organizations meeting in Jerusalem, 1 July 1976.
58. Cited in Shenhav, 2006, 159.
59. Shapira, 2014, 370.
60. Abdulhaq, 2016, 27.
61. Miccoli, 2013, 197-8. The group publishes a regular bulletin and maintains an active presence on the Internet: https://www.aspcje.fr/
62. Picard, 2007, 3.
63. Rubin, 2012, 138-9.
64. Shenhav, 2006, 142; 31; 131; 164-5.
65. Roumani, 2003, 46.
66. Roumani, 2003, 45-6.
67. Hillel, 1985, cited in Shenhav, 2006, 132.
68. Roumani, 2003, 72.
69. Sion, 2015, 423.
70. Mayer, 1987, 202-4.
71. Roumani, 2003, 43.
72. Picard, 2017, 18.
73. Family history related by Jacob Bousso for the *Out of Egypt* celebratory booklet, printed in 2019.
74. El-Shamaa, 25 May 2019.
75. Roumani, 2003, 77.
76. Aharoni, 1987, 193-4.
77. Miccoli, 2015, 170.
78. Miccoli, 2013, 197.
79. Meital, 2017, 192.
80. Oppenheim, 2003, 429.
81. Julius, 2018, location 142 (Kindle edition)
82. *The Economist*, 'Out of the Shadows, the Last Jews of Egypt'. 09/2017, Vo. 424, No. 9057.
83. Barda, unpublished manuscript, 20.
84. Sion, 2015, 424.
85. Roumani, 2003, 72.
86. Quoted in Fischbach, 2008, 13-4.

Appendix: Jewish Egyptian Voices

As I carried out my research for this book, I was eager to include a range of voices, of experiences, of being Jewish and Egyptian. The many academic and other works I consulted offered me some scope to do this, and the chapters above cite the experiences of a variety of Egyptian Jews.

However, I was particularly delighted to find a booklet, *Out of Egypt*, which was assembled by Zachary Edinger of the Congregation Shearith Israel in New York in 2019, where Rabbi Albert Gabbai, himself one of the contributors, leads the congregation. This wonderful work contains the beautifully recounted memories of a number of Egyptian Jews, whose accounts mirror the bitter-sweetness of my own experiences. Several of the contributors have been kind enough to grant permission to reprint their narratives, which echo in the most personal of ways the points raised in the preceding chapters. I also include a narrative by Allegra Hodara, which was originally published in *Moment* magazine in 2002. All of the narratives are included with heartfelt thanks to the contributors.

Vivette Ancona

My parents both came to Egypt between the two world wars, my father from Aleppo, Syria and my mother from Lausanne, Switzerland. The similarities between them were quite extraordinary: both my grandfathers were called Isaac and both my grandmothers were called Rachel, and I had an Uncle Joseph on each side. Moreover, both my grandmothers were their husbands' second wives and both my grandfathers were Torah scholars, one studying with a Rav in Poland till his death, and the other in Jerusalem for more than twenty years. Both families had been wealthy, but wars and other upheavals had destroyed their wealth and my parents had no family money to rely on.

My mother was the youngest of three and had come to Egypt with her brother to live with their oldest sister. Regine, my mother's sister, had married in Lausanne a doctoral student in clinical pathology, who had come to Egypt to open a medical diagnostic lab after he graduated. He was of

Georgian origin but his family had emigrated to the Middle East, some to what was then Palestine and some to Egypt.

My parents both went to French schools in Cairo, my mother to the Lycée and my father '*chez les Frères*' (a school run by Catholic monks).This was my father's first foray into secular education, as in Aleppo, he had attended the *kitab* from the age of two and a half. Indeed, the main reason his family had come to Egypt was for the secular education. My father stayed only about two years '*chez les Frères*'. Given his family need, he started working at age fourteen for a publishing house, where he spent decades (leaving it only when he left Egypt), and quickly rising to the top. Without attending a single class because of his work schedule, he did his French Baccalauréat and obtained his law degree from the Université de Paris, which had an extension school in Cairo. My mother stayed in school, though she was very busy helping her sister. She too went to the Université de Paris law school extension school. She was the only woman in the class, and the faculty would not answer her questions until one of the young men in the class said he needed the answer too! Unlike many women of her time, she had learned to drive, in her brother's yellow convertible. It was his pride and joy, but when my mother collided with the corner of the building in which they lived with their sister, his only question to her was whether she was hurt and he ignored the damage to his car.

My parents met on a *felucca* (boat) outing on the Nile organized by a Jewish social club for young people, called Les Essayistes. My parents' romance was carried on in secret for four years. No dates allowed, of course, and my father, laden with the financial responsibility for his family, did not feel he could get engaged. Their 'dates', given the times, were unorthodox. For example, my mother would go to buy chicken for her sister's household in the *souk* opposite the building where my father worked. Buying chicken was not an easy affair: the live chicken had to be chosen and the *shohet* called for to kill it etc. etc. In the meantime, my parents saw each other, of course purely by chance! Eventually, my grandparents encouraged my father to get engaged, which my parents did after my mother passed her final exams. They were married two months later in the garden of my aunt Regine's house. At least four Sephardi Rabbis, besides my grandfather, officiated. I do not know whether this was usual or whether it was due to my grandfather's standing in the community or even to the fact that, given that my mother was Ashkenaz, this was a 'mixed' marriage!

My parents moved in to a small but new apartment in the centre of Cairo. Their windows overlooked the Egyptian Museum of Antiquities. A few years later, my grandparents moved into an apartment in the building next door. My father continued to support his siblings, until his sisters were married and his brothers self-sufficient. He supported his mother until she died a few months before he did. I was not born for some years as my mother had some health issues. After my birth we moved to an apartment on the island of Gezira, where the front windows faced the Nile and the back windows the sports club.

Though my mother had a law degree (quite extraordinary for the time and place), she never practised law. She wrote articles for the local French press before the war but later spent much of her time volunteering for various organizations, particularly for a school run by a Jewish charitable organization called 'La Goutte de Lait'.

My parents spoke French to each other, and to their siblings, though my father continued to speak Arabic to his mother. They had a very large group of friends and entertained a lot. Indeed, I remember my father complaining that we never sat down to a meal just the four of us (my parents, my brother, and I). Their friends were of all nationalities and religions. They were, of course, very close to their families. Whenever they gave a party, they invited not only their siblings but also their siblings' in-laws. My uncle Joseph Liverant, my mother's brother, who married late, was a fixture every Friday night, walking in with gifts under his jacket for me (my brother was not yet born). My grandmother would stay with us for weeks at a time. Since she played cards every afternoon, my mother gave card parties for her friends when she was with us. I also remember a period when my cousin Rikki and my father's youngest sister, who were the same age, came to lunch every school day. Their English convent school was close to our apartment.

Until the1950s, Cairo was a major stop on tours by performing arts companies such as the Comédie Française and La Scala opera house. My parents enjoyed the theatre, the opera, and the symphony, but they drew the line at going to hear Wilhelm Furtwängler, who had conducted the Berlin Philharmonic during the war, when he came to Cairo after the war.

Though my childhood was idyllic to me, the times were not always so for my parents. My father, given his position in the largest publishing company of the Middle East, was quite prominent. It did not stop him from being arrested at the beginning of World War Two, as an enemy alien. My father's family had gone to Aleppo from Italy several generations before as traders. My father was still Italian, and that did not sit well with the Brits, who had taken control of Egypt at the time. His friends got him out after four days and he went back to work, doing business with the Brits for the publishing house. The Brits returned the favour, giving him two seats on the train that was carrying the diplomatic corps out of Egypt ahead of the anticipated Nazi invasion. Their destination was India, but they stopped in Palestine where they spent several months in a German convent in Bethlehem which had been evacuated by the nuns, and returned to Egypt after the Germans were defeated at El Alamein. During their absence, one of my father's sisters, who, recently married, lived with her in-laws, moved into our apartment.

This was not the first time my father was an enemy alien. As a baby, he was deported from Aleppo to Cyprus during the First World War. (My uncle, Joseph Ancona, was born in Cyprus.) In the years after the creation of the State of Israel, our home was searched more than once by the police. However, these searches were conducted in a relatively civilized manner. My brother remembers my mother having coffee with the police captain in the living room while his men searched the house. The police captain asked my mother to identify her closet and ordered his men not to search among 'the lady's things'.

In 1948, my father's youngest brother was arrested and spent a year in a detention camp in the desert. Many of his friends were arrested with him and the mothers would take turns driving to the camp with home-cooked food for all the detainees *and* their guards. My father arranged his release, but it was only on condition that he would leave Egypt right away. I remember seeing my uncle in handcuffs at the train station on his way to Alexandria to board a boat for France. In Paris, he lived with his sister and her family, who had left earlier, in a tiny apartment.

My parents sent my brother and me to English schools in Cairo from age five. The schools were very diverse, both by nationality and religion. Both my brother and I, as it happened, had two best friends in school: one Muslim and one Christian. We are both in touch with them to this day. As Jews, we were not discriminated against in any way. The only time it mattered was after School Assembly in the morning. The Christians were required to attend morning prayer so, after announcements were read and attendance was taken, the Assistant Headmaster would bellow 'Muslims and Jews fall out' and we were given more time in the playground as the Christians filed in for prayers. Though my parents considered sending us away earlier, it was not till the late 1950s that we were sent to England to continue our education because all English teachers had been expelled from Egypt after the Suez war. I got my first degree at the University of London. My brother, to the disgust of his very British Headmaster at his very British boarding school, turned down a place at Cambridge University to come to MIT.

My parents remained in Egypt. Indeed, for a while they could not leave as both could not get exit visas at the same time. After the publishing house was nationalized by the socialist President of Egypt, Gamal Abdel Nasser, my father assumed he should go home. The colonel who had been deputized to take over the publishing house found him packing up and told him that the Raiss (i.e. the Chief, Abdel Nasser), wanted him to stay to continue to manage the business. Of course, he stayed. So a Jew, and one who was very well known to be a Jew and very active leader in Jewish affairs, such as the Jewish Hospital and the Jewish Community Council, continued to manage the largest publishing house in the Middle East. My parents came to see my brother and me in England separately. It was not until 1961 that they managed to get exit visas together. They gave a huge party so that everyone could see that they had not dismantled their apartment, and were driven the next morning to the airport by the driver, who then took the car back to the garage to await their return. They never went back.

My parents would have liked to immigrate to the US at that time, but, as it happened, my father went to work for an Italian publishing house. Over the next twenty years, he worked his way to the top, in Milan, and then Paris, as he succeeded in turning the publishing house from a major Italian fixture to a European one. My brother and I completed our education in the US, he finished all but his dissertation for the PhD at MIT and got an MBA from Harvard. I completed the PhD in Economics at Columbia.

In 1980, my parents decided to spend a larger part of the year in New York. They bought an apartment and went synagogue-shopping. They fell in love with Shearith Israel, and particularly enjoyed the Friday night service, to which they walked every week, hand-in-hand. After my father's death, my mother came to Shearith Israel most Shabbat mornings. One of her closest friends from Egypt, Joyce Mosseri, was a member, too, which helped. My brother was married in the Small Synagogue. My daughter was married under Shearith Israel auspices and her son's Brit and daughter's naming were at Shearith Israel. My daughter's children are twins, and Phil Sherman, who officiated at the combined ceremony, managed to make my granddaughter's naming as consequential as my grandson's Brit. I so appreciated it.

All of my parents' descendants are Americans, but the descendants of my father's siblings are in Israel and France. The descendants of my mother's siblings are even more scattered: in the US, the UK, Switzerland, and Australia. Fortunately, my Aunt Regine's granddaughter, Yasmine Ergas, is a member of Shearith Israel. Her mother, Rikki (Rachel) Ergas, who came to live in the US late in life, is buried in our cemetery.

I sit in my mother's seat upstairs and love the music and the formality of the services in our beautiful sanctuary. I also find the customs we have for *nahalas* very personal and comforting. Most of all, I love the wonderful friends I have made at Shearith Israel over the almost 38 years I have been attending services.

Jacob Bousso

My name is Jacob Bousso and I was born in Cairo. I always said that coming to this country [America] was the best thing that ever happened to me, because coming here opened opportunities for me that I had never imagined possible when I was growing up as a teenager in Cairo.

We left Egypt in 1966, which was already late, considering the rising tensions, but luckily, we left before the 1967 war. My friend Rabbi Albert Gabbai can attest to what happened to his family after the Six-Day War. My oldest sister had already left about a year before, right after she got married.

There was an old Turkish law that was still on the books in Egypt that said one's nationality was acquired from the father's side. My mother was born in Cairo, but her father was born in Syria; therefore, legally, she was not Egyptian. My father was born in Beirut, which was at that time part of Syria. He moved to Egypt at a very young age; therefore, he was not Egyptian. So my three sisters and I were not considered to be Egyptians. None of us were officially 'Egyptians'; our family's status was 'stateless'. There were many of us in Egypt with that status.

When we left Egypt, I was about 17. I have good memories of my childhood in Egypt. Socially, my experiences were very positive. Politically, it was a different story, but socially, I had a wonderful relationship with my friends and schoolmates who were Jews, Christians, and Muslims. My sisters and I went to a French Lycée. Unlike the school system in the US where students move from room to room to attend various classes where they meet different students, the system at the Lycée was such that students remained in the same room for the whole school year (unless they needed to go to lab or gym), and teachers were going from class to class. As a result, one stayed the entire school year with the same schoolmates, and then moved with them, from year to year, and from one grade to another. So I developed very strong bonds with my friends. In fact, until today, I get together with my friends from kindergarten who happen to be living in the Northeast and Canada. We are regularly on the phone and on e-mail, we meet in person once or twice a year, and we have a great time. They have remained my very dearest and closest friends.

I socialized with a small circle of friends and relatives on a regular basis. It included Jews, Christians and Muslims. We went out together; we went to the movies, we attended parties, and we played soccer together. We basically had a good time.

During the month of August, my father would take us to Alexandria. Cairo is blisteringly hot in August. I have fond memories of the warm days we spent at the various beaches along the Mediterranean Sea, and the dancing on the beach after sunset. We listened to music from England, France, and the United States. But I also enjoyed listening to Arabic songs by famous Egyptian singers; in fact, I still enjoy listening to them today.

Politically, it was a different story. Starting in 1948, antagonism and discrimination against Jews became more prevalent. Gradually, we were told that we could no longer go the tennis club where we had been going for years. The chances of my being accepted at a university were almost nil.

The Curriculum at the Lycée involved classes in French. Arabic was another subject, just like English was introduced later as another subject. Gradually, the government made it mandatory that all subjects be taught in Arabic, and French became another subject. I was at a terrible disadvantage because, although we spoke the language fluently, we hardly spoke it at home. We had a woman who came every day to help with the housework, and we spoke Arabic with her, and that was the only time we spoke Arabic at home. However, having to study history, geography, and biology in Arabic was a challenge for me. Keep in mind that there were many people in Egypt who did not speak Arabic. They were English, French, Italians, Greeks, and so on. When I lived in Egypt, I have to say, I never felt at home because, as tensions intensified, it always felt like it was a temporary situation. It was clear that it was time for us to go. The question was where…

My father's side of the family left Egypt in the early 1950s and had gone mostly to Israel, except for one sister who went to France and who still lives in Paris. There was no contact between Egypt and the state of Israel, so communication with our relatives in Israel had to be through a third party. The news from our Israeli family were scarce.

My mother's side of the family had gone to France, England, the United States and Brazil. My oldest sister was already living in Brooklyn. The question for us was: Where should we go? Which part of the family were we going to join?

I was hoping from all the options that it would be the United States. I had seen the US through the lens of Hollywood and I was just enamoured with it. I wanted so much to speak English so I could understand the dialogue at the movies, but that was impossible, the actors just spoke too fast. So I had no choice but to read the sub-titles. I was so driven to learn English that I went to an English school three times a week after the Lycée, just to improve my English. In my history book, I was fascinated by the chapter about American history. I thought it was an incredible story. The colonies people were saying 'No taxation without representation.' I said, 'These are my kind of people.' Until today, I am a Revolutionary War junkie. The Revolutionary War is one of the most significant events in the history of civilization. It simply is amazing how a bunch of dysfunctional pedestrians could come together and create something so significant. I was in love with this country even before I arrived here.

So where should we go? News from our relatives in the US was always more encouraging than from our relatives in other places. My sister was already here. Also, my mother was very close to her younger sister, who was already living with her family in Brooklyn. Her sister agreed to be our sponsor and guarantor, and so we left on our journey that would end up in New York. I was delighted that they had made that decision. Immigrating to the US was very stringent in those days, and we had to go through a very rigorous process that took us through France for a period of several months, while our paperwork was being processed by the HIAS (Hebrew Immigration Aid Society). We were grateful to the French government for assisting Egyptian Jews with that process.

Now my father was very hesitant about leaving. He was convinced that things would go back to normal in Egypt again; all we had to do was wait it out. It was clear that this was not going to happen. I can understand how he felt, considering that he was already 52 at the time and he faced the challenge of having to move to another country where he hardly spoke the language. I know I would be reluctant too. But I am glad that he came around. The fact that my sister was already here helped him come around. Otherwise, we would have still been there in 1967.

A word about my father. He was in the import-export business and had access to the customs (until he was told he was not allowed there anymore because he was Jewish). Given his position, he helped many Jewish families with the shipping of their luggage. Whenever possible, he would arrange to have as many families as possible take with them a Torah scroll from one of the synagogues. He would arrange it so the people at the customs would look the other way and let it go through. It was his way of saving the numerous scrolls that were sitting in the Cairo synagogues. In the 1950s, there were thirty-nine Sephardic synagogues in Cairo alone, and at least one Ashkenazi synagogue that I can remember. Today, it is impossible to take the scrolls out; the Egyptian government considers them to be 'Egyptian relics'. Many of the scrolls are still sitting inside the arks of empty synagogues.

We took a Torah scroll with us when we left. It made its way in a duffle bag from Egypt to France and then to the United States. When we arrived here, we had a new box built for it. One day, we walked it to Ahi Ezer Synagogue in Brooklyn, in front of a parade of music, singing and dancing in the street, from Avenue Z to Avenue X on Ocean Parkway. At that time, the synagogue operated from a small garage. Regrettably, one day the synagogue caught fire and the scroll was destroyed.

When we left Egypt, although we left whatever assets we had behind, we were lucky to have had the luxury to plan and to pack for the trip. Etty's family had to leave overnight with their clothes on their backs and had no chance to plan for the trip. Her father was told he no longer could work at 'Tissue Castro', a textile company where he had been for years. Someone was appointed to take his position. Her family left for France, where they lived for seven years, waiting for their turn to immigrate to the United States on the quota system. They could feel the pressures of antisemitism in France; Etty and her friend Annie Benzaken were the only Jewish girls at the Lycée Claude Debussy and Etty's mother was fired from her job because she asked to take off for Yom Kippur. She was told that she did not have to bother coming back if she took off. Her mother's side of the family came from Syria; her father's side of family can trace its origins to Castillo in Spain; this is how they adopted their family name 'Castel'.

The deal was that Jews could leave Egypt, as long as they left their assets behind. Since we didn't have many assets, this ended up being the best deal we ever made.

When we lived in France, I went to the Lycée while we were waiting for our visa. I was struggling. The environment was very different, less friendly, and less personal. My school mates were not exactly welcoming to immigrants from North Africa. They were especially antagonistic to those who emigrated from Algeria. I enjoyed living in Paris, but again, I did not feel at home; I knew it was a temporary situation. I have enjoyed Paris much more when I went back in later years, especially when I was back to visit our relatives with Etty, Joseph and David.

When we came to New York, the minute I set foot on the ground, I felt at home. I had this feeling that I always belonged here. It's very hard to explain. It was strange to see all these brick buildings in Brooklyn, yet I felt at home.

Etty and I met the year after I arrived and we started dating. Everything was going well, my life was off to a good start, until came the draft and Vietnam. That was 1968, the height of the Vietnam War.

I was drafted into the US Army. I was just getting my bearings as I was starting my new life. In those days, many people were finding all sorts of ways to dodge the draft, by moving to Canada or claiming to be conscientious objectors. I felt that I had spent too much time of my life waiting to come to the US, and I was not about to jeopardize that situation. So I went into the Army, assuming that I could not be sent outside of the US because I did not have a green card, only to find out that US military bases everywhere in the world are considered to be US soil; therefore, from the Army's point of view, I was not leaving US soil. I didn't know that, and I ended up serving 14 months in Vietnam. I was lucky to come back, and in one piece. Yet, I objected to the Army about the fact that I was not a citizen yet, and that I had no green card. 'No problem', said the Army, 'we can swear you in without a green card'.

I figured if I am going to work and pay taxes like every American, if I am going to serve the country and risk my life like every American, then I should be able to vote like every American. So I was sworn in and I became a citizen before the rest of my family; they had to first wait five years before they could secure their green card. I went to architecture school, got married and started a family.

My introduction to Shearith Israel came shortly after Etty and I moved down the block from the synagogue. I was walking to work one day, and a gentleman standing outside asked me if I was Jewish. When I told him I was, he asked if I could come inside and complete a Minyan.

Although the service was close to the one I grew up with, I found it to be solemn and rigid. The choir sings beautifully, but it can be intimidating and not easy to sing along. Over time, I got used to it, and now I very much enjoy the services, especially the morning Minyan.

Shearith Israel has managed to cater to a variety of people coming from all over the world. We met many people and made many friends who have been amazingly supportive to our family during very difficult times. After the tragic death of our beloved son David, Shearith Israel provided us with tremendous emotional support, which was very helpful and very much appreciated. Today, we are very happy to be part of the Shearith Israel.

I would like to express my gratitude to my parents who took the leap of faith by leaving everything behind at an advanced age in their lives and starting all over again. In fact, I have a lot of respect for all those of my parents' generation who did the same thing and moved to places where they hardly spoke the language. They didn't make it about themselves; they did it to secure the future of their families. I would also like to express my gratitude to this country that has adopted Etty and me as teenagers. We both took circuitous routes to come here, but we met right here in Brooklyn; and I am so glad we did. It was a life changer for me. I love this country, I served it well, and I will forever be grateful to it.

Lucienne Carasso Bulow

Sham El Nessim, a spring holiday that goes back to Ancient Egypt, was an occasion for the family to get together, especially after my father, Léon Guédalia Carasso, and my uncle Joseph (Josy) de Botton were released from internment three months after the Suez Canal crisis. We gathered at my Uncle Josy and Aunt Viviane Nahmias's to celebrate our being together again, while knowing that our remaining days in Egypt were numbered. My maternal grandmother, Sol Arditi de Botton, who was the lynchpin of our family, was born in Alexandria and had declared that she would never leave Egypt. We all had to wait until she passed away before we would leave. In the case of my parents and I, we left in August of 1961.

My parents, Fortunée de Botton and Léon Guédalia Carasso, were both born in Alexandria, Egypt. So was I. Their families all came to Alexandria from Salonika in the Ottoman Empire between the third portion of the nineteenth century and the early twentieth century. They could all trace themselves back to Spain and spoke Judeo-Spanish. Actually, my paternal grandparents, Guédalia Carasso and Lucia (Lea) Barzilai, were Spanish citizens. My grandfather was given the nationality around 1903.

My maternal great grandparents Arditi came to Egypt about 1880. The family was from Livorno (Leghorn), but some members subsequently went to Salonika. My great grandfather, Mercado Joseph Arditi, was a banker and, like many Europeans, was attracted by the forward-looking policies of Muhammad Ali Pasha and the expected boom of the Suez Canal. My great grandmother was Signorou Angel. They had three sons, Isaac, Jacques, and Albert who, I understand, were born in Salonika while my grandmother Sol, her sisters Regina and Ida, and their younger brother, Salomon were all born in Alexandria. My grandmother, her sisters and younger brother spoke Italian as well as Spanish and French.

My maternal grandparents de Botton were Meir de Botton and Graziella Cohenca. I am not sure when they came to Alexandria from Salonika.

I believe that my grandfather, Judah de Botton, was born in Alexandria. He had two sisters, Rachel, who married Salomon Orsini, and Matilde, who married Jacques Angel.

My grandparents, Judah de Botton and Sol Arditi had seven children:

Mario, who married very late in life Rosine/Esther, who converted to Judaism; they did not have any children.

Yvonne, who married Léon Moréno, also didn't have any children, they were in some ways my second parents,

Odette, who married Amedeo Piperno. They were the parents of Sergio and Roberto Piperno.

Joseph, who married Viviane Nahmias. They were the parents of Gerard, Yves, and Isabelle de Botton.

Marcel, who married Emma Shamaa. They were the parents of Mireille and Sarah de Botton.

My mother Fortunée and her twin sister Georgette, who married Felix Halifi. Georgette died very young and did not have children.

Sergio Piperno lives in Florence and Roberto Piperno lives in Rome. Gérard, Yves, Isabelle, Mireille and Sarah de Botton all live in Paris.

On the Carasso side of my family, my paternal grandmother Lucia Barzilai Carasso came to Alexandria to join her family while pregnant with my father. My father's sister, Rachel, who was seven years older than he, was born in Salonika. I believe that my grandmother left Salonika to join her siblings and because the Balkan war was erupting. The Greeks were fighting to take over Salonika, which they eventually succeeded in doing. My grandfather did not join her. I found out that he had obtained a *laissez-passer* in the summer of 1912 but was probably prevented from leaving, because the Greeks took control of the city in September or October. He was apparently inducted into the Greek army. My cousin, Luna Barzilai Rosenfeld, told me that he had been wounded and walked with a limp. To my father's chagrin, his father never registered him as a Spanish citizen in the Spanish Consulate of Alexandria. My father never spoke of his father.

Both my mother and my father grew up without fathers. My grandfather, Judah de Botton, who worked in Tanta – I believe in the cotton industry – in order to be able to support his large family, died young leaving my grandmother Sol a widow at the age of 35 with seven children. My mother and her twin sister were two years old. My oldest uncle, Mario, became the head of the family at the age of thirteen.

My grandmother was unable to cope with the tragic situation. She got sick and all the children rallied around her. My aunt Yvonne became the surrogate mother. My grandmother at first sought help from her brothers, who were well off, but eventually my uncles and aunts had to fend for themselves. It was decided that the boys would go to school so they could get good jobs, whereas the girls would stay home. My mother and her twin sister were mortified not to go to school.

With time, the family prospered. My uncles studied accounting and eventually founded a successful company in import and export of coal, pharmaceuticals and industrial products. My father started in the paper industry, then traded in chemicals. He eventually discovered his passion: ships and the shipping business. After I was born, he obtained a ship agency. He represented Italian, Portuguese, and Brazilian lines, but his main business was a Spanish liner company named Naviera el Exportación Agricola, Madrid.

We led a very comfortable and tight family life. My parents and I lived with my Nonna Sol first in a villa that we also shared with my Uncle Marcel and his family, but eventually we moved to apartments. We opened a door between two apartments, and Nonna Sol lived in one apartment with her 'dame de compagnie' and my parents and I lived in the other one. Eventually, my Nonna Carasso had to be operated on for cataracts, and she moved in with us. My cousins lived very close to us in Mustapha Pasha. I used to bicycle to their villa almost every afternoon. I went to movies, mostly American movies, three or four times a week.

As I was growing up, everyone in the family spoke Judeo-Spanish (Ladino) although we all went to French schools and spoke French as our native language. We also spoke Italian, Arabic, and knew some Hebrew. My Nonna Carasso, however, only spoke Spanish or Greek. Inasmuch as I did not know enough Greek, I had to speak to her in Spanish. She almost spoke in Ladino proverbs. She had a proverb for every circumstance.

For school, I went to a Jewish school, the Lycée de l'Union Juive pour l'Enseignement, which was a Jewish private school. After 2 November 1956 when the Suez Canal Crisis occurred, all French and British teachers were expelled and most of my classmates left the country. The next year, I went to Catholic school, Notre Dame de Sion, where French nuns were not affected by the expulsion decree. The school curriculum changed a great deal after the new policies of the Nasser government were implemented.

My uncle's business was nationalized and a sequester took over his office. My father's agency was taken over by his Muslim shop chandler. We slowly started to liquidate everything. My Nonna Sol passed away in the fall of 1960. After I finished my school year and obtained my secondary diploma in Arabic, we left on the *Massalia*, which transported many refugees from Egypt. My cousins had left for Paris earlier. My parents and

I went to Genoa because my father needed to be in a port. He established his business in our new, large apartment while we applied for a visa to emigrate to the United States. One year later, we obtained the visa under a special programme for stateless political refugees and arrived in New York in September 1962. For our first Yom Kippur in New York, we attended the downstairs service at Shearith Israel run by Rabbi Battan, who was also from Egypt. It was a relief to find a service which felt familiar. We then moved to the East Side, and I started my college career at Hunter College.

After we left Egypt, my father always had his office at home, and I would help him in his work.

We tried several synagogues for Kippur, but eventually concluded that Shearith Israel was home. Upon graduation from Hunter, I was awarded a Woodrow Wilson Fellowship and went to Yale University where I obtained a Ph.D. in French literature. When I returned to New York and taught at Stern College for Women and York College of CUNY, I started to attend book discussions at Rabbi Marc and Gilda Angel's home. There, I met my husband, George.

After teaching for two years, I noticed that I was already repeating myself and decided to switch fields. I got into the shipping business by taking a typist job. I worked for two international agricultural products trading companies. I was promoted and became the first woman maritime arbitrator in the world. I eventually was elected president of the Society of Maritime Arbitrators, Inc.

I have had a long connection with Shearith Israel. Our children, Harris and Alessandra, celebrated their Bar and Bat Mitzvahs here. I am a past president of the Shearith Israel League. One of my proudest achievements has been to produce the three CDs of the Historic Music of the Spanish and Portuguese Synagogue in the City of New York. It was a labour of love which has tied me irrevocably to Shearith Israel.

Alain Farhi

My paternal grandfather, Hillel Farhi, was born in 1868 in Damascus to a Sephardic prestigious family whose ancestors, originally from Catalonia (ca 1302), arrived in Syria in 1731.He visited Egypt for the first time in 1899. Shortly after receiving his MD degree from London, he returned to Egypt and married Esther Setton from Aleppo. Hillel died in Cairo in 1940 after a long career as Chief Doctor of the Royal Egyptian Railways. In addition to his private practice, Hillel was also a prolific author of religious essays, commentaries, books and articles in literary newspapers. He translated into classical Arabic the daily prayer book (Siddur Farhi) as well as the High Holidays prayer books and the Haggadah. This endeavour had finally allowed Jews of Arab countries to understand their prayers and it allowed the Arab countries to better understand their Jewish countrymen. These books remain to this day the only ones ever published with an Arabic translation.

My father, Azar Farhi, was his eldest son. Like many Jewish boys of his generation, he was educated at a Jesuit school. In their quest for the best education for their children, Jewish families did not hesitate to send them to a Catholic parochial school. They did not perceive it as a threat to their Jewish principles and community. Azar studied law and was intending to practice at the International Courts (Tribunaux Mixtes). But upon graduation, the International Courts were abolished. Foreign residents in Egypt could no longer be judged according to the laws of their country of origin. Egyptian laws became the rule of the land, applied to all residents.

My father had to pivot and choose a new career. He started Peerless, a knitting factory for T-shirts, underwear and socks. With Nasser's policy of economic strangulation of the Jewish community, my father's business was nationalized in 1963. Shortly after, he was asked to lead as general manager for the conglomerate of the all the nationalized knitting factories. And life went on until June 1967. He married my mother, Antoinette Harari, in 1943 and lived in Garden City near the Nile.

My maternal grandparents were both born in Aleppo. My grandfather, Ibrahim Harari, came to Egypt in the early 1900 to seek his fortune. He had a business importing British woollen fare.

My parents had four children. I am the eldest son. We all went to the Lycée Français du Caire de Bab El Louk, a secular private school where most Jewish families sent their children. Children of well-to-do Muslim and Christian families were sent there as well. The curriculum was rigorous and most teachers were French nationals. Wednesday afternoons were reserved for sports and boy scouts' activities when we were bused to the Méadi track and field complex. Most kids knew each other but rarely socialized after school hours because of heavy loads of homework. We socialized on Sundays, our only day off before 1957. After the October War in 1956, the Egyptian Ministry of Education took over the direction of the school. The French administrators and teachers were expelled and 50 per cent of the curriculum was taught in Arabic, a language we spoke fluently. Classmates from the Lycée have remained close friends whether they emigrated or stayed in Egypt.

Our religious education was done by our parents. Sit-down dinners on Friday nights and for the high holidays were the big events. For my bar mitzvah, rote learning was supervised by a rabbi during private sessions. During the winter, we all met for Friday night service at the downtown synagogue Sha'ar Hashamayim, commonly known as Temple Ismaélia, to plan our activities for Saturday evening and Sunday.

Like most teenagers in Cairo, my social life was centred around going to the movies, biking, card games, backgammon and sports. I was an avid swimmer and fencer (saber). Every Sunday morning, I would go horseback riding in the desert around the Pyramids and the Sphinx in Giza. We had to avoid any political discussions as it would bring our parents aggravations and reprisal from the authorities, so our social gatherings were mostly spent dancing to American, French, and Italian songs. I have fond memories of the three long months of summer vacations my family took in Alexandria, a city bordering the Mediterranean Sea.

After graduation in 1961, I went to Paris to study engineering. My family (parents, two sisters and a brother) stayed in Cairo. Having kept my Egyptian passport (very unusual for a Jew after 1956), I did return to Cairo for several summer visits.

On June 6, 1967, my father, brother and our Farhi relatives were spared the automatic round up of Jews by Nasser. My future father-in-law was summarily expelled as he held an Italian passport. During the Six-Day War, my family hunkered down and left in July, abandoning all of their assets. After sailing from Alexandria to Marseille, they arrived in Paris to wait for a US authorization facilitated by the HIAS to immigrate as refugees. On 29 February 1968, we landed at Idlewild airport in freezing weather and were driven by my maternal uncle to Brooklyn in his huge American car to start our American life.

In December 1974, Jeannine Toueg and I were married at the Spanish Portuguese Synagogue in a ceremony officiated by the late Rabbi Louis Gerstein (z'l).

Jeannine's parents, Maurice Toueg and Sarina Sabbagh, were both born in Egypt with their ancestors arriving at the turn of the 19th century from Iraq and Aleppo, respectively. A description of her mother's apartment and life in Cairo at that time can be found in Lucette Lagnado's book *The Man in the White Sharkskin Suit*. Jeannine and her family left Egypt in June 1967. As Italian citizens, they resided in Milano for a few years before immigrating to NYC. Maurice Toueg owned a construction company in Cairo and imported textiles in Italy.

In 1988, we were posted overseas, returning to the US only in 2005. We joined Congregation Shearith Israel in 2010 as we were often in Manhattan for the Jewish Holidays.

Jeannine and I have two children: Philippe and Sabrina and three grandchildren: Hannah, Theo and Nico. Philippe and his wife Libby live in San Francisco; and Sabrina and her husband Adam live in Brooklyn.

Rabbi Albert Gabbai

To tell my personal story in Egypt is really to tell the story of many of my coreligionists. I was blessed of being born a Jew to parents who came from different backgrounds, as were many Jews who came to Egypt from the mid-nineteenth century. I am one of ten siblings. It was wonderful to be part of such a large family. Our father was born in Baghdad to a family of rabbis and learned sages (the name 'Gabbai' goes back to Talmudic times; see T. Sanhedrin where it says 'Kol Gabbai Kasher', 'every gabbai is honest'). As a child, he came down to Egypt with his family, like many others, to find fortune there. He traded in silk shirts. Our mother came from a family from Leghorn, Italy. They met in Egypt.

Like many of the Jews in Egypt, our culture was French (and Italian and English and Greek). Her mother, my grandmother, was born in Salonika, Greece. Her family spoke Spaniolit (Ladino) and many of her sisters married in the Ashkenazi community.

So, we were sent to French school, the Lycée Laique (secular) Français or the Collège de la Salle (French Catholic school). Just imagine: An observant Jew, in a French Catholic school, in a Muslim country! The majority of the students were Jews, but we made friends very naturally and easily with all, Jews, Christians and Muslims alike. We had a wonderful easy life with a lot of privileges.

When Nasser's Pan Arab nationalism swept the whole Middle East, life became very difficult for the Jews. Like many others we started leaving Egypt. First, four of our brothers left and went to the US where they became US citizens. Although the Egyptian government was very happy to expel us and kick us out, they made our life miserable by giving us a hard time to get out. (There is a prevalence of contradictions in the Arab world.)

When I was in high school in June 1967, we were supposed to get out that summer. We were just waiting to be granted the exit visa that was so coveted, yet so difficult to obtain. When the Six-Day War broke out, my three brothers and I were rounded up by the secret service and put in a prison camp (thank God they did not touch the women). Yet, they would not tell our mother of our whereabouts.

Three years passed until, under pressure from the outside, we were let go. We were taken from the prison camp to the airport, inside the plane to fly to Paris. (From extreme confinement to extreme freedom!)

It was about a year later, when I arrived in New York, on a snowy night in January. I still remember the melody played at the Kennedy airport: 'If I were a rich man...' It was a dream come true to finally arrive in America and be reunited with my family.

When I became a student at Yeshiva University, I went to the library to look at the micro-films of the *New York Times* to see what was going on while I was in that horrible hole for three years. I discovered (not a bit surprised) that there were constant demonstrations at the Egyptian delegation at the United Nations in New York demanding the release of the Jews in prison camps in Egypt. I was not surprised by these demonstrations by our fellow Jews because, as the Talmud says, 'The Jewish people is like the human body, if a limb hurts the whole body hurts.' No doubt that we can say that this effort contributed to our freedom.

Roberto Salama

Many Egyptian Jews, especially from Alexandria, had a connection with Livorno, Italy. Jews from Tuscany began settling in Egypt already in the early nineteenth century. Our family's connection to Italy is documented starting with Salomone Salama, who lived in Alexandria together with his wife Mira in the 1830s. But his marriage certificate was registered with the Commune de Livorno, as were the birth and death certificates of his sons and daughters, including my great-grandparents, Lazzaro and Elena Salama.

My grandfather, Umberto Salama, lived in Egypt, but he too had an Italian connection, having served in the Italian Army during World War I. He left Egypt in 1933 for Venezuela. Unfortunately, he died at an early age in 1938 leaving my grandmother Claire Anzarut, a widow with three young sons. After WWII, they moved from Venezuela to Bolivia where my grandmother's relatives, the Anzarut and Attie families (originally from Syria) had settled.

My father Ricardo and his older brother, Lazaro, remained in Bolivia. They went into business and had families of their own. Their younger brother (my uncle) emigrated to the US in the early 1960s. My brother David and I later left Bolivia to study abroad.

The synagogue in Bolivia where we grew up was built and financed by an Alexandrian Jew named Isaac Antaki. The Antakis had come to Bolivia from Kobe, Japan where they owned a successful textile business importing cotton from Egypt and exporting silk to Europe.

Bolivia has always been a safe haven for Jews. Even though the community is very small now, it once numbered close to 8,000. The synagogue was inaugurated in 1947.

My wife, Jadranka (Adrienne) and I came to New York in 1979. We have two children, Jessica and Allen. We became members of Shearith Israel, and our children went to the Talmud Torah, studied with Rabbi Hayyim Angel and with Rabbi Ira Rohde, and had their bar and bat mitzvah celebrations at Shearith Israel, where we are still members today. Allen is now a Senior in college and Jessica recently made Aliyah to Israel.

L. Gilles Sion

I was born in Cairo in 1956, just a few weeks before Egypt's Suez war with France, the UK and Israel erupted. Although my father's family had been in Egypt for more than a century, within six months we had joined a second exodus of Jews from Egypt, as we made our way, first to North America, and then to Switzerland, for a new life far from Cairo's muezzins and minarets.

My father, Elie Sion, was born in Cairo in 1923, the last of eight children, one of whom had died in early childhood. His father, Léon, was a lawyer, born to a proudly French family that had emigrated to Egypt from Algeria, then a *département* of France. One of the scions of the family had supplied jute bags to the French engineering company that excavated the Suez Canal in the mid-nineteenth century.

My father's mother, Latifa Sourour, had emigrated to Cairo as a child from Beirut, and married my grandfather, much to the chagrin of my grandfather's siblings, who as French-Egyptian 'grandees' looked askance at poor immigrants from the Levant. During the hot Cairo summers, the family vacationed in huts in Ras-el-Bar, where the Nile delta met the Mediterranean, and travelled through Palestine to the mountains of Lebanon.

My grandfather died at 49 after a short bout with typhoid fever, leaving my grandmother to care for her seven children, with the help of my father's older brother Marcel, also a lawyer, who practised in the so-called mixed courts (which adjudicated disputes involving foreign nationals in Egypt). Like most good Jews in Cairo, my father and his siblings attended Jesuit schools, where the language of instruction was French. He excelled at math and eventually enrolled in the engineering school of Cairo University. On graduating, he joined the Tractors and Engineering Co., which served as the Egyptian distributor for York, the US air conditioning manufacturer.

My mother, Jeanette Kamri (who everyone knew as Jean), was born to a modest family. Her father, Ovadia (Albert), had emigrated to Egypt from Urfa, in what is now southeastern Turkey. Legend has it that he walked to

Beirut, where he caught a steamer to Alexandria because, he had heard, the streets of Egypt were paved with gold (another *goldene medine*).

Her mother, Latifa Dayan, came from a family of Aleppan Jews who had also emigrated to Cairo for economic reasons. After my Uncle Henri was invited to study at the Rabbinic Seminary of Rhodes, my mother was offered a scholarship to attend the Lycée Français of Cairo, and, not to be outdone by her brother, persuaded my observant grandfather to let her attend the secular school, where classes met on Saturdays.

Her mother died when she was in grade school, but even after her extended maternal family emigrated to Palestine, she persevered, earning the French *Baccalauréat* in math. She learned English and then Spanish, eventually joining the marketing department of TWA, the US airline, which after the war had established a regional headquarters in Cairo.

My parents were introduced by a mutual friend at the famed Groppi, a Swiss establishment where the well-heeled European community of Cairo sipped tea and coffee amidst fresh French and Italian pastries. Quite the modern couple, they married in Paris, where my mother had been stationed with TWA, and eventually moved into an apartment in the Zamalek neighbourhood of Cairo, not far from the Gezira Sporting Club, where old English *colonialisme* still reigned.

They lived what by all accounts was a charmed life, but after Gamal Abdel Nasser's *coup d'état* in 1953, they knew their days in Egypt were numbered. In December 1956, after US Secretary of State John Foster Dulles had strong-armed the French and the British to withdraw their troops from the Suez Canal, an Egyptian police officer knocked at our door to serve expulsion papers on my father, a French citizen. Although not expelled as a Jew, when my father reported to the local town hall, the civil servant looked at his papers and, in disbelief, exclaimed 'French... and Jewish?'

That expulsion order sent my father to North America to look for employment with York, the company whose equipment he had been distributing in Egypt. He was offered a position to do the same in an unlikely locale – the Bahamas. Leaving behind all belongings except for the few family jewels that could be sewn into the hems of dresses, my mother and I joined him in Nassau, where we lived for 18 months before my father found a position in New York.

For the next few years, extended family arrived from Egypt, all looking for a new life in America; at one point, my parents told me, there were seven people living in our one-bedroom apartment in Bayside, Queens. In 1961, my father was asked to open York's first office in Europe, and we moved to

Geneva, where I spent my childhood and my parents lived most of the rest of their lives.

For many years, my parents had a love-hate relationship with their Egyptian heritage. They spoke French but resorted to Arabic to intone their favorite love songs or to 'discreetly' insult a bad taxi driver.

While inveighing against Nasser and cheering Israel's military successes, my father would spend his evenings listening to records of the legendary Umm Kalsum, and no dinner left him quite as satisfied as the *béléhat* (torpedo-shaped meatballs) and *fassulia béda* (white beans) he grew up with.

My mother, who shed the tell-tale rolling r's of Egyptian Jews to adopt the proper French of the local genevois, took to saying that her birth and upbringing in Egypt were a 'geographical mistake'. And yet, with time, both reconciled themselves to their past, eventually returning to Egypt, with me, on more than one occasion after Egypt and Israel signed a peace treaty in 1978.

In the late 1980s, coming full circle, my father established an air conditioning manufacturing joint venture just outside of Cairo with one of his former business associates. On his last return to Egypt in 2008, not long before his passing, we could not pry him away from lively conversations, over obligatory cups of Turkish coffee, with his former colleagues and friends.

My heritage had also come full circle in 1981, when, during a year of graduate study in Brussels, I met Lina Ajami, whose mother's maiden name, Dayan, was the same as my maternal grandmother's. Lina's family had followed a similar peripatetic path, from Aleppo, to Beirut (where Lina was born), to Israel and finally to Belgium. Distant cousins, it seemed, we quickly bonded, and were married in 1985 by Rabbi Marc Angel at Shearith Israel. We, too, use Arabic to insult bad cab drivers (though, we have learned, that is a more perilous proposition today in New York City), but also to keep secrets from our children, Elliot, Jake and Jessica, all of whom have been to Egypt with us and my late father, and have sworn to learn the language so we can no longer keep those secrets from them. And no Shabbat dinner is complete without the *béléhat* and *fassulia béda* that my father loved so much.

Allegra Hodara

The following text was originally published as 'An Exodus from Egypt' in *Moment* magazine in October 2002, written by the magazine's editor,

Hershel Shanks. Mr Shanks had previously written about a visit he had made as a young man to Egypt, where he had met and spent some time with a young woman, Allegra, whose father was a well-to-do man who owned a button factory. Through the article, he was able to make contact with her again, and she contributed information about her family's story:

***

To give you a slight idea what happened to us, on 5 June 1967, when the Six-Day War started, the Egyptian authorities came to take my father to jail. A week later, they took my brother (at 4 in the morning). My mother was in very bad shape, and I was going around, asking for help from different foreign embassies in Cairo. We were finally able to leave with Spanish passports. The Spanish consul himself went to jail to pick up my father and my brother, as well as six other Jewish prisoners... on 5 June 1967, we all left on a Spanish cargo ship called the *Beni-Casim*. We were penniless, but the most important thing is that we were all together.

The young people slept on the floor. We left the few cabins to the parents. The shop went all around the Mediterranean to load and discharge merchandise – Beirut, Latakia, Malta, Cyprus and Athens. We ended up in Civitavecchia, a port near Rome. We were cared for by Jewish organizations at Ostia Lido, where we stayed for six months – until we got visas to go to the States (my brother was already there).

We got an apartment in Brooklyn, the same apartment where my mother still lives. We all got jobs – my mother, my sister, my brother, and of course my father and me. I got a job as a messenger at Blue Cross Blue Shield, taking documents from one department to another. My father found a job in the mail department of Chase Manhattan Bank. He was not even hired full-time because he had a heart murmur, so he worked per hour without benefits.

[With respect to the family's button factory] the Egyptian man, who actually worked for my father, took everything. But we wouldn't have been able to leave Egypt for money or valuables, in any case. We were entitled to take with us only five Egyptian pounds.

[My father was arrested] simply because he was a Jew. They had no reason whatever to arrest an honest citizen with no political involvement of any kind, a peaceful man who minded his own business. It was a real nightmare for my father, my brother, and all the other arrested Jewish men. They were treated very, very badly. They tortured them. The idea was to 'break them' and remove any possible dignity they might still have.

Atrocious things happened in this jail. The Egyptians were apparently trained by some Nazis living in Egypt. I remember when we were on the ship, at night my father would wake up screaming and crying. He had lost a lot of weight, and he looked terrible.

You must understand that it is very difficult for me to go back in the past and recall all these horrible memories that are hidden within myself. I am writing these lines with tears in my eyes. I must stop for a moment.

Unfortunately, my father passed away in 1977. He was never the same man as he was in Egypt. This last episode in Cairo destroyed him. They managed to break him.

Bibliography

Abdalla, A., *The Student Movement and National Politics in Egypt, 1923–1973* (Cairo: The American University in Cairo Press, 2008).

Abdelmonem, M.G., 'The Modern Ordinary: Changing Culture of Urban Living in Egypt's Traditional Quarters at the Turn of the Twentieth Century', *Middle Eastern Studies*, 52, 5 (2016), pp.825-44.

Abdulhaq, N., *Jewish and Greek Communities in Egypt* (London and New York: IB Taurus, 2016).

Abecassis, F. and Faü, J.F., 'Les Karaïtes: une Communauté Cairote à l'heure de l'État-nation', *Égypte/Monde Arabe*, 11, 1 (1992), pp.47-58.

Abecassis, F., 'Girgis Salama, Histoire de l'enseignement Etranger, 1963', *Égypte/Monde Arabe*, 18-19, 1 (1994), pp.521-7.

Aharoni, A., 'The Image of Jewish Life in Egypt in the Writings of Egyptian Jewish Authors in Israel and Abroad', in S. Shamir (ed.), *The Jews of Egypt : A Mediterranean Society in Modern Time*s (Abingdon: Routledge, 1988), pp.192-8.

Aharoni, A., 'The Forced Migration of Jews from Arab Countries', *Peace Review*, 5, 1, (2003), pp.53-60.

Aharoni, A., 'Memories of Egypt', *Palestine -Israel Journal of Politics, Economics and Culture*, East Jerusalem 15/16, 4, 1 (2008/2009), pp.165-9.

Al-SayidMarsot, A.L., *Egypt in the Reign of Muhammad Ali* (Cambridge: Cambridge University Press, 1984).

Arad, D., 'Welfare and Charity in a Sixteenth-Century Jewish Community in Egypt: A Study of Genizah Documents', *Al-Masāq*, 29, 3 (2017), pp.258-72.

Barda, R., *The Migration Experience of the Jews of Egypt to Australia, 1948-1967: A Model of Acculturation*, PhD thesis, University of Sydney, Sydney, (2013).

Barda, R., *The Modern Exodus of the Jews From Egypt*, Http://www.nebidaniel.org/documents/Whence Hence by R.Barda.doc, accessed 25 January 2020.

Bareket, E., 'Head of the Jews in Spain in Comparison to Head of the Jews in Egypt', *Journal of Islamic and Middle Eastern Multidisciplinary Studies: Matha*, 3, 3 (2013).

Behar, M., 'What's in a Name? Socio-Terminological Formations and the Case for "Arabized-Jews"', *Social Identities* 15, 6 (2009), pp.747-71.

Behar, M. and Ben-DorBenite, Z., 'The Possibility of Modern Middle Eastern Jewish Thought', *British Journal of Middle Eastern Studies*, 41, 1 (2014), pp.43-61,

Beilin, Y., *Israel: A Concise Political History* (London: Weidenfeld and Nicolson, 1992).

Beinin, J., *The Dispersion of Egyptian Jewry: Culture, Politics, and the Formation of a Modern Diaspora* (Oakland, CA: University of California Press, 1998).

Beinin, J., 'Egypt: Society and Economy, 1923-1952', in M.W. Daly (ed.), *The Cambridge History of Egypt* (Cambridge: Cambridge University Press, 1998), pp.309-33.

Ben Israel, M., 'How Profitable the Nation of the Jews Are' in L. Wolf (ed.), *Menasseh ben Israel's Mission to Oliver Cromwell: Being a Reprint of the Pamphlets published by Menassah ben Israel to promote the Re-admission of the Jews to England, 1649-1645*(Cambridge: Cambridge University Press, 1901/2012), pp.81-9.

Brenner, L., *Zionism in the Age of the Dictators* (London: Croom Helm, 1983).

Brilliant, M., *Portrait of Israel* (New York: American Heritage Press, 1970).

Bosworth, C.E., 'Christian and Jewish Religious Dignitaries in Mamluk Egypt and Syria: Qalqashandi's Information on Their Hierarchy, Titulature and Appointment', *International Journal of Middle East Studies*, 3, 2 (1972), pp.199-216.

Bulletin All. Isr. 1881, pp.64-69; 1892, pp.28-29 cited in http://www.jewishencyclopedia. com/articles/6237-fornaraki-affair, accessed on 7 March 2020.

Cochran, J., *Education in Egypt* (Abingdon: Routledge and Kegan Paul, 1986).

Cohen, M., *Jewish Self-Government in Medieval Egypt: The Origins of the Office of Head of the Jews, c. 1065-1126* (Princeton, NJ: Princeton University Press, 1980).

Cohen, M., *The Voice of the Poor in the Middle Ages: An Anthology of Documents from the Cairo Geniza* (Princeton, NJ: Princeton University Press, 2005).

Cohen, M., *Poverty and Charity in the Jewish Community of Medieval Egypt* (Princeton, NJ: Princeton University Press, 2005).

Cohen, S., 'Prejudice and the Unexamined Life: A Neuro-Psychoanalytic Framework for the Repressed Conflict between Ethnic and National Identities Among Arab-Jews in Israel', *International Journal of Applied Psychoanalytic Studies*, 8, 4 (2011), pp.325–40.

Cohn-Sherbok, D., *Israel; the History of an Idea* (London: SPCK, 1992).

Crecelius, D., 'Egypt in the Eighteenth Century', in M.W. Daly (ed.), *The Cambridge History of Egypt* (Cambridge: Cambridge University Press, 1998), pp.59-86.

Daly, M.W. (ed.), *The Cambridge History of Egypt* (Cambridge: Cambridge University Press, 1998).

De Aranjo, A., *Assets and Liabilities: Refugees from Hungary and Egypt in France and in Britain, 1956-1960*, PhD thesis, University of Nottingham, Nottingham (2013).

Deeb, M., 'Bank Misr and the Emergence of Local Bourgeoisie in Egypt', *Middle Eastern Studies*, 12 (1976), pp.69–86.

Deeb, M., 'The Socioeconomic Role of the Local Foreign Minorities in Modern Egypt, 1805–1961', *International Journal of Middle East Studies*, 9, 1, (1978), pp.11–22.

Dershowitz, A., *The Case for Israel* (Hoboken, NJ: Wiley, 2003).

Dulska, A.K., 'Abrahamic Coexistence in the Twelfth Century Middle East? Jews among Christians and Muslims in a travel account by a Navarrese Jew, Benjamin of Tudela', *Journal of Beliefs & Values*, 38, 3 (2017), pp.257-66.

Economist, The,'Out of the Shadows, the Last Jews of Egypt', 9 September 2017, (424, 2017, 9057).

Eden, A., *The Memoirs of Sir Anthony Eden: Full Circle* (London: Cassell & Company, 1960).

Edinger, Z., *Out of Egypt: Celebrating Egyptian Jewish Heritage at Shearith Israel*, (Philadelphia: Self-published, 2019).

El-Kodsi, M., *The Karaite Jews of Egypt 1882-1986* (New York: Mourad El-Kodsi, 1987).

El-Shamaa, M., 'Six women are all that remain of a once-thriving Jewish community in Cairo', *Arab News*, 25 May 2019.

Fargeon, M., *Les Juifs En Egypte Depuis Les Origines Jusqu'à Ce Jour* (Cairo: M. Fargeon Self-Published, 1938).

Fischback, M.R., 'Palestinian Refugee Compensation and Israeli Counterclaims for Jewish Property in Arab Countries', *Journal of Palestine Studies*, 38, 1 (2008), pp.6-24.

Gat, M.,'The IDF and the Mass Immigration of the early 1950s: Aid to the Immigrant Camps', in E. Karsh (ed.), *Israel: The First Hundred Years* (London: Frank Cass, 2002).

Gerber, J.S., 'History of the Jews in the Middle East and North Africa from the Rise of Islam until 1700', in R. Spector Simon, M. Laskier and S. Reguer (eds), *The Jews of the Middle East and North Africa in Modern Times* (New York: Columbia University Press, 2003), pp.3-18.

Gerges, F., *Making the Arab World: Nasser, Qutb, and the Clash That Shaped the Middle East* (Princeton, NJ: Princeton University Press, 2018).

Gilbert, M., *Israel: A History* (London: Harper Perennial, 2008).

Ginat, R., 'Jewish Identities in the Arab Middle East: The Case of Egypt in Retrospect', *International Journal of Middle East Studies*, 46, 3 (2014), pp.593-6.

Goitein, S.D., *Jews and Arabs: Their Contacts Through the Ages* (New York: Schoken Books, 1974).

Goldberg, H.E., 'From Sephardi to Mizrahi and Back Again: Changing Meanings of "Sephardi" in Its Social Environments', *Jewish Social Studies*, 15, 1 (2008), pp.165-88.

Gorgas, J.T., 'The Limits of the State: Student Protest in Egypt, Iraq and Turkey, 1948–63', *British Journal of Middle Eastern Studies*, 40, 4 (2013), pp.359-77.

Govrin, N., 'The Encounters of Exiles from Palestine with the Jewish Community of Egypt during World War I, as Reflected in their Writings', in S. Shamir (ed.), *The Jews of Egypt: a Mediterranean Society in Modern Times* (Abingdon: Routledge, 1987) pp.177-91.

Haag, M., *Alexandria: City of Memory* (London: Yale University Press, 2004).

Halamish, A., 'Zionist Immigration Policy Put to the Test', *Journal of Modern Jewish Studies*, 7, 2 (2008), pp.119-34.

Halbertal, M., *Maimonides: Life and Thought* (Princeton, NJ: Princeton University Press, 2014).

Hanna, N., 'Ottoman Egypt and the French Expedition: Some Long-Term Trends', in I.A., Bierman (ed.), *Napoleon in Egypt* (New York: Ithaca Press, 2003), pp.5-13.

Hastings, F., 'The Unsung Savior of Cairo's Jewish Community', *Haaretz*, 21 July 2019.

Hernon, I., *Assassin! 200 years of British Political Murder* (London: Pluto Press, 2007), p.161.

Herrmann, S., *Israel in Egypt* (London: SCM Press Ltd, 1973).

Israel-Pelletier, A., 'Edmond Jabès, Jacques Hassoun, and Melancholy: The Second Exodus in the Shadow of the Holocaust', *MLN*, 123, 4 (2008), pp.797-818, 976.

Julius, L., *Uprooted: How 3000 Years of Jewish Civilisation in the Arab World Vanished Overnight* (London and Chicago: Vallentine Mitchell, 2018).

Kabalo, P., 'Israeli Jews from Muslim Countries: Immigrant Associations and Civic Leverage', *Contemporary Review of the Middle East*, 9, 6 (2009).

Kalimi, I., 'Medieval Sephardic-Oriental Jewish Bible Exegesis; the Contributions of Saadia Gaon and Abraham ibn Ezra', in I. Kalimi, *Fighting Over the Bible: Jewish Interpretation, Sectarianism and Polemic from Temple to Talmud and Beyond* (Leiden: Brill, 2017), pp.231-49.

Kasher, A., *The Jews in Hellenistic and Roman Egypt: The Struggle for Equal Rights* (Tubingen: JCM Mohr, 1985).

Krakowski, E., *Coming of Age in Medieval Egypt: Female Adolescence, Jewish Law, and Ordinary Culture* (Princeton, NJ: Princeton University Press, 2018).

Krämer, G., '"Radical" Nationalists, Fundamentalists and the Jews in Egypt; or Who is a Real Egyptian?' in G.R. Warburg and U. Kuperferschmidt (eds), *Islam, Nationalism and Radicalism in Egypt and Sudan* (New York: Praeger Publishers, 1983).

Krämer, G., 'Political Participation of the Jews in Egypt Between World War I and the 1952 Revolution', in S. Shamir (ed.), *The Jews of Egypt : A Mediterranean Society in Modern Times* (Abingdon: Routledge, 1987), pp.68-82.

Krämer, G., *The Jews in Modern Egypt, 1914-1952* (London: IB Tauris, 1989).

Landau, J.M., *Jews in Nineteenth-Century Egypt*. (New York/London: New York University Press/University of London Press, 1969).

Landau, J., 'Ritual Murder Accusations in Nineteenth-Century Egypt', in Landau, J., *Middle Eastern Themes* (London: Frank Cass, 1973).

Landau, J., 'Abu Naddara: An Egyptian Jewish Nationalist', *The Journal of Jewish Studies*, 3, 1 (1952), pp.30-4.

Lagnado, L., *The Man in the White Sharkskin Suit: My Family's Exodus from Old Cairo to the New World* (New York: HarperCollins, 2007).

Lane, E.W., 'An Account of the Manners and Customs of the Modern Egyptians 1833-1835', *Natali*, 2 (1836), pp.344-49.

Laskier, M.M., 'Egyptian Jewry under the Nasser Regime 1956-1970', *Middle Eastern Studies*, 31, 3 (1995), p.581.

Laskier, M.M., *The Jews of Egypt, 1920-1970: In the Midst of Zionism, Anti-Semitism and the Middle East Conflict* (New York: NYU Press, 1999), p.287.

Lassner, J., *Jews, Christians, and the Abode of Islam: Modern Scholarship, Medieval Realities* (Chicago: University of Chicago Press, 2012).

Lavie, D., 'Lost Jewish property in Arab countries estimated at $150 billion', *Israel Hayom*, 16 December 2019.

Layton-Henry, Z., *The Politics of Immigration: Race and Race Relations in Postwar Britain* (Hoboken, NJ: Wiley-Blackwell, 1992).

Lev, E., 'Drugs Held and Sold by Pharmacists of the Jewish Community of Medieval (11–14th centuries) Cairo According to Lists of Materia Medica found at the Taylor–Schechter Genizah collection, Cambridge', *Journal of Ethnopharmacology*, 100, 2 (2007), pp.275-93.

Levick, A., 'Remembering the Ethnic Cleansing of Egypt's Jews', *The Algemeiner*, 15 January 2020.

Lewis, B., *The Jews of Islam* (Abingdon: Routledge & Kegan Paul, 1984).

Lewis, B., *Cultures in Conflict: Christians, Muslims and Jews in the Age of Discovery* (Oxford: Oxford University Press, 1995).

Maged, M., 'The Jewish Community in Cairo Down to Five after President's Mother Dies', *Egypt Independent*, 19 July 2019.

Mahmoud, R., 'What reopening the Eliyahu Hanavi Synagogue means for Egypt', *Al-Monitor*. 22 January 2020.

Mayer, T., 'The Image of Egyptian Jewry in Recent Egyptian Studies', in S. Shamir (ed.), *The Jews of Egypt : A Mediterranean Society in Modern Times* (Abingdon: Routledge, 1987), pp.199-204.

Meital, Y., 'A Jew in Cairo: the Defiance of Chehata Haroun', *Middle Eastern Studies*, 53, 2 (2017), pp.183-97.

Meron, Y., 'The Expulsion of Jews from Arab Countries and the Attitudes of the Palestinians Towards It', *State, Government, and International Relations,* 35 (1992), pp.37-56.

Miccoli, D., 'A Fragile Cradle: Writing Jewishness, Nationhood, and Modernity in Cairo, 1920–1940', *Jewish Social Studies,* 21, 3 (2016), pp.1-29.

Miccoli, D., 'Moving Histories. The Jews and Modernity in Alexandria 1881-1919', *Issues in Contemporary Jewish History,* 2 (2011), pp.149-71.

Miccoli, D., 'Another History: Family, Nation and the Remembrance of the Egyptian Jewish Past in Contemporary Israeli Literature', *Journal of Modern Jewish Studies,* 13, 3 (2013), pp.321-39.

Miccoli, D., 'Moses and Faruq. The Jews and the Study of History in Interwar Egypt 1920s-1940s', *Issues in Contemporary Jewish History,* 4 (2012), pp.165-80.

Miccoli, D., 'Digital Museums: Narrating and Preserving the History of Egyptian Jews on the Internet', in E. Trevisan Semi, Miccoli, D. and Parfitt, T. (eds.), *Memory and Ethnicity: Ethnic Museums in Israel and the Diaspora* (Newcastle: Cambridge Scholars Publishing, 2013), pp.195-223.

Miccoli, D., *Histories of the Jews of Egypt : An Imagined Bourgeoisie, 1880s-1950s* (Abingdon: Routledge, 2015).

Modrzejewski, J.M., *The Jews of Egypt: From Rameses II to Emperor Hadrian* (Edinburgh: T&T Clark, 1995).

Nadler, A., 'The 'Rambam Revival' in Early Modern Jewish Thought; Maskilim, Mitnagdim, and Hasidim on Maimonides Guide of the Perplexed', in J.M. Harris (ed.), *Maimonides after 800 Years: Essays on Maimonides and His Influence* (Cambridge, MA: Harvard University Press, 2007).

Negrine, R., 'Are Jews Who Fled Arab Lands to Israel Refugees, Too?' *Media History,* 19, 4 (2013), pp.450-63.

Nissim, L., 'Ethno-religious Fundamentalism and Theo-ethnocratic Politics in Israel', *Studies in Ethnicity & Nationalism,* 14, 1 (2014), pp.20-35.

Oppenheim, J.M.R., 'Egypt and the Sudan', in Spector Simon, R. (ed.), *The Jews of the Middle East and North Africa in Modern Times* (New York: Columbia University Press, 2003), pp.409-30.

Petricioli, M., 'Italian Schools in Egypt', *British Journal of Middle Eastern Studies,* 24, 2 (1997), pp.179–91.

Picard, A., 'Like a Phoenix: The Renaissance of Sephardic/Mizrahi Identity in Israel in the 1970s and 1980s', *Israel Studies,* 22, 2 (2017), pp.1-25.

Oppenheim, R.,. 'Egypt and the Sudan', in Spector Simon, R., *The Jews of the Middle East and North Africa in Modern Times* (New York: Columbia University Press, 2003), pp.409-30.

Reich, B., *A Brief History of Israel* (New York: Facts on File, 2005).

Daniel, R., 'The Arab League's Propaganda Campaign in the US Against the Establishment of a Jewish State (1944-1947)', *Israel Studies,* 25 (2020), pp.1-25.

Rossant, C., *Apricots on the Nile: A Memoir with Recipes* (New York: Washington Square Press, 1999).

Roumani, M., 'The Sephardi Factor in Israeli Politics', *Middle East Journal,* 42, 3 (1988), pp.423-35.

Roumani, M., 'The Silent Refugees: Jews from Arab Countries', *Mediterranean Journal,* 14, 3 (2003), pp.41-77.

Rubinstein, H., Cohn Sherbok, D., Edelheit, A. and Rubinstein, W. D., *The Jews in the Modern World: A History since 1750* (London: Hodder Education, 2002).

Rubin, B., *Israel; An Introduction* (London: Yale University Press, 2012).

Russell, M., 'Competing, Overlapping, and Contradictory Agendas: Egyptian Education under British Occupation, 1882–1922', *Comparative Studies of South Asia, Africa and the Middle East*, 21, 1–2 (2001), pp.50–60.

Rustow, M., *Heresy and the Politics of Community: The Jews of the Fatimid Caliphate* (New York: Cornell University Press, 2008).

Sachar, H., *A History of Israel from the Rise of Zionism to our Time* (New York: Knopf, 2006).

Saleh, M., 'Public Mass Modern Education, Religion, and Human Capital in Twentieth-Century Egypt', *The Journal of Economic History*, 76, 3 (2016), pp.697-735.

Sezgin, P.D., 'Jewish Women in the Ottoman Empire' in Zohar, Z., *Sephardic and Mizrahi Jewry: From the Golden Age of Spain to Modern Times* (New York: New York University Press, 2005), pp.216-35.

Shamir, S., 'Preface' to Shamir, S. (ed.), *The Jews of Egypt: A Mediterranean Society in Modern Times* (Abingdon: Routledge, 1987), pp.xii-xx.

Shamir, S., 'The Evolution of the Egyptian Nationality Laws and Their Application to the Jews in the Monarchy Period', in Shamir, S. (ed.), *The Jews Of Egypt: A Mediterranean Society in Modern Times* (Abingdon: Routledge, 1987), pp.33-67

Shapira, A., *Israel: A History* (London: Weidenfeld and Nicolson, 2014).

Shenhav, Y., 'Ethnicity and National Memory: The World Organization of Jews from Arab Countries (WOJAC) in the Context of the Palestinian National Struggle', *British Journal of Middle Eastern Studies*, 29, 1 (2002), pp.27-56.

Shenhav, Y., *The Arab Jew: A Postcolonial Reading of Nationalism, Religion, and Ethnicity* (Redwood, CA: Stanford University Press, 2006).

Shindler, C., *A History of Modern Israel* (Cambridge: Cambridge University Press, 2008).

Shmuelevitz, A., 'The Jews in Cairo at the Time of the Ottoman Conquest: The Account of Capsali', in Shamir, S. (ed.), *The Jews Of Egypt: A Mediterranean Society in Modern Times* (Abingdon: Routledge, 1987), pp.3-8.

Shohat, E., 'Sephardim in Israel: Zionism from the Standpoint of its Jewish Victims', *Social Text*, 19, 20 (1988), pp.1-35.

Shohat, E., 'Rupture and Return: Zionist Discourse and the Study of Arab Jews', *Social Text*, 21, 2 (2003), pp.49-74.

Shokeid, M., 'Cultural Ethnicity in Israel: The Case of Middle Eastern Jews' Religiosity', *AJS Review*, 9, 2 (1984), pp.247-271.

Sion, B., 'Pilgrimage, Healing Practices, and Tourism at Maimonides's Synagogue in Cairo', *Worship*, 89 (2015), pp.407-424.

Smallman-Raynor, M. and Cliff, A.D., 'The Diffusion of Cholera in Egypt, 1947: a Time-space Analysis of One of the Largest Single Outbreaks in the Twentieth Century', *Journal of Historical Geography*, 54 (2016), pp.24-37.

Snir, R., 'Who Needs Arab-Jewish Identity? Fragmented consciousness, "inessential solidarity," and the "coming community" 1 (Part 1)', *Journal of Modern Jewish Studies*, 11, 2 (2012), pp.169-188.

Stillman, N.A., 'The Jews of the Medieval Islamic West: Acculturation and its Limitations', *Journal of the Middle East & Africa*, 9, 3 (2018), pp.293-300.

Thornhill, M.T., 'Informal Empire, Independent Egypt and the Accession of King Farouk', *The Journal of Imperial and Commonwealth History*, 38, 2 (2010), pp.279-302.

Tignor, R., 'The Economic Activities of Foreigners in Egypt, 1920–1950: From Millet to Haute Bourgeoisie', *Comparative Studies in Society and History*, 22, 3 (1980), pp.416-449.

Toledano, E., *State and Society in Mid-Nineteenth Century Egypt* (Cambridge: Cambridge University Press, 1990).

UN General Assembly, Convention Relating to the Status of Refugees, 28 July 1951, United Nations, Treaty Series, 189, pp.37-84.

Weil, P., 'Racisme et Discrimination dans la Politique Française de L'immigration 1938-1945/1974-1995', *Vingtième Siècle,* 47 (1995), p.80.

Winter, M., 'Egyptian Jewry during the Ottoman Period as a Background to Modern Times', in Shamir, S. (ed.), *The Jews Of Egypt: A Mediterranean Society in Modern Times* (Abingdon: Routledge, 1987), pp.9-14.

Zamkanei, S., 'Justice for Jews from Arab countries and the Rebranding of the Jewish Refugee', *International Journal of Middle East Studies,* 48 (2016), pp.511-530

Zamir, L., *Cooking from the Nile's Land* (Tel Aviv: 1982).

Index of Names

Lightning Source UK Ltd.
Milton Keynes UK
UKHW021630190821
389121UK00005B/198